Robert de La Sizeranne

Ruskin and the religion of beauty

Translated from the Countess of Galloway

Robert de La Sizeranne

Ruskin and the religion of beauty
Translated from the Countess of Galloway

ISBN/EAN: 9783337131296

Hergestellt in Europa, USA, Kanada, Australien, Japan

Cover: Foto ©Lupo / pixelio.de

Weitere Bücher finden Sie auf **www.hansebooks.com**

RUSKIN

AND THE

RELIGION OF BEAUTY

RUSKIN

AND THE

RELIGION OF BEAUTY

TRANSLATED FROM THE FRENCH OF

R. DE LA SIZERANNE

BY

THE COUNTESS OF GALLOWAY

"*To have pleasure rightly*"

LONDON
GEORGE ALLEN, 156, CHARING CROSS ROAD
1899
[*All rights reserved*]

Printed by BALLANTYNE, HANSON & Co.
At the Ballantyne Press

TRANSLATOR'S PREFACE

THESE three essays on Ruskin and the Religion of Beauty appeared first in the *Révue des Deux Mondes*, and were subsequently published in the form of a book which has, I believe, been widely read in France. Perhaps those who already belong to the band of Mr. Ruskin's disciples and admirers,—those who acknowledge the power of his thought in everyday life—will be disappointed to find nothing very new or original in M. De La Sizeranne's picturesque study of the Master, but it will, I hope, be interesting to them as well as to others to note the impression made upon a foreigner by a personage who, not to mention that he is among the greatest of our stylists in prose, has permanently influenced the opinion of the English-speaking people in matters of Art. With all the keen critical feeling of his race M. De La Sizeranne has, I think, made a compact and concise statement of the fundamental ideas of Mr. Ruskin's teaching, and I shall be satisfied if my translation gives some of those, who have neither opportunity nor leisure to study the writings fully themselves, a definite conception of the doctrine and dogma of the author of *Modern Painters*. The judgment of one outside ourselves is valuable when we are anxious to divine the charm by which we are attracted: and even if it should be true that Ruskin like Carlyle wrote for an epoch and a generation which is rapidly passing away, this may be all the more reason for looking at his works from the standpoint of one who came under the spell at a distance of time when their form, colour, and perspective could be appreciated as a whole and not only in parts. Every one no doubt recognises in Ruskin a worshipper of the beautiful. I do not think, however, that it has hitherto been generally admitted that his Lectures on Political Economy, visionary and impossible as they appear to many, are the logical outcome of his Religion of Beauty, and surely there are already signs among us of progress on the lines he has persistently advocated for so many years. I have been asked what is meant by the Religion of Beauty. The answer will be found in these pages. It is a religion that should appeal alike to rich and poor. It is not a substitute for the Christian Faith, on the contrary it is a protest against the religion of

Self, of Materialism, and of Worldly Advancement, and it is but a branch growing out of the Igdrasil or World Tree of the religion of Christ. It teaches that the beautiful in Nature is precious because it is the expression of God's Love and Power on earth. It teaches that where there is no truth there can be no Art and no life—and for the work of daily duty its commandment is that of the great German poet—
Im Ganzen, Guten, Schönen, Resolut zu leben.

M. A. A. GALLOWAY.

1899.

INTRODUCTION

SOME years ago I was at Florence on the 7th of March, which is the feast of St. Thomas Aquinas. In the cloisters of Santa Maria Novella, greatest of all Dominican churches, are certain frescoes by Taddeo Gaddi and Simone Memmi, representing St. Thomas in triumph surrounded by his consistory of the seven celestial and the seven terrestrial sciences. What better day then, said I, to try and attain a sense of his contribution towards the schooling of human thought? Moreover the sun chanced to be shining brilliantly that morning on the domes of the "city of lilies," and sun is the one thing needful if all the several faces in the frescoes are to be distinguished, whether of apostles or of allegorical animals,—the Lord's hounds tearing the wolves of heresy,—or of wise men from Boethius, who resembles a leper, back even to Tubalcain, like nothing so much as an ourang-outang.

Wishing to be alone, I went as early as nine o'clock, and found the cloister deserted. The freshness of the morning and the monastic calm of the place made it a delicious resort. The grass, ever fading yet ever springing, gleamed green through the old fourteenth-century arches. The sacristan, intent equally on my peace and his own pocket, had closed the door with a wealth of bolts. Long silences followed the occasional clashing of the bells. . . .

For some little time I had been sauntering along that pavement of tombstones, which fringes the *Chiostri Verdi*, and I was approaching the Spanish Chapel, when a soft sound, rising and flowing, fell upon my ear, a murmur of words—speaking, reading —as in prayer. Had I been forestalled? Suddenly in the luminous shadow I perceived outlines of girlish forms, youthful with Giottesque profiles, wearing sailor hats and little white veils, and all carrying bunches of mimosa in their hands. They were clustering together before the *Triumph of St. Thomas Aquinas*, and one of them was reading:

"Optavi et datus est mihi sensus,
Invocavi et venit in me spiritus sapientiæ,
Et præposui illam regnis et sedibus."

Then the voice resumed the English text:
"I prayed and the Spirit of Wisdom came upon me. . . . The personal power of Wisdom; the σοφία or Santa Sophia, to whom the first great Christian temple was dedicated. The higher wisdom, governing by her presence, all earthly conduct, and by her teaching, all earthly art, Florence tells you, she obtained only by prayer."

She read on for some time, passing from eloquent generalisations on the necessity of discipline in human thought to minutest observations on the fingers or the hair of this or that personage in the fresco, noting where they were retouched, studying the attitudes and the draperies, contrasting the calm air and dignity of the figure of Rhetoric with the extravagant gestures of the common people of Florence—"They try to make lips of their fingers," insanely hoping to "drag by vociferation whatever they would have out of man and God."

The audience listened intently, forming face with the precision of a Prussian platoon towards this figure or that, as the small red and gold book directed them. At times the voice rose even to invocation; the muffled strains of an organ sounded from afar, the faint perfumes of flowers were wafted by like incense, and, touched with shafts of sunlight, the golden-tipped mimosas shone like tapers in their midst. I observed that the pilgrims had stationed themselves on the very sepulchral slab of those Spanish Ambassadors who give the chapel its name; and the words they were reading seemed like a tuft of flowers springing from the dust of the past. What then was this book? What this unknown liturgy? Who the priest of this Religion of Beauty? The sacristan, returning a moment, muttered a name—RUSKIN.

Another year, in London, after attending a Congress of Economists, I was resting in one of those Gothic drawing-rooms where sobriety is wed to comfort, and the claims of taste are satisfied without sacrifice of ease. The conversation turned on the transformation wrought in everything by machinery, and especially in textures and embroideries which were formerly products of art, the work of thoughtful minds, and much more enduring in olden times when linen descended as patrimony from generation to generation. The machine-made textures of to-day, it was observed, do not last,—"for example, such as these little napkins," said one of the guests (needless to explain we were at tea.)—"But," answered our hostess, "you forget that this is Langdale linen."—"And my coat," said the master of the house, "is cloth made by the St. George's Guild." This was accepted as conclusive.

It was then that I first heard of a pretty little cottage in Westmoreland where the thread is spun on the old wheels of our grandmothers, and with the old looms woven by men into cloth. This handmade fabric costs from two to six shillings a yard, and the money produced by its sale is paid into a bank, and the profits are divided among the workers at the end of the year. The household linen was all made there; while the coat of my host, the economist, was made of cloth carded, spun, and woven at the St. George's Mill at Laxey in the Isle of Man. Only the natural agency of water, working the mill, assists the human hand. Moreover the colour does not fade, for it is undyed, being natural to the black sheep of the island. Many English ladies have their stuffs made there, for they are very durable, and they have been manufactured without the smoke, noise, or ugliness of machinery, among trees and green fields, in defiance of progress and of all the social and industrial movements of the age. And when I asked who was the founder of this guild, who the Titan or madman who had undertaken thus to turn the century back upon itself, I received in answer the name that I had heard in the *Chiostri Verdi* at Florence—RUSKIN.

Here then was a man, at our very doors, just across the Channel, who held such empire in the British mind that he could attune it to the ecstatic visions of the Early Masters, and impose on life, style, economy, and even dress, ideas that were frankly retrograde. Fifty-four years ago he burst upon the world, armed with a book, and dashed into a conflict which speedily made him famous; and since that epoch, in the threefold guise of writer, orator, and patron of village industries, he has stood forward preaching a threefold doctrine of æsthetics, morals, and social reform, or, rather let us say, talking at random over every subject under the sun, while his words have been collected with pious care, like drops of a martyr's blood, by admirers, male and female. His books, printed in large numbers notwithstanding their high price, diffused his ideas on nature, art, and life throughout Great Britain, and pirated editions sowed the seed away in the far West. The author's profits on this æsthetic venture amounted to £4000 a year, and that profit was dedicated to promote the social venture of which he dreamed. There were founded Ruskin Reading

Societies in London, Birmingham, Manchester, Glasgow, to discuss his views, a journal to announce them, a special press, a *Ruskin House* in London to spread them abroad. At the same time artists occupied themselves in engraving his drawings, and writers in writing his life though he was yet alive, in expounding his doctrines though he had not done writing them, and in making selection from his works of *Ruskiniana*, of Birthday-books, of Guides to Museums, as well as of books for prize-givings. Already the railway time-tables for the Lake District advertised the hotels from which "the residence of Professor Ruskin" could be seen in the distance among the trees; while, during strikes, passages from the works of the great æstheticist were thrown into the discussion. Mr. Frederick Harrison described him only the other day as "the brightest living genius, the most inspiring soul still extant among us"; and not long ago the Principal of a college for girls declared at a school function that it was the writings of Ruskin that would make the nineteenth century famous to posterity.

Who is this man? What is his work? Apart from the merely curious interest that one cannot but feel, answers to these questions will be imperative to the future history of art. I set myself, therefore, to probe them more deeply than was possible by the perusal of the excellent study published by M. Milsand thirty-five years ago, at a time when Ruskin had written only one third of his works, lived only one half of his life and revealed only one aspect of his thought. It seemed to me that for my purpose I ought not only to read and study those, who knew him best, and above all his most chosen disciple Mr. W. G. Collingwood, but more than that I must retrace through Europe and through the history of "Æsthetic" the path the master had trod. In Switzerland, at Florence, at Venice, at Amiens, on the banks of the Rhine or of the Arno, everywhere where he had worked I too worked after him, sometimes sketching over again the sketches whence he had drawn his theories and his examples, waiting for the same light he had waited for, always seeking, as it were, on the eternal monuments the fugitive shadows of his thought. Then for several years I delayed to write until his system dawned upon me no longer as a delicious medley but as a harmony of great lines, like those Alpine mountains which he loved so well. In their midst all is but chaos; gradually, as we recede, they blend and unite till they stand on the horizon, only a "little blue film" yet "itself a world."

PART III.—HIS ÆSTHETIC AND SOCIAL THOUGHT

CHAP.	PAGE
Introduction	143
I. Nature—§ 1	146
,, § 2	155
,, § 3	168
II. Art—§ 1	178
,, § 2	193
,, § 3	210
,, § 4	221
III. Life—§ 1	236
,, § 2	242
,, § 3	259
,, § 4	272
Appendices	297

PART I
HIS PERSONALITY

A

RUSKIN

PART I

HIS PERSONALITY

CHAPTER I

CONTEMPLATION

THE guardian of the gates of Schaffhausen was awakened one summer night in 1833 by the noise of a postchaise. He sulkily opened or half opened the barriers at the entreaty of the belated travellers, and the carriage passed through in such haste that it smashed one of its lamps, and at once disappeared into the town. When it reached the hotel a courier alighted, and with him an English gentleman with his wife, a little girl, a boy of fourteen, and a maid; and all quickly sought their rooms. The following day was Sunday, and they would have to be up in the morning for Church.

The names which the hotel-keeper wrote the next day on his list would have revealed nothing to any one, and the information he obtained about the new arrivals from the courier, Salvador, was quite commonplace. If he had been told that the gentleman in question was Mr. John James Ruskin, who had his name writ fair on a brass plate in Billiter Street as the head of the firm Ruskin, Telford & Domecq, that he was one of the largest sherry importers of his day and among the most scrupulous merchants of his country, that the lady accompanying him was his wife *née* Miss Margaret Cox, the boy his only son John, and the little girl, Mary, an orphan niece, and that they all were Tory and Jacobite in politics and Presbyterian in religion, this bare statement of facts would have seemed fraught with little interest for the history of Art. It might have been added also that the family was somewhat unsociable, giving itself up entirely to the contemplation of the beauties of Nature, while æsthetical enthusiasm was its principal characteristic.

The city merchants would assuredly have been vastly astonished had they been made aware that Mr. John James Ruskin, so exact in his counting-house, so punctual in his payments, and so good a judge of sherry, cherished the aspirations of an artist. But the fact is, that within his own doors he was at once transformed into an enthusiastic and imaginative being. He would rapidly wash in a water-colour, or, taking up some new writing of Walter Scott's, or some old piece of Shakespeare, would read it aloud to his wife and son in a rhythmic and impassioned voice. In

I. CONTEMPLATION

bygone years night had often found him stooping over engravings of Prout or Turner, or with maps of Switzerland or Italy open under the lamp, dreaming of journeys not at that time to be accomplished, to the lands where mountains gleam so white and waves sleep so blue.

When Mrs. Ruskin came on the scene her persuasive eloquence recalled him to that preoccupation of moneymaking, which Englishmen are so fain to call their duty. Mrs. Ruskin was a first cousin of her husband, and by four years his senior. Having known her from childhood, it was borne in on him one day that she was exactly the kind of wife he needed. He told her so, and arranged with her that they should postpone their marriage until the family debts were paid, the business well established, and the horizon free from clouds. They waited nine years. At last came an evening when, perceiving that he had a credit balance to his account, Mr. John James Ruskin listened to the dictates of his heart. The young people were married after their supper, and so secretly that the servants discovered it only the next day when they left together for Edinburgh. Such a strange blend of phlegm and sensibility—of romantic fidelity and practical common sense—gave Mr. Ruskin his distinct individuality among his fellow-merchants, and enabled him to save the honour of his family by paying all his father's debts, and to bequeath to his son at the same time two hundred thousand pounds and that worship of Nature which was to become the most marked characteristic of the great writer.

To the child that Nature was revealed only on rare occasions, as a queen appearing on high days and holidays. He used to see her either when visiting his aunts at Croydon, where the view was so beautiful that he cried out to his astonished mother it seemed as if his eyes were coming out of his head,—or at Perth, where the gardens stretching down to the river Tay first enchanted his view. Then the black curtain of London fog fell again upon these visions. But later, when his parents left the town for the suburbs and settled on the edge of the Surrey slopes at Herne Hill, the beauty of inanimate things became more familiar to him. From his father's windows on one side he could see a rich undulating country of green meadows and trees, with houses sprinkled here and there in the foreground, and on the other side his eye could range over London and beyond it towards Windsor and Harrow. The simple comfortable house was surrounded by a garden with well-trimmed lawns sloping to an orchard full of cherries and mulberries, "decked with magical splendour of abundant fruit; fresh green, soft amber, and rough bristled crimson bending the spinous branches; clustered pearl and pendent ruby joyfully discoverable under the large leaves that looked like vine," altogether a delicious garden which seemed a terrestrial paradise to the child. "All the fruit was forbidden, and there were no companionable beasts." His instinctive taste for

I. CONTEMPLATION

form and colour was no longer restricted to tapestry designs and constructions in brick. "In the garden when the weather was fine, my time there was chiefly passed in the same kind of close watching of the ways of plants. I had not the smallest taste for growing them, or taking care of them, any more than for taking care of the birds, or the trees, or the sky, or the sea. My whole time was passed in staring at them, or into them. In no morbid curiosity, but in admiring wonder, I pulled every flower to pieces till I knew all that could be seen of it with a child's eye."

As shy and retiring in society as successful in business, Mr. John James Ruskin lived much alone, happy in the companionship of the romantic and legendary creations of his favourite authors. His wife, who had been brought up amongst people inferior to the Ruskins, was not at home amongst her new connections. Too intelligent to ignore the fact and too proud to submit to it, she determined to renounce the world,—a religious and devoted mother who kept the *Christian Treasury* on her table and the hatred of the Pope in her heart, abhorring the theatre and adoring flowers, uniting the spirit of Martha to that of Mary, indefatigable, well regulated, living only for her husband and her son. To avoid separation from the latter during his university career, she brought herself to live a stranger in Oxford, watching continually to save him from all pain, even should she unman him, and from all danger, at risk of taking from him the power to avoid it. Each day with order and regularity she gave him a Bible lesson, and revealed to him by degrees that light of the Old and New Testament which has ever shone on the summits of his achievement. The child had not a conception of what care was. The Ruskins never spent more than the half of their income, and were free from all money troubles. Finding all their joy in admiration, they were ignorant of the pangs of jealousy and ambition. To live in a cottage and to taste the "healthy delight of uncovetous admiration" in visiting Warwick Castle was a greater happiness to them than "to live in Warwick Castle and have nothing to be astonished at." Their even temperaments were warmed to enthusiasm only by ideas or by the contemplation of Nature. "Never," says their son, "had I heard my father's or mother's voice once raised in any question with each other. I had never heard a servant scolded." "Under such gentle discipline there reigned in this house peace, obedience, and faith."

Shielded from all external trouble, the artistic taste of the boy was refined into a sort of ecstatic habit which was encouraged by the perpetual novelty of travel. Every year Mr. J. J. Ruskin started in the month of May on a business tour. His wife, who never allowed him to encounter fatigue alone, went with him; little John was seated between them on the portmanteau, with the maid in the dickey behind; and the whole family posted off. Every evening, when his commercial business was over, Mr. J. J. Ruskin took his son out to see the ruins, the castles or the

I. CONTEMPLATION

cathedrals on their route. They read poetry, they made drawings. At five years old, John visited the Scottish lakes; at six years he went to France, and at Paris was present at the fêtes of the coronation of Charles X.; he saw the field of Waterloo; and then he returned to England, taking notes and sketches. He described the colleges and chapels and music at Oxford, the tomb of Shakespeare, and a pin manufactory at Birmingham, drew sketches of Blenheim or of Warwick Castle; and thus explored the world in all its attractive and picturesque variety, at an age when little French boys worry their heads over the dead names on their maps. Not long after we find him writing verses comparing Skiddaw and the Pyramids, which certainly would not be attributed to an ordinary child of ten years.

"The touch of man
Raised pigmy mountains, but gigantic tombs.
The touch of Nature raised the mountain's brow
But made no tombs at all."

At Herne Hill he passed the long winter months dreaming over Turner's illustrations to Rogers' *Italy*, and a violent desire took possession of him to know in what *aliquas partes materiæ* the great seer had seen his vision. In the valleys of Clifton or of Matlock in Derbyshire he made collections of minerals, calculated heights, and watched reflections. And all that he perceived with a mind so precocious and overflowing, he loved with a heart strangely virgin and void; for he had little sentiment for his family. "My mother herself, finding her chief personal pleasure in her flowers, was often planting or pruning beside me, at least if I chose to stay beside *her*. . . . Her presence was no restraint to me, but also no particular pleasure, for, from having always been left so much alone, I had generally my own affairs to see after." Sixty years afterwards he sadly exclaims, "I had nothing to love. My parents were in a sort visible powers of nature to me, no more loved than the sun and the moon." And as a child he knew no one else. Even when travelling the Ruskins lived apart from their fellows and preferred watching the great poet Wordsworth from behind the pillar of a church, to asking for an introduction. "We did not travel for adventures, nor for company, but to see with our eyes, and to measure with our hearts." Their mode of travelling enabled them to see everything thoroughly, and their ignorance of foreign languages prevented them from regarding the people from any other than the picturesque point of view. They found a peculiar charm in the very fact of being unable to understand the speech of those around them. For so they noted each gesture but for its beauty, each voice but for its music, and neither one nor the other for its significance.

Trained in this special manner, all the child's faculties tended to one result—an acute sensibility, a power of minute analysis of landscape and figures. He could not love his little cousin because she had ringlets, which are not in accordance with true taste.

I. CONTEMPLATION

Should he be taken to pay a visit, he would give no attention to the guests, but think of nothing but the pictures which decorated the room. Presently at Oxford he could not bear the sight of certain of his tutors and comrades, because their features were not strongly enough marked, and he listened only to such professors as were endowed with some resemblance to the "Erasmus" of Holbein or the "Melancthon" of Dürer. With a talent for geometry, that science of dimensions that can be seen and touched, he stopped short on the threshold of algebra, for it only deals with the relations of abstract terms. His estimate of things depended entirely on their relation to his idea of beauty and the pain or pleasure communicated by them to the eye; and it is easy to understand how any strong æsthetical impression received at this period of his youth, would determine his whole life. If the full glory of Nature should once open out before him, —not in her grey northern raiment but in the blue blazonry of the south, not with painted face and tired head as in the vicinity of large towns, but in all the naked majesty of her first savageness,—then hers he would be mind and heart and soul, and theirs who, like Turner, should have revealed her to him.

This ardour without an assured object, this hope for one knows not what, this flame that burns without giving light,—have we not all had experience of these when at twenty we have begun to ask what shall be done with our years? This was the state of young John Ruskin's mind at fourteen, when he arrived that summer's night at Schaffhausen, with his father, his mother, and his cousin Mary. He had longed eagerly for this journey. At Strasburg it had been a question between Basle and Schaffhausen. "Schaffhausen," he cried. "My impassioned petition at last carried it, and the earliest morning saw us trolling over the bridge of boats to Kehl, and in the eastern light I well remember watching the line of the Black Forest hills enlarge and rise, as we crossed the plain of the Rhine. 'Gates of the Hills,' opening for me a new life to cease no more, except at the Gates of the Hills whence one returns not." Let us now hear how he relates his impressions of Eternal Beauty. It seems as though we hear the tremor in his voice even after fifty years.

"It was past midnight when we reached the closed gates. None of us seemed to have thought the Alps would have been visible without profane exertion in climbing hills. We dined at four as usual, and the evening being entirely fine, went out to walk, all of us—my father and mother and Mary and I. We must have still spent some time in town-seeing, for it was drawing towards sunset when we got up to some sort of garden promenade—west of the town I believe, and high above the Rhine, so as to command the open country across it to the south and west. At which open country of low undulation, far into blue, gazing as at one of our own distances from Malvern of Worcestershire, or Dorking of Kent — suddenly— behold—beyond! There was no thought in any of us for a moment of their being clouds. They

I. CONTEMPLATION

were clear as crystal, sharp on the pure horizon sky, and already tinged with rose by the sinking sun. Infinitely beyond all that we had ever thought or dreamed—the seen walls of lost Eden could not have been more beautiful to us; not more awful, round heaven, the sacred walls of Death. Thus in perfect health of life and fire of heart, not wanting to be anything but the boy I was, not wanting to have anything more than I had; knowing of sorrow only just so much as to make life serious to me, not enough to slacken in the least its sinews; and with so much of science mixed with feeling as to make the sight of the Alps not only the revelation of the beauty of the earth, but the opening of the first page of its volume, I went down that evening from the garden-terrace of Schaffhausen with my destiny fixed in all of it that was to be sacred and useful. To that terrace, and the shore of the lake of Geneva, my heart and faith return to this day, in every impulse that is yet nobly alive in them, and every thought that has in it help or peace."

From that moment the contemplation of Nature was to absorb his whole life. It would be no longer a distraction, a flirtation with the vague and marvellous, but a vocation, a progress towards the attainment of the ideal. All his first essays, written between the ages of fifteen and twenty, in the scientific journal of the time, the *Magazine of Natural History*, on the causes of the colour of the Rhine water, on the stratification of Mont Blanc, on the convergence of perpendicular lines, or on meteorology, are signed *Kata Phusin* (according to Nature). The history of Ruskin's career is the history of his relations with Nature, and of the journeys which year by year he undertook in the company of his parents during two-thirds of his lifetime, and, when they were dead, alone. He does not have recourse to Nature as a refuge from weariness and disenchantment, or as a distraction for weary hours, but he goes in the full force of his age as to a goddess who gives joy to youth. She is not only the consoler in love, she is his love itself.

" I had a pleasure, as early as I can remember, and continuing till I was eighteen or twenty, infinitely greater than any which has since been possible to me in anything; comparable for intensity only to the joy of a lover in being near a noble and kind mistress, but no more explicable or definable than that feeling of love itself. I never thought of Nature as God's work, but as a separate fact of existence. This sentiment was, according to its strength, inconsistent with every evil feeling, with spite, anger, covetousness, discontent, and every other hateful passion, but would associate itself deeply with every just and noble sorrow, joy, or affection.

"Although there was no definite religious sentiment mingled with it, there was a continual perception of sanctity in the whole of Nature from the slightest thing to the vastest; an instinctive awe, mingled with delight; an indefinable thrill, such as we sometimes

I. CONTEMPLATION

imagine to indicate the presence of a disembodied spirit. I could only feel this perfectly when I was alone; and then it would often make me shiver from head to foot with the joy and fear of it, when after being some time away from the hills, I first got to the shore of a mountain river, where the brown water circled among the pebbles, or when I saw the first swell of distant land against the sunset, or the first low broken wall, covered with mountain moss. I cannot in the least describe the feeling; but I do not think this is my fault, nor that of the English language, for I am afraid no feeling is describable. If we had to explain even the sense of bodily hunger to a person who had never felt it, we should be hard put to it for words; and this joy in nature seemed to me to come of a sort of heart-hunger, satisfied with the presence of a great and holy Spirit. . . . The feeling cannot be described by any of us that have it. Wordsworth's 'haunted me like a passion' is no description of it, for it is not *like*, but *is*, a passion; the point is to define how it differs from other passions, what sort of human, pre-eminently human feeling it is that loves a stone for a stone's sake and a cloud for a cloud's. A monkey loves a monkey for a monkey's sake, and a nut for the kernel's, but not a stone for a stone's. I took stones for bread."

To examine these stones more closely, he passed long months in Italy or in Switzerland. He would have liked to establish his home at Chamounix, above the Châlet of Blaitière, but the rising flood of tourists chased him away. He then proposed to buy from the Commune of Bonneville the summit of the Brèzon, but the peasants of the place, astounded at the idea of a purchaser for barren rocks and goat pasture, suspected that the *milord* had divined the existence of some treasure, and discouraged him by their excessive demands. He consoled himself by changing his sky but not his love. "A study in the rose-garden of San Miniato and in the cypress avenue of Porta Romana, remain to me, for memorials of perhaps the best days of early life."

For long this passion preserved him from all others, and when those others came it kept him sane. Until he was seventeen the intense unremitting application of mind and heart towards the Beautiful had preserved him from the seduction of what the world mostly means by Beauty. This romanticism of the Lake School however, which Englishmen either have pre-eminently or not at all, is very apt to develop into a disease; and the day that the young anchorite of Herne Hill raised his head from his books and saw before him the face of a young girl, smiling in the first blush of sixteen years, he fell desperately in love. She was a daughter of his father's partner, M. Domecq, called Adèle; and this name became familiar to the readers of *Friendship's Offering*, wherein the young man published verses which he addressed to all the world, not venturing to address them to the only reader for whom he cared. When told of the passion of this awkward young geologist, this timorous troubadour, the young woman only laughed aloud. "On any blessed occasion of *tête-à-tête* I endeavoured to entertain my Spanish-born, Paris-bred, and Catholic-hearted mistress with my own views upon the subject of the Spanish Armada, the battle of Waterloo, and the doctrine of Transubstantiation," says Ruskin in his *Præterita*. Mrs. Ruskin was indignant that her son, a sound and instructed Tory, of the straitest sect of Georgian evangelism, should love a Frenchwoman, and still worse a Catholic; and, wounded in all her deepest sentiments and traditions by what seemed to her a monstrous affection, she obstinately opposed all idea of the marriage. The hopeless passion however lasted four years, years that tried terribly the frail organism of the enthusiastic thinker. Expecting to die of love, he wrote some lines, pathetic enough, and called them "The Broken Chain." But we do not die of love; broken chains are forged anew, and it is perhaps the most melancholy part of such sorrows that they prove so passing. One fine day it was announced that Adèle had married, and the young man was taken away across Europe in the hope that he would leave by its highways some of his painful memories, and something of the image that he carried in his heart. He carried them in turn to the banks of Loire, into the mountains of Auvergne, and to the galleries of Florence and Rome. Each site he visited was like a picture deprived of the one figure which animated it, and in each smiling face, among the thousands of golden frames, he was seeking the reflection of other

B

features, possibly less beautiful, but more adored. At last, when again he saw the Alps, he seemed to take on new life. "It was not only the air of the Alps braced him," says Mr. Collingwood, "but the spirit of mountain-worship stirred him as nothing else would." He has himself related in his *Præterita* how a year later he was cured by the contemplation of Nature. At Fontainebleau, one day, ill and feverish, he made his way painfully to the Forest, and stretching himself at the roadside, under some young trees, tried to sleep. "The branches against the blue sky began to interest me, motionless as the branches of the tree of Jesse on a painted window." And he realised that his death was not to be that day, and began to draw with care a little aspen-tree which was on the other side of the road. Yet he found nothing at Fontainebleau worth seeing. The "hideous rocks" of Evelyn were not ugly enough to cause the least emotion, nor of value but as specimens to carry away, had they been worth the transport.

"And to-day I missed rocks, palace, and fountain all alike, and found myself lying on the bank of a cart-road in the sand, with no prospect whatever but that small aspen-tree against the blue sky. Languidly, but not idly, I began to draw it; and as I drew, the languor passed away; the beautiful lines insisted on being traced, without weariness. More and more beautiful they became, as each rose out of the rest, and took its place in the air. With wonder increasing every instant, I saw that they composed themselves by finer laws than any known of men. At last the

I. CONTEMPLATION

tree was there, and everything that I had thought before about trees, nowhere."

Like all great passions this love of Nature, which filled Ruskin's life with great joys, added to these also sorrows unknown to others. When the prospect is framed no longer by the accustomed flowers of his youth he is miserable. "Scarce all the hyacinths and heath of Brantwood redeem the loss of these to me, and when the summer winds have wrecked the wreaths of our wild roses, I am apt to think sorrowfully of the trailings and climbings of deep purple convolvulus which bloomed full every autumn morning round the trunks of the apple-trees in the kitchen garden." If, returning to a favourite landscape, he finds it changed and disfigured by increased facilities of locomotion, by a port or a railroad, by such modern improvements as a tea-garden or an hotel, it is an outrage on his Best Beloved.

"You have despised nature; that is to say, all the deep and sacred sensations of natural scenery. The French revolutionists made stables of the cathedrals of France; you have made racecourses of the cathedrals of the earth. Your one conception of pleasure is to drive in railroad carriages round their aisles, and eat off their altars. You have put a railroad bridge over the falls of Schaffhausen. You have tunnelled the cliffs of Lucerne by Tell's chapel; you have destroyed the Clarens shore of the Lake of Geneva; there is not a quiet valley in England that you have not filled with bellowing fire."

Indeed if the unhappy æstheticist wished to experience over again the impressions of his youth, and wandered to the slopes of Herne Hill, where he dreamed his first dreams, he no longer recognised anything around him.

"The view from the bridge on both sides was, before railroads came, entirely lovely; westward at evening, almost sublime, over softly wreathing distances of domestic wood;—but the tops of twenty squares miles of politely inhabited groves. On the other side, east and south, the Norwood hills, partly rough with furze, partly wooded with birch and oak, partly in pure green bramble copse, and rather steep pasture rose with the promise of all the rustic loveliness of Surrey and Kent in them, and with so much of space and height in their sweep, as gave them some fellowship with hills of true hill-districts. Fellowship now inconceivable, for the Crystal Palace, without ever itself attaining any true aspect of size, and possessing no more sublimity than a cucumber-frame between two chimneys, yet by its stupidity of hollow bulk, dwarfs the hills at once; so that now one thinks of them no more but as three long lumps of clay, on lease for building."

If he wishes to follow the quiet pathway where he composed his *Modern Painters*—a pathway running by a field where the cows used to browse, and so warm that invalids sought refuge there even in March, when all other walks would have been death—he finds it a street.

"Since I last composed or meditated there, various improvements have taken place; first the neighbourhood wanted a new church, and built a meagre Gothic one with a useless spire, for the fashion of the thing, at the side of the field; then they built a parsonage behind it, the two stopping out half the view in that direction. Then the Crystal Palace came, for ever spoiling the view through all its compass, and bringing every show-day from London a flood of pedestrians down the footpath, who left it filthy with cigar-ashes for the rest of the week: then the railroads came, and expatiating roughs by every excursion train, who knocked the palings about, roared at the cows, and tore down what branches of blossom they could reach over the palings on the enclosed side. Then the residents on the enclosed side built a brick wall to defend themselves. Then the path got to be insufferably hot as well as dirty, and was gradually abandoned to the roughs, with a policeman on watch at the bottom. Finally, this year, a six-foot high close paling has been put down the other side of it, and the processional excursionist has the liberty of obtaining what notion of the country air and prospect he may between the wall and that, with one bad cigar before him, another behind him, and another in his mouth."

When Nature herself changes, he complains more gently, but still as if of infidelity. "Yes," he writes from England to a friend who is in the Alps, "Chamounix is as a desolated home to me. I shall never I believe be there more: I could escape the riffraff in winter and early spring; but that the glaciers should have betrayed me, and their old ways know them no more, is too much. Please give my love to the big stone under the Breven, a quarter of a mile above the village, unless they've blasted it up for hotels." He returned all the same to the Alps in 1882. "I saw Mont Blanc again to-day, unseen since 1877; and was very thankful. It is a sight that always redeems me to what I am capable of at my poor little best, and to what loves and memories are most precious to me."

This mystic reverie of contemplation, rapture, and ecstasy whether of joy or sorrow, is the principal feature in the individuality of Ruskin. Once immersed in it nothing rouses him. Events take place around him without his giving them so much as a thought. Sometimes he has passed weeks without so much as knowing what agitated his country. Khartoum fell with the heroic Gordon; the news had not reached him, and when the Soudan was mentioned, he thought of the figure painted by Giotto at Santa Croce, to face St. Francis of Assisi, and asked curiously, "But who is the Soldan of to-day?" Even family events did not seem to deserve attention. Whilst in the Alps he heard of the death of his cousin Mary, the companion of his youth and of his early travels, but he did not pause in his endeavour to reproduce the effect of sunrise on Montanvert, and the "aerial quality of Aiguilles." Even in his old age he remains ever the

I. CONTEMPLATION

same—the boy his mother soothed in childish illness by bidding him think of the sky and seas of Dover. The close of *Præterita* reveals no melancholy echo of what the aged Petrarch described as "the superfluous cares, the futile hopes and the unlooked-for events," which had agitated him during his life on earth. No trace of this—but a last note on the infinite and marvellous forms assumed by the "upper cirri" of the sky in the pure air of Kent and Picardy when not "disturbed by tornado nor mingled with volcanic exhalation," and a thrill of joy in the thought that the clouds which float over the English coasts are as full of beauty as those which hover round the Alps. And in those final pages where speaking of himself he might have betrayed or grieved over the secret dramas of his life, the great enthusiast does not seem to avert his gaze for an instant from the radiant horizons of Eternal Nature, the sum of all he has loved on earth.

CHAPTER II

ACTION

THIS dreamer is also a man of action. Like those pious cavaliers, depicted by the Early Italian Masters, though Ruskin holds a flower, he has a sword at his side; and this feature distinguishes him clearly from the art-critics or the poets of the Lake school, who for the most part were satisfied to pass comments upon pictures, or encomiums upon Nature, without a thought of bettering the one, or championing the other. Such was not the faith that was in Ruskin; like a soldier who fires a shot from afar, he projected an idea in a pamphlet or a book, and forthwith plunged into the thick of the fray to support it with his own person, and, as it were, to grapple with the realities of things.

For example, he wrote that the taste for Art must be spread among the masses. No one would listen to him. So he determined to give drawing-lessons himself in the evening to an adult school, and for four years, from 1854 to 1858, with Rossetti to teach the figure-drawing, Ruskin subjected himself to the task of rekindling fading zeal and guiding incapable hands in the arts of landscape sketching and of

II. ACTION

decoration. In 1876 he founded with his own and his friends' money a Museum of Art for Sheffield, the chosen city of artisans and cutlery, and filled it with delicate and carefully chosen exhibits, amongst others a picture by Verrochio, who was himself a worker in iron. He established his museum in a cottage situated on a hill among green fields, away from the centre of industry. The valley of the Don with the woods of Wharncliffe Crags opened below the windows, and invited the eye to roam from illuminated missals of the thirteenth and fourteenth centuries to a distance gleaming in golden sun,—from show-cases, studded with onyx, various crystals, amethysts, displaying the beautiful colours which enrich the earth, to coloured plates reproducing the birds of all countries, which are the life of the sky. By pictures on the walls, recalling the most beautiful buildings of the world (among others St. Mark's of Venice), the visitors were transported to an ideal country, and might forget for a moment the gloomy frontages and smoky chimneys of Sheffield. Later the collection was moved into the town itself, and the Ruskin Museum for Working Men is now to be found in Meersbrook Park, in a house presented by the Municipality.

In like manner when Ruskin was chosen in 1869 to occupy the Slade Professorship at Oxford, he felt that he could not lecture profitably on painting without showing pictures, or on architecture without exhibiting architectural designs, to support his theses and enrich his arguments. So he added to the Slade

Collection a School of Drawing, and a series of original drawings, from Tintoret to Burne-Jones, which could be copied, and specimens by his own hand after the Old Masters, which might be studied. He organised this collection in 1872, in the Oxford Galleries which face towards Beaumont Street, and gave a donation of £5600 for the maintenance of the school and the salary of the professor who was to teach there. For thirteen years he devoted himself to promoting the worship of the Beautiful in the intellectual sanctuary of Great Britain, until on a fatal day the University authorities sanctioned vivisection in their midst in spite of his opposition. He could not tolerate this cruel and hideous practice; useless, he said, to science, since learned men had for ages done without it; useless to art, since the Greek sculptors never studied anatomy; and he nobly resigned his professorship. But the Museum remains. A few undergraduates and many young women profit daily by the Ruskin teaching. The materials are admirably arranged for the education of the eye and mind, and the drawings, ingeniously enclosed in mahogany cabinets with ivory labels, are at the service of all pupils. Oxford is now a centre of art, thanks to her graduate who signed his name to *Modern Painters*.

But what avail a few examples of plastic beauty in academies, if the whole world is growing ugly, and the folk from the country, abandoning that healthy toil which develops their muscles and deepens their ruddy tints, crowd together in towns and enervate themselves by guiding machines until they become machines themselves moving mechanically to the hand of a master? What avails it to collect in museums pale reflections of fair landscapes while industrial buildings and factories, which wither the grass on the earth and spread a pall of smoke across the sky, destroy Nature's own more beautiful originals? The amateur—the æsthete—is content to worship the Beautiful in museums and particular churches where none but the converted congregate; but ugliness must be attacked and wrestled with in the use of every day, and having exiled it from our dreams, we must drive it from our waking life.

"We will try," says Ruskin, "to take some small piece of English ground, beautiful, peaceful, and fruitful. We will have no steam engines upon it, and no railroads; we will have no untended or un-thought-of creatures upon it; none wretched, but the sick; none idle, but the dead. We will have no liberty upon it, but instant obedience to known law, and appointed persons; no equality upon it; but recognition of every betterness we can find, and reprobation of every worseness. When we want to go anywhere, we will go there quietly and safely, not at forty miles an hour in the risk of our lives; when we want to carry anything anywhere, we will carry it either on the backs of beasts, or on our own, or in carts, or boats; we will have plenty of flowers and vegetables in our gardens, plenty of corn and grass in our fields—and few bricks. We will have some music and poetry; the children shall learn to dance to it and sing it;—perhaps some of the old people in time may also. . . . Little by little, some higher art and imagination may manifest themselves among us; and feeble rays of science may dawn for us. Botany, though too dull to dispute the existence of flowers; and history, though too simple to question the nativity of men; nay—even perhaps an uncalculating and uncovetous wisdom, as of rude Magi, presenting, at such nativity, gifts of gold and frankincense."

It was in May 1871, during the days of the Commune, that Ruskin dreamed this dream. Sometime afterwards, with some idea of realising it, he founded the St. George's Guild.[1] The experiment failed, as socialistic experiments always do in simple agriculture. A farm of eight or nine acres was indeed purchased near Totley for £2000, and other possessors of barren pastures or of uncultivated and useless rocks promptly welcomed an opportunity of disposing of them to promote the good of the greatest number. Thus the association soon had lands at Barmouth, at Bewdley in Worcestershire, and other places. When, however, it was discovered that no member of the Guild understood agriculture, and that it would be vain even for one who knew all the secrets of Proserpina to found an agricultural colony

[1] This account of the foundation of St. George's Guild is somewhat too picturesquely described, and must not be taken as a statement of literal facts. See *Fors Clavigera*, Letter 52, and Appendix.—*Editor's Note.*

II. ACTION

if he had not put hand to plough, Ruskin turned to the communists and sought their co-operation, offering them lands whereon to try their theories of society, provided they were willing to apply his ideas of æsthetics. Furthermore, he did not oblige them for the present to coin special money after the fashion of the Florentine florin, nor yet to dress themselves like the three Switzers of the Rütli. The communists consented to a conference, and Ruskin came to it in a postchaise with gorgeous postillions, so as to avoid benefiting the unsightly railroad. It was at Sheffield that he met his new allies. There were twenty of them of at least twenty different sects, and between this worshipper of the Beautiful and the reformers of society, between the Tory partisan of all aristocracies, and the levellers of the fourth estate, between this mind free as air, and those brains working rigidly to a system, the interview was most extraordinary. Not only did they come to no agreement, but it is very doubtful if each understood what the other meant. Nevertheless, Ruskin confided to them the lands of the St. George's Guild, and stepping again into his postchaise, disappeared with his gorgeous postillions and his picturesque revival of eighteenth-century lordliness, in a cloud of dust, leaving the group of Deists, Nonconformists, and Quakers, not only astounded but vastly disconcerted. For the first time it dawned upon them that no more than Ruskin did they know anything of agriculture; and like every other proprietor they ended by engaging a farmer.

The farm was a failure, and instead of the dreamed-of paradise, they established a tea-shop. Thus neither the theories of the communists, nor those of Ruskin, were tested in the province of agriculture.

But the master had his revenge in an industrial enterprise. He heard that in the picturesque valleys of Westmoreland the small rural industries were disappearing daily. There was no more wood-carving, no more spinning, no more weaving of the good cloth of olden days. The machine, which stupidly rotates, obeying the pestilential breath of steam, was ousting all the pretty motions of the hand which are governed by the living breath of man. Ruskin rushed to a new battlefield to fight a great fight with modern machinery. One of his passionate admirers, Mr. Fleming, vowed he would re-establish the spinning-wheel. But it was not easy to find one, for that wheel at which Margaret sits and sings, "Quel est donc ce jeune homme?" was at the London Opera House, and not available. The whole Langdale district was searched, and advertisements appeared in the local newspapers. At last a wheel was found belonging to an old dame who had not touched it for fifty years; and immediately, as in the fairy tale where the princess finds the spindle which wounds her and causes her to fall asleep for a hundred years, the entire valley reassumed the aspect of a past century. A loom was next discovered, but all in pieces, and how should it be put together? Fortunately a drawing of the loom which is carved on the campanile of Giotto—

II. ACTION

the Shepherd's Tower—restored the tradition of the Middle Ages, even as presently some lines of the Odyssey were to teach the Ruskinians to bleach the cloth they had prepared. Perhaps this cloth was a little rough; but there was consolation in these words of the *Seven Lamps:* "It is possible for men to turn themselves into machines, and to reduce their labour to the machine level; but so long as men work as men, putting their heart into what they do, and doing their best, it matters not how bad workmen they may be, there will be that in the handling which is above all price. It will be plainly seen that some places have been delighted in more than others, that there have been a pause and a care about them, and the effect of the whole, as compared with the same design cut by a machine or a lifeless hand, will be that of poetry well read and deeply felt to that of the same verses jangled by rote." And in very truth after a short time this linen, that was first made at Langdale and soon after at Keswick, procured a real livelihood for the old women and for the hardy workers of the village. Fashion came to the rescue, and they say Ruskin Linen sometimes figures even now in wedding trousseaux.

Another voice was heard from the Isle of Man, crying that wool-spinning was ever on the decrease. The women were leaving their wheels and their cottages to go and work in the mines. The young girls no longer learned to spin, although the black sheep of the island still gave wool and their durable homespun textures were in demand on all sides. Ruskin takes the field, finds capital, builds a mill at Laxey, and, with his lieutenant Mr. Rydings, starts the necessary machines for carding wool and bleaching cloth. Machines did we say? but machines worked by the direct forces of Nature, not by artificial force, machines of which the motive power is in conformity with æsthetics and such as were immortalised by Claude Lorraine in his *Molino*. "It is to be carefully noted that *machinery* is only forbidden by the Guild where it supersedes healthy, bodily exercise, or the art and precision of manual labour in decorative work; but that the only permitted *motive power* of machinery is by natural power of wind or water (electricity, perhaps, not in future refused); but *steam* absolutely refused, as a cruel and furious waste of fuel to do what every stream and breeze are ready to do costlessly" (*Fors*). Because there was no longer an æsthetic coinage like the beautiful florin of Florence, money was not to be used. The farmers were to bring their wool to be stored in the mill, and they were to be paid in cloth or in knitting thread for home work, or in wool prepared for the spinning-wheel. These bold reactionary ideas did not shipwreck the industry of Laxey homespuns. Moreover they are only retrograde at first sight. For they open mysterious vistas into the coming age; and when Ruskin tells us that all industry is to borrow its motor-force from the winds and rivers, the question suggests itself whether this æstheticist has not found in his dreams a formula for all future mechanics, to be applied as soon as the huge latent power of the rivers and winds, subdued and diverted in the form of electricity, shall be pressed into the service not only of the riverside folk and mountaineers, but of the whole world.[1]

And if outside among the indifferent multitude Ruskin strenuously sought to make public life conform to æsthetical laws, even more strenuously would he endeavour to make his own life conform to those laws. He is none of those priests, who, to use his own expression, "go and dine with the rich and preach to the poor." At Brantwood, his home on Coniston Lake, he devised a very costly reclamation of land in order to entice the peasants away from the toil of towns which degraded while it attracted them. He himself set the example of muscular labour by building a little port on the lake with some of his disciples in the intervals of translating Xenophon, and by repairing with his pupils at Oxford a road near Hinksey. No laughter deterred these strange road-makers who broke more pickaxes and took more time than any ordinary labourers would have done. The master himself took lessons in carpentering and in housepainting, in some of which phases he resembles Tolstoi, of whom he said: "He will be my successor," and who in his turn said of Ruskin, "He is one of the greatest men of this century." Pursuing his contest with machinery to the bitter end, he

[1] The above account does not seem to agree in all details with that of Mr. George Thomson, given in the Appendix to this volume.

banished gas from his house, and opposed with all his might the introduction of a railroad to Ambleside through the picturesque country of the Lakes in which he lived. The hatred of steam inspired him with startling arguments. Do you wish to know, he cries to his fellow-citizens, what is the purpose of a railway? Here it is:

"The Town of Ulverstone is twelve miles from me, by four miles of mountain road beside Coniston lake, three through a pastoral valley, five by the sea-side. A healthier or lovelier walk would be difficult to find. In old times, if a Coniston peasant had any business at Ulverstone, he walked to Ulverstone; spent nothing but shoe-leather on the road, drank at the streams, and if he spent a couple of batz when he got to Ulverstone, 'it was the end of the world.' But now he would never think of doing such a thing! He first walks three miles in a contrary direction to a railroad station, and then travels by railroad twenty-four miles to Ulverstone, paying two shillings fare. During the twenty-four miles' transit, he is idle, dusty, stupid; and either more hot or cold than is pleasant to him. In either case he drinks beer at two or three of the stations, passes his time between them, with anybody he can find, in talking without having anything to talk of; and such talk always becomes vicious. He arrives at Ulverstone, jaded, half-drunk, and otherwise demoralised, and three shillings, at least, poorer than in the morning."

If the Master did not allow the train to carry his

II. ACTION

person he did not even use it to transport his books, if anywise that might be helped. The volumes that his publisher sent from the publishing house at Orpington to his house in London travelled by road.

With Ruskin action follows speedily upon the idea. His watchword is—To-day. He writes as he fights, to obtain results—evident—immediate—decisive. The first thing that a visitor observes on entering the National Gallery in London is the crystalline sheen on the pictures there, and he will quickly see that all are under glass, like water-colours. The smoky atmosphere of London renders this precaution necessary, but it was not adopted until Ruskin had suggested it in a letter to the *Times* in 1845. Another striking point is the extraordinary wealth of pictures by Early Italian Masters. Five rooms devoted to the Schools of Siena and Florence contain pictures of exquisite purity by Botticelli, Filippo Lippi, Benozzo Gozzoli, Perugino, Ghirlandajo, Pinturicchio, whereas our gallery in the Louvre gives us nothing like the same opportunities of study. Now in 1845 the London collection possessed very few examples of these masters; but there to-day is the answer to Ruskin's cry of reproach when he returned from Italy. Still more in the Turner Room do we perceive the triumphant success of his campaign in favour of the great painter of landscape; and if we descend to the basement where are preserved the drawings and water-colours, down to the slightest sketches, from the same hand as *Dido at Carthage*, we shall understand that

Modern Painters was not published in vain. Nor in vain were written the *Stones of Venice* and the *Seven Lamps of Architecture*, for English architecture has, largely owing to their influence, been entirely transformed since those books appeared. A sober Gothic, gay Dutch colouring and a picturesque variety has succeeded to the pseudo-Greek style. The architects of the Oxford Museum, Sir Thomas Dean and Mr. Woodward, complied expressly with the precepts of Ruskin, in that they allowed the workmen to design the details of the ornamentation themselves, to decorate in their own fashion the capitals and the spandrils; and designs of English fern, which show the inexperience but also the independence of the stonecutter, replace 'ready-made' *acanthi* of the classic style. It was at Oxford too that a group of young and enthusiastic artists tried, under the direction of Ruskin, to paint in fresco the library of the Union Debating Society. Time has since destroyed these experiments, made under bad material conditions, but it was not therefore all in vain that the Master of the *Laws of Fiésole* animated with his holy fire men like Dante Rossetti, William Morris, Munro, Millais, Hunt, Woolner, Prinsep, and Burne-Jones. All those among this group, who were then unknown, have since made their name, and the note of enthusiasm sounded at that time by Ruskin vibrates still, though the colours on the walls of the Union have long since faded away.

His disciples do him honour. One of them, M.

II. ACTION

Giacomo Boni, has undertaken the preservation of monuments in Italy, and administers his trust according to the precepts of Ruskin. From the latter's drawing-classes for adults have come artists of all sorts, engravers, draughtsmen, decorators, woodcarvers, such men as George Allen, W. H. Hooper, Arthur Burgess, Bunney, E. Cooke, W. Ward, who continue up to the present time to aid the Master with their labours. The early pre-Raphaelites whom he defended have triumphed. The neo-pre-Raphaelites, like Burne-Jones, whom he encouraged from the beginning, are above the fluctuations of opinion and have taken their place, so to speak, in history. Two of the landscape painters he most praised, Hook and Brett, are certainly among the first, if not quite the first, of their country. It may be boldly stated that at least one half of the higher art of our day in England is due to Ruskin, thanks as much to his immense authority over artists as to his enormous influence upon the public. Great artistic energy cannot produce great art unaided; there must be amateurs to admire, to encourage, to understand, and, if one dare say the word, to support it. Ruskin multiplied these amateurs by the hundred. He taught his countrymen to appreciate Nature, to look at and to love pictures. Even his enemies cannot deny this. Long ago Miss Brontë wrote: "I have lately been reading *Modern Painters*, and have derived from the work much genuine pleasure, and, I hope, some edification; at any rate it has made me feel how ignorant I had previously been on the subjects which it treats. Hitherto I have had only instinct to guide me in judging of art; I feel now as if I had been walking blindfold—this book seems to give me new eyes." And not Miss Brontë alone says so, but all those in England who in the last forty years have learnt that "a thing of beauty is a joy for ever."

Although he has not succeeded, as he hoped, in reinstating Beauty as a factor in national life, he has by aiming over-high succeeded none the less in attaining certain ends. For instance in 1854 he penned a vigorous diatribe against the Crystal Palace, "this cucumber frame with two chimneys," and in censuring the expenditure on the new architecture in glass and iron he suggested a society for the preservation of old stone monuments. The Crystal Palace was not destroyed, but the proposed society was founded. In like manner if engines have not been pulled to pieces nor railroads destroyed, England has learnt that a landscape has a value merely for the pleasure it gives to the eye, and that a picturesque oasis may be a source of wealth. So much so that once a few years ago artists were summoned to give evidence before a committee of the House of Lords as to whether a certain valley would be disfigured, by a projected railroad. If all the rich people in England have not sold their London houses in order to take up their abode in and restore old palaces of Verona, at least one, whose name is great in poetry, realised at Venice the dream of the great æstheticist. Finally the Ruskinian propaganda in favour of picturesque costumes and the masques of olden time has not failed as completely as might be supposed. Any one who asks permission to enter the Girls' College of Whitelands in Chelsea on the first of May will find the chapel and the hall decorated with flowers, flowers sent by old pupils from all parts of England; for the return of Spring is celebrated on that day. One-hundred-and-fifty pupils, assembled in the hall, have elected by ballot a Queen of May. She is chosen not for her beauty, or for her learning, but because she is beloved. Here she comes! Her companions form a double row and hold out palms, which arch over her head as she passes. She is crowned with flowers, dressed in an archaic costume designed by Kate Greenaway, and decorated with a golden cross designed by Burne-Jones. Behind her walks the Queen of the past year, her head wreathed with forget-me-nots. She mounts her throne and her companions pass in front of her to salute and receive their presents, which are no other than the works of Ruskin, beautifully bound. You may almost hear these clustering flowers murmur together the words written in the pages of *Sesame and Lilies:* "And whether consciously or not, you must be in many a heart enthroned: there is no putting by that crown; queens you must always be; queens to your lovers; queens to your husbands and your sons; queens of higher mystery to the world beyond, which bows itself and will ever bow, before the myrtle crown, and the stainless sceptre of womanhood. But it is little to say of a woman, that she only does not destroy where she passes. She should revive; the harebells should bloom, not stoop, as she passes." The prizes are distributed after no competition, for the Master holds rivalry in horror. The Queen disposes of them by right of her sovereignty, to this one because she is faithful to her friends, to that one because she delights in music, to that other because she is always merry, to this last because the Queen loves her well. And it is especially charming, writes a witness, to see the Queen's grateful smile when a special friend passes by and kisses her hands on receiving the book. The praises of the King Eternal sung at chapel in the morning have preceded this homage to the Queen of a day. And in the evening if she, who has received as a prize the Ruskin Birthday-Book, should open it at the first day of May, she will find there, not as in the socialist newspapers recriminations against the law of daily toil, but these words of the Master: "If, resolutely, people do what is right, in time they come to like doing it."

Doubtless it will be said that this insignificant protest of a remote school in London against the apathy of the mass and the ugliness of all things is but of little moment. But of the pupils in this school, who are all educated to be teachers, already more than one has instituted in her village Ruskin's æsthetical festival. The wreaths of flowers may fade, but the seed sown ten years ago will blossom afar off, even in Ireland, and each first of May will bring before this little band of disciples, visions, not of gloomy meetings where black-coated doctrinaires preach a doctrine of "Union against Labour," as in M. Béraud's picture of *La Salle Graffard*, but of a day of peace and joy and bright garments, when no socialistic creeds are proclaimed but the gospel of Nature, whose firstfruits gathered in spring are due to the long hard dark travail of winter—Nature, whose lessons are not those of idleness, but of toil, not of revolt against human laws, but of obedience to those divine laws, which we may disown but we cannot disobey.

CHAPTER III

EXPRESSION

THE man who has accomplished these things, smiles even in his sorrow, is sympathetic even when he tyrannises, and noble even when he hates. We have seen him standing in ecstasy, like one of Fra Angelico's angels, in a meadow-land dazzled by the flowers of the field; and we have seen him in battle, his muscles braced like one of Michael Angelo's figures withstanding the onslaught of a multitude. Let us now examine him as we might examine a portrait by Holbein of a face in repose, so tranquil that we can count the faintest wrinkles, so clear that we may follow every line of their maze. Perhaps in considering him in his private life, in his immediate and personal surrounding, we shall find that Dante might have said of him also:—

> "And if the world knew his heart,
> After having praised him much
> It would have praised him yet more."

But the world knew it not. Vexed by his militant enthusiasm, it has taxed him with intolerance, and annoyed with his child-like joy at being his own personal witness to those beauties and truths which

III. EXPRESSION

he proclaimed, it has called him presumptuous. Ruskin's enthusiasm for these truths, as they were borne in upon him one by one, it calls contradictory, his admiration for all great work it calls inconstancy, his zeal it calls tyranny, his generosity it calls egoism. The word which most correctly and comprehensively describes all these characteristics and explains Ruskin—the quality which forms the third great feature of his personality—is outspoken sincerity and frankness, or, as he himself terms it from its old derivation, Franchise.

"To be ἐλεύθερος, *liber* or *franc*, is first to have learned to rule our own passions; and then, certain that our own conduct is right, to persist in that conduct against all resistance, whether of counter-opinion, or counter-pain, or counter-pleasure. To be defiant alike of the mob's thought, of the adversary's threat, and the harlot's temptation,—this is in the meaning of every great nation to be free; and the one condition upon which that freedom can be obtained is pronounced to you in a single verse of the 119th Psalm, 'I will walk at liberty, for I seek Thy precepts.'" This rugged and independent frankness towards others made him sometimes lose all sense of proportion and forget all politeness. When some one told him that he had been much interested in his writings he answered shortly, " I don't care whether they have interested you; have they done you any good?" He answered in French to a lady president of the Society for the Emancipation of Women who asked for his countenance, "You are nothing but a set of fools in this matter." He wrote to the students of Glasgow who offered to nominate him for the Rectorship of the University in opposition to Mr. Fawcett and the Marquis of Bute, but begged of him a statement of his political ideas,—at least so much that they might know whether he was for Mr. Disraeli or Mr. Gladstone—"What in the devil's name have you to do with either Mr. Disraeli or Mr. Gladstone? You are students at the University, and have no more business with politics than you have with ratcatching. Had you ever read ten words of mine (with understanding) you would have known that I care no more either for Mr. Disraeli or Mr. Gladstone than for two old bagpipes with the drones going by steam, but that I hate all Liberalism as I do Beelzebub, and that, with Carlyle, I stand, we two alone now in England, for God and the Queen." Just what he thinks he boldly states, without heeding the effect, and without consideration for his own admirers. A clergyman, who had run into debt by building a church at Richmond, appealed to Ruskin for money. He wrote to him:—

"BRANTWOOD, CONISTON, LANCASHIRE,
May 19*th*, 1886.

"SIR,—I am scornfully amused at your appeal to me, of all people in the world, the precisely least likely to give you a farthing. My first word to all men and boys who care to hear me is, 'Don't get into debt. Starve and go to heaven—but don't borrow. Try first begging,—I don't mind, if it is really needful, stealing. But don't buy things you can't pay for.'

"And of all manner of debtors, pious people building

churches they can't pay for are the most detestable nonsense to me. Can't you preach and pray behind the hedges—or in a sand-pit—or a coal-hole—first?

"And of all manner of churches thus idiotically built, iron churches are the damnablest to me. And of all the sects of believers in any ruling spirit—Hindoos, Turks, Feather-idolaters, and Mumbo-Jumbo, Log and Fire-worshippers, who want churches, your modern English Evangelical sect is the most absurd, and entirely objectionable and unendurable to me. All of which they might very easily have found out from my books—any other sort of sect would!—before bothering me to write it to them. Ever, nevertheless, and in all this saying, your faithful servant,

"JOHN RUSKIN."

This is the abrupt side of his frankness, where spring more briars and brambles than beneficent and nourishing herbs. But we may observe that the Master did not spare himself any more than he spared others. Often in *Præterita* he speaks of the "follies and absurdities" of his youth: he derides his own pompous style in *Modern Painters*, and the period when, if he had to tell any one their house was on fire, he would not have said, "Sir, your house is on fire," but "Sir, the abode in which I presume you passed the days of youth is in a state of inflammation." He boldly reprints his writings, mutilated, in confession of his errors, and having spoken of Mr. Gladstone, whom he scarcely knew, with the audacity which was usual to him, he suppressed the violent sentences in the next edition, and left a blank space in record of his unjust judgment. He does no more than justice to himself and also to the futility of literature. In 1870, when his friends entreated him to write to the King of Prussia and beg him to divert his guns from those Gothic cathedrals of France which he was wont to admire most in the world, he refused, calling his friends "vain persons who imagine that a writer has any power of intercession" with a sovereign so little sentimental as he of Germany. Nevertheless he subscribed largely to the famine fund in Paris with Archbishop Manning, Sir John Lubbock, and Professor Huxley. The moment that it struck him that criticism of art cannot seriously improve the art of a country, nor even improve the character of any but the most mediocre works, he did not pause to reflect that such an avowal could be turned against himself, and against the thirty volumes into which he had put all his life, but loudly proclaimed what he had just discovered. "You sent for me to talk to you of art; and I have obeyed you in coming. But the main thing I have to tell you is—that art must not be talked about. The fact that there is talk about it at all, signifies that it is ill done, or cannot be done. No true painter ever speaks, or ever has spoken much of his art. The greatest speak nothing." Here we have one of those frequent sentences of his which have seemed inconsistent, and which have caused the Master of the *Stones of Venice* to be considered a Bonghi or a Chamberlain

III. EXPRESSION

in art criticism. Certainly he has contradicted himself, for the simple reason that he has thought differently on the same subject at different times. We all do that, but we do not all say we do it, and moreover, we do not generally rush into print at fifteen, and few of us at sixty-eight write with our mental vigour unimpaired. Ruskin was in haste to write his thoughts without reservation, and he was still thinking even as he wrote. He did not wait to write until certain that his views were finally formed, even as later he did not stop writing when he found that they were still fluid. Wherever he thought to find a fresh light he advanced towards it, and having sometimes gone forward without prudence he has come back without shame, having only one thing in view, namely Truth. Where his armour is weak, the armour of many another author would be weak equally had he the same sincerity. In thought every one of us is inconsistent; let us not blame Ruskin overmuch if he is inconsistent also in utterance.

But his "franchise" did him good service when it opened his eyes to all the wretchedness which lies below the ivory tower of the dilettante and the æsthete, and pointed out his plain duty to descend and offer help. We have seen his sincerity lead him to diatribe; now let us see it lead him to charity. Being during March 1863 in the Alps at Mornex, Ruskin in that splendid and restful scenery examined his conscience and asked himself if he had the right to gratify in peace his passion for nature. He wrote to a friend: "The loneliness is very great; and the peace in which I am at present is only as if I had buried myself in a tuft of grass on a battlefield wet with blood—for the cry of the earth about me is in my ears continually. . . . I am still very unwell, and tormented between the longing for rest and lovely life, and the sense of this terrific call of human crime for resistance, and of human misery for help." Then he tears himself away from his egotistical contemplation, calling to mind that there are at least as many peasants as painters in a landscape. He would look no longer at Turner, but would read the economists; and he found them ridiculous with their universal optimism, and even went to Manchester itself to deliver a vehement onslaught on the theory of *laissez-faire* and *laissez-passer*. And he wrote *Fors Clavigera*, a monthly letter to artisans of all classes, and developed therein his gospel of society. But he is not one of those who think to speak is to act. He admitted loyally that he was wrong, to give advice instead of example, and proceeded forthwith to found and endow St. George's Guild, to give Miss Octavia Hill houses for working men's dwellings, and to subscribe everywhere to special schemes. And the searching sincerity which with him knows no bounds finds vent in vigorous words: "I am trying to reform the world," said he one day in his rooms at Oxford to one of his friends, "and I suppose I ought to begin with myself. I am trying to do St. Benedict's work, and I ought to be a saint. And yet I am living between a Turkey carpet

III. EXPRESSION

and a Titian, and drinking as much tea" (taking his second cup of tea) "as I can swig."

"This is just what we feel ourselves," writes to him a lady admirer. "I will join St. George's Guild whenever you join it yourself. Above all things, you urge our duties to the land, the common earth of our country. You speak of the duty of acquiring, if possible, and cultivating the smallest piece of ground. But (forgive the question), where is your house and your garden? I know you have got places, but you do not stay there. Almost every month you date from some new place, a dream of delight to me; and all the time I am stopping at home, labouring to improve the place I live at, to keep the lives entrusted to me. And when I read your reproaches, and see where they date from, I feel as a soldier freezing in the trenches before Sebastopol might feel at receiving orders from a general who was dining at his club in London. Again I agree with you in your dislike of railways, but I suspect you use them, and sometimes go on them. *I never do.* You see you are like a clergyman in the pulpit in your books; you can scold the congregation, and they cannot answer; behold the congregation begins to reply."

The prophet did not flinch from this sharp attack. He inserted the letter of the recalcitrant member in the next number of *Fors* and answered it. "She tells me first that I have not joined the St. George's Company, because I have no home. It is too true. But that is because my father, and mother, and nurse, are dead;

because the woman I hoped would have been my wife is dying; and because the place where I would fain have stayed to remember all of them, was rendered physically uninhabitable to me by the violence of my neighbours—that is to say by their destroying the fields I needed to think in, and the light I needed to work by. Thirdly my correspondent doubts the sincerity of my abuse of railroads, because she suspects I use them. I do so constantly, my dear lady; few men more. I use everything that comes within reach of me. If the devil were standing at my side at this moment, I should endeavour to make some use of him as a local black. The wisdom of life is in preventing all the evil we can, and using what is inevitable for the best purpose. I use my sicknesses for the work I despise in health; my enemies for the study of the philosophy of benediction and malediction; and railroads for whatever I find of help in them—looking always hopefully forward to the day when their embankments will be ploughed down again, like the camps of Rome, into our English fields." Sarcasm can hardly be deaf to such a cry of distress; but the Master has withheld nothing which could give support to the irrepressible sallies of his detractors.

It was to be his lot to direct this brilliant and penetrating force of observation into the recesses of his own heart, and conscience; into the home of all unacknowledged feelings and all unexpressed doubts, where all light wounds and where all wounds kill. It was to be his lot to apply it where analysis can be

III. EXPRESSION

least endured; to both Faith and Love. He has in *Præterita* dissected his first passion in terms cold and mordant as steel: "I wonder mightily now," he cries with the regret of a devotee, "what sort of a creature I should have turned out, if at this time love had been with me instead of against me; and instead of the distracting and useless pain, I had had the joy of approved love, and the untellable incalculable motive of its sympathy and praise," but loyal to the Eternal purpose he added at once: "It seems to me such things are not allowed in this world. The men capable of the highest imaginative passion are always tossed on the fiery waves by it; the men who find it smooth water and not scalding, are of another sort." Faith he still thought to possess, if not exactly that which he had gleaned from reading the Psalms in the orchard at Herne Hill, at any rate such as his admiration for George Herbert and the Vaudois had given him. He recollected that on one Sunday at Gap he had broken the Sabbath by climbing after church among his beloved mountains, and this victory of his passion for nature over his religious duty haunted him afterwards as a cruel memory. Twelve years later he took to drawing on Sundays. By degrees disgust with the narrowness of those sects which he had been taught to love, a clearer understanding of the æsthetical beauty of that catholicism which he had been taught to abhor, and the doubts which science sets in all our paths, plunged him in the agnosticism which Mallock, his disciple, has described in his *New Republic:* "Am I a believer? No, I am a doubter too. Once I could pray every morning, and go forth to my day's labour stayed and comforted. But now I can pray no longer. You have taken my God away from me, and I know not where you have laid Him." By a strange chance it was at the most acute moment of this perpetual but unavowed torture that love came to him and forced him to look with open eyes into himself, and to put his sincerity to a test which was most painful. He was at Oxford. A young lady, for whom his attachment was known, and who even passed as his betrothed, was dying. Her religious sentiments had revived during the last years of her life, and for some time past she had refused to entertain any further thought of marriage with an unbeliever. He asked to see her again. She sent "to ask him whether he could yet say that he loved God better than he loved her." Ruskin scanned his mind as closely as any sailor the horizon on a murky night, but no light showed him safety either on the shores of that Presbyterianism which he had just left, or on those of that catholic Christianity,[1] where some years later he was to find a haven. Loyally and bravely he answered No, and the door closed upon him.

The man who denounced his own weaknesses to himself so frankly did not hesitate to rejoice in his own work when it seemed to him good. His may not have been modesty as the hypocrites of society

[1] In the widest sense. It is clear that the Roman Catholic Church is not here included.

understand it, but modesty it was as we may understand it in him. Modesty for Ruskin does not consist in doubting his own capacity or in hesitating to maintain his own opinion, but in understanding aright the relation between what he is capable of and what others are capable of, and in measuring exactly and without exaggeration his own worth. For modesty is the "measuring virtue, the virtue of modes or limits. Arnolfo is modest when he says he can build a beautiful dome at Florence. Dürer also, who wrote to some one who found fault with his work, 'Sir, it cannot be better done,' for he was convinced of it, and to say anything else would have been a want of sincerity. Modesty is so pleased with other people's doings, that she has no leisure to lament her own; and thus, knowing the fresh feeling of contentment, unstained with thought of self, she does not fear being pleased, when there is cause, with her own rightness, as with another's, saying calmly: 'Be it mine, or yours, or whose else it may be, it is no matter;—this also is well.'" In writing these lines Ruskin intended to declare his opinion; he has succeeded in reproducing his personality. For no one was less greedy of admiration or more prodigal of encouragement. *Modern Painters* was respectfully dedicated not to a prince, not to a great writer, but to the "Landscape painters of England, by their sincere admirer." "Contrast his career as a critic," says Mr. Collingwood, "with that of other well-known men, the Jeffries and the Giffords, not to mention writers of a later date; and note that his error has been always to encourage too freely, not to discourage hastily." This characteristic will hardly perhaps commend Ruskin to such of our younger critics as are only too ready to score through and through with their pens the sum of an artist's lifelong labour; but they may well lay it to heart. If by any chance Ruskin believed himself in duty bound to chastise an artist, whose private character he honoured, he would chastise him, but at the same time write a private letter expressing sorrow, and an earnest hope that "this may make no difference to our friendship." Whereby he brought on himself the following reply from a certain artist: "My dear Ruskin, the first time I meet you I shall knock you down, but I hope that will make no difference to our friendship."

The fervour and the simplicity of his enthusiasm are equally proverbial. Every new artist whom he studies, every important book which he analyses, he desires his audience to accept as the greatest and the most perfect of all time, wholly oblivious that he has already assigned this unique throne to a hundred other such. At one time it was a pleasantry among the philistines of Oxford to ask the admirers of Ruskin who was "the greatest painter in the world" for the current day? "Yesterday it was Carpaccio. . . ." The professor would rave also about his pupils' works, attributing to them a thousand imaginary merits. For instance he announced that he had met a young American lady who could draw so admirably, that, having previously declared no woman could draw, he

III. EXPRESSION

was now tempted to believe that no one could draw but a woman. And the same day he discovered two young Italians so deeply imbued with the spirit of their Early Schools that "no hand like theirs had been put to paper since Lippi and Lionardo."

This enthusiasm vents itself sometimes in a comic outburst. The disdain of the Master for the instruction usually given in national schools may be easily conceived,—pedantic dogmatism without thought of promoting manual skill or exciting artistic taste in the workman! One day a mason, employed in building some addition to Brantwood, was in need of money and asked for an advance. Ruskin gave it and asked him to sign a receipt. Much hesitation and confusion followed this natural request, and at last the workman exclaimed in his own dialect: "Aa mun put maa mark!" He did not know how to write; upon which Ruskin sprang up, held out his two hands to the astonished mason and cried: "I am proud to know you! Now I understand why you are such a perfect workman."

Some of these unexpected and paradoxical features might almost lead one to imagine that the Master hid his real self behind a mask, and that his originality was a cloak in which he enveloped himself after the fashion of the "æsthetes," whom he considered personal enemies, and strongly and continuously condemned. It was nothing of the kind. His "franchise," while it led him into the most direct contradictions and the strangest exaggerations, preserved him from all affection. No man could have lived more simply than he the domestic life of a gentleman-farmer, a kind and courteous neighbour, keeping his ice-house cold and his hot-house hot, so as to give ice or grapes to the villagers when they needed it, but maintaining nothing in his costume, his manners, or his home that could surprise them,—no " æsthetic " affectation of dress, furniture, or architecture. He wore no slouch felt hat like William Morris nor carried in his hand the sunflower of a *Cyril* or of a *Vivian*. He wished everything to be beautiful but above all appropriate to its use. "Do not use golden ploughshares, nor bind ledgers in enamel. Do not thrash with sculptured flails: nor put bas-reliefs on millstones," said he to his disciples. He lived with the old mahogany furniture of his parents. He insisted that St. George's Mill at Laxey should be so solid and comfortable as thoroughly to fulfil its function as a mill, without any superfluous decoration. His own house at Brantwood is simple, ample, comfortable, adorned with creeping plants but devoid of any exquisiteness of style; nothing is in bad taste, but nowhere is a symptom of affectation.

His simple good-humour and personal modesty have struck all those who have had any intimacy with him. "I will tell you," writes Mr. James Smetham to a friend, after a visit to Denmark Hill, in 1858,—"that he has a large house with a lodge, and a valet, and footman and coachman, and grand rooms glittering with pictures, chiefly Turner's, and that his father and mother live with him, or he with them. His father is a fine old

III. EXPRESSION

gentleman, who has a lot of bushy grey hair, and eyebrows sticking up all rough and knowing, with a comfortable way of coming up to you with his hands in his pockets, and making you comfortable, and saying, in answer to your remark, that 'John's' prose works are pretty good. His mother is a ruddy, dignified, richly dressed old gentlewoman of seventy-five, who knows Chamouni better than Camberwell; evidently a good old lady, with the *Christian Treasury* tossing about on her table. She puts 'John' down and holds her own opinions, and flatly contradicts him; and he receives all her opinions with a soft reverence and gentleness that is pleasant to witness. I wish I could reproduce a good impression of 'John' for you, to give you the notion of his 'perfect gentleness and lowlihood.' He certainly bursts out with a remark, and in a contradictious way, but only because he believes it, with no air of dogmatism or conceit. He is different at home from that which he is in a lecture before a mixed audience, and there is a spiritual sweetness in the half-timid expression of his eyes; and in bowing to you, as in taking wine with (if I heard aright) 'I drink to thee,' he had a look that has followed me, a look bordering on tearful."

But in public lecturing he charmed his audience by that same sort of personal magnetism that made him so many friends amongst the London workmen and the peasants at Coniston. Look for instance at him in the professorial chair at Oxford in 1870. For some time past the room has been filled to overflowing, every corner carried by assault by students who have deserted the other classes or their luncheons or, what seems still more incredible, their cricket in order to hear him. They fill the windows, are standing even on the cupboards. Here and there are ladies, occasionally as numerous as the students, some of them Americans who have crossed the Atlantic to see the man whom Carlyle calls "the Ethereal Ruskin." The doors remain open, blocked by the crowd overflowing into the passage. Now the Master appears, and all Oxford receives him with acclamation. Those who have never seen him, raise themselves on tiptoe and catch glimpses of a tall thin figure accompanied, like a philosopher of Athens, by a train of disciples. This is not perhaps quite orthodox, but Ruskin seems to occupy the Chair of Heterodoxy. His thick hair is long and fair, his eyes are clear and blue and changing as a rippling sea, his mouth is fine, ironic, and more mobile than a resilient bow, his complexion is bright, and his eyebrows are strongly marked. The whole countenance speaks alike of enthusiasm and of sarcasm, reflecting equally the passion which burns or the contemplative habit which soothes, the face of a fighter and of a seer. He bows slightly and ceremoniously, recognises friends scattered in the audience, disposes around him a quantity of odd and whimsical articles, minerals, coins, drawings, photographs, his "diagrams," as he calls them, to be used in his demonstration; then he throws aside his long black professor's gown, and his academic character disappears with it. For now he wears a blue-skirted coat with large white cuffs, a spreading

III. EXPRESSION

"Gladstone" collar, and a voluminous blue cravat, his most distinctive mark; quite simply dressed, however, with quiet old-world elegance and neither rings nor trinkets.

He begins, and at first it seems as if a clergyman were preaching a sermon in the hall—for he is reading passages written with much care, marking his cadences, balancing his periods, restraining his gesture, and subduing his glance. Little by little, as he reads over his own words, he grows animated. Exaltation returns as on the day he wrote them. He forgets the dead pages which lie before him on the table and looks at the living faces of his listeners. Do they agree with him up till now? He cannot go on without knowing. He asks them, makes them lift their hands in sign of agreement, and, emboldened, he attacks the heart of his subject, improvises, pauses to show a diagram. It may be the head of a lion by a pseudo-classic sculptor with which he compares a tiger's head, drawn by Millais in the Zoological Gardens. At the incongruous sight there is loud laughter. But this is not enough, the Master must give a pictorial description of things; he lets himself go and loses all restraint. If he is speaking of birds he imitates those which fly and those which strut. If he would explain that the art of engraving is the art of scratching, he imitates the cat's use of its claws. The audience would howl down any one else, but it feels that here is a man speaking under the influence of an idea, not declaiming but crying aloud a truth which he has discovered but a moment ago. It is not of himself that he makes an exhibition but of his subject. He heaps observation on observation, he multiplies arguments. Botany, geology, exegesis, philology, all is good which serves to prove his thesis. Now he no longer pleads but prophesies, and those who are taking notes give up co-ordinating them. He has lost his thread but he has gained his audience. The confused succession of lucid and ingenious thoughts at once puzzles and enthrals. What is it—instinct? science? imposture? genius? Who can say? But we listen and delightedly follow this jolting jerking road, which is always winding and at each turn opens to us some new valley, some unexpected horizon. At last we seem to be near the summit; as we climb the view opens more and more, and amidst loud applause the lecture which began with microscopic details ends with a grand first principle. From the humble village hidden in the hollow of a valley our guide, with the edelweiss for his badge, has conducted us by a thousand windings to a lofty peak whence we may look out over all a world.

But one day the guide himself halted at the foot of the mountains he had so often ascended. And now let us look at the old man, whose voice resounds no longer in public, in his retreat at Brantwood, among the rocks and wild wood (*brant-wood*) on the edge of Coniston Lake, where he went to live after the death of his parents because nothing there could trouble his dreams: "Ruskin," writes Mrs. Thackeray Ritchie,

III. EXPRESSION

"seems to me less picturesque as a young man than now in his later days. Perhaps grey waving hair may be more becoming than darker locks, but the speaking earnest eyes that must have been the same, as well as the tones of that delightful voice, with its slightly foreign pronunciation of the 'r,' which seemed so familiar again when it welcomed us to Coniston long, long after. Meeting thus after fifteen years I was struck by the change for the better in him; by the bright, radiant, sylvan look which a man gains by living among woods and hills and pure breeze. . . . That evening, the first we ever spent at Brantwood, the rooms were lighted by slow sunset crosslights from the lake without. Mrs. Severn sat in her place behind a silver urn, while the master of the house, with his back to the window, was dispensing such cheer, spiritual and temporal, as those who have been his guests will best realise,—fine wheaten bread and Scotch cakes in many a crisp circlet and crescent, and trout from the lake, and strawberries such as grow only on the Brantwood slopes. Were these cups of tea only, or cups of fancy, feeling, inspiration? And as we crunched and quaffed we listened to a certain strain not easily to be described, changing from its graver first notes to the sweetest and most charming vibrations. . Who can ever recall a good talk that is over? You can remember the room in which it was held, the look of the chairs, but the actual talk takes wings and flies away. . . . The text was that strawberries should be ripe and sweet, and we munched and marked it then and there; that there should be a standard of fitness applied to every detail of life; and this standard, with a certain gracious malice, wit, hospitality, and remorselessness, he began to apply to one thing and another, to dress, to food, to books."

And already legends have grown up around the great charmer. It is said that one day he entered a jeweller's shop in London, and being recognised, all the precious stones were spread before him and he was begged to reveal their mysteries. And standing there in the midst of the listening ladies, the author of *Deucalion* spoke. He spoke with the knowledge of the Dwarf who stole the Rhine-gold but with the charm of the Rhine-maidens who guarded it. He told his hearers the secret of the ruby—in heraldry *gules*—which is the Persian rose, colour of love and joy, and of all life on earth, the flower from whose bud was modelled the alabaster box of precious ointment that the Magdalen poured over the feet of the Saviour. And the secret of the sapphire—in heraldry *azure*—which is the type of joy and love in heaven, a stone of one nature with the ruby but another colour. I will lay thy foundations with sapphires, says the Scripture. And the secret too of the pearl, which is the subduing of light, symbol of patience, colour of the dove that carries the news that the waters are abating—the *marguerite* in Norman heraldry—grey, an inferior colour in arms, but of great price—for humility opens the gates of Paradise, and we are told that though the walls are of jasper each door is a pearl. He told of the dark and gradual birth of gems in the depths of the earth or the sea, and then turning towards the fine ladies he spoke to them to this purpose :—

"Are we right in setting our hearts on these stones, loving them, holding them precious? Yes, assuredly, provided it is the stone we love, and the stone we think precious; and not ourselves we love, and ourselves we think precious. To worship a black stone, because it fell from heaven, may not be wholly wise; but it is half-way to being wise; half-way to worship heaven itself. Or, to worship a white stone because it is dug with difficulty out of the earth, and to put it into a log of wood, and say the wood sees with it, may not be wholly wise; but it is half-way to being wise; half-way to believing that the God who makes earth so bright, may also brighten the eyes of the blind. It is no true folly to think that stones see, but it *is* to think that eyes do not; it is no true folly to think that stones live, but it *is* to think that souls die; it is no true folly to believe that, in the day of the making up of jewels, the palace walls shall be compact of life above their corner-stone, but it *is* to believe that in the day of dissolution the souls of the globe shall be shattered with its emerald, and no spirit survive, unterrified, above the ruin. Yes, pretty ladies, love the stones, and take care of them; but love your own souls better, and take care of *them*, for the day when the Master shall make up His jewels."

Leaving words such as the jeweller's fair clients had never heard at rout or ball yet ringing in their ears, the prophet was gone. He had marched off to a pastry-cook's, where still he talked on while he lunched, and those present left their sandwiches and their buns and grouped themselves silently about him to receive the spiritual food which he was pleased to dispense.

So tradition will have it that he taught not only in the synagogues, but also in the public places in the midst of profane life and vulgar cares. It tells us also that he appeared suddenly wherever there was an artist soul to be comforted, or a flame of enthusiasm to be kept alight. One morning in the Louvre two diligent readers of his works, who had never seen him, were standing before the *Walk to Emmaus* which one of them was endeavouring to copy. An old man approached and entered into conversation, and speaking of the picture of Rembrandt, confessed that he had once copied it himself. He grew excited, renewed his youth in recollection of the heroic days of art, and a gleam which thrilled the two disciples passed across his eyes. He invited them to breakfast at his hotel, and only in the breaking of bread did they discover that they were in the presence of the Master. It was Ruskin. And surely they said to each other as they went away, like the pilgrims in the old picture they were looking at two hours before, "did not our hearts burn within us while he talked with us," and opened to us the Holy Gospel of Art?

It is related also that one night at Rome Ruskin

III. EXPRESSION

dreamed that he had become a Franciscan monk, and that he had devoted himself to that great community which he had extolled in his chapter on Santa Croce. A little while after this dream, as he was going up the steps of the Pincio, he was accosted by an old beggar sitting on the steps. He gave him alms and was about to continue his way when the beggar seized his hand and kissed it. Ruskin bent over and embraced the old man. The next day the latter, with tears in his eyes, came to see him in all his rags, and begged him to accept a precious relic, a piece of brown cloth which he assured him had belonged to the robe of St. Francis. Was not this the saint himself, says a biographer, who appeared to one who had learned of him to interpret the voices of Nature? Be that as it may, Ruskin remembered his dream and went at once on a pilgrimage to the convent of the saint at Assisi, dreaming of great things to be done. But he found Assisi haymaking, so in the end he also made hay.

He could have chosen no more fitting patron-saint, and we can compare him to no purer model. Like St. Francis, Ruskin has performed some very pretty miracles. He made his philosophy heard not indeed of the birds but of smart ladies—perhaps the greater feat. He caused no roses to spring in the snow, but he grafted on cold British souls rosy flowers of enthusiasm upon which one chances still. He did not order the seasons, but once, when he had asked the painters to paint apple-trees in bloom, the walls of an

Academy were apple-blossom from end to end. Such at any rate are the tales, and the tender recollection that the Master has left with some, the rapturous smiles he has called to the lips of others, have perhaps given rise to many such legends. Be that as it may, it is in any case not the common lot even for great men to be veiled, while yet alive, in the gracious cloud of legend; and only on the highest summits for the most part are the mists wont to gather.

Will not this "Old-Man of Coniston," think you, loom loftier yet when death has added her supreme and holy darkness to the profane mists of fiction? It may be then that the countless tourists for whom Ruskin has made bread of the stones of Venice, and flowers of the jewels of Pallas Athene, will bethink them to visit the shrine, where he lived who woke so many souls to life, and where shone the fire whence so many torches took their flame. It may be also that those very railroads, which he fought so obstinately, will bring worshippers of the Beautiful from all parts of the world. And even it may be that if ugliness eventually should triumph, as everything seems to augur, with science for its accomplice and political economy for its ally, we shall deem this man but a hero of fable, who alone against all a world, fought not for Truth, who has her prophets, nor for Justice, who has her apostles, nor for Religion, who has her martyrs, but for an ideal that has had no other champion and perhaps will know no other victory—the ideal of the Beautiful.

PART II
HIS WORDS

PART II

HIS WORDS

OF the many surprises which Mr. Ruskin's personality occasions, none is greater than his popularity. A nineteenth-century philosopher, whose works are read by the masses, is not common clay. But when that philosopher happens also to be an æstheticist, works of art forming the subject or the pretext of his writings, the phenomenon is altogether amazing. For of all literature, art-criticism is by a strange irony just that on which authors like best to embark, but which readers most distrust, convinced as they have been by long and conclusive experience that they will find it to consist mostly in a superficial and pedantic verbiage. And if in order to explain to some extent the popularity of Ruskin's books and the charm they have even for women and children, we add that in reality they do not all deal with questions of art, but often also with the most stirring problems in public economy, the phenomenon becomes a miracle, and the explanation more strange than the fact.

The better to find a more satisfactory explanation, let us hear Ruskin's own words, and let us listen to these, moreover, not with the intention of discovering the guiding thought which runs through and co-ordinates them, but, for the moment, without system and at random, so as to detect the new processes, the manifold aspects, the hidden and devious ways of the method whereby Ruskin has inclined the least artistic people in the world towards æsthetical thought, and this religion of beauty. Let us mark them all, words alike of his twentieth year and words of his seventy-sixth year, words persuasive, words romantic, words passionate. Ruskin is at once man of letters, orator, and guide: and there are words of his that float back into the memory by the fireside in winter when the logs crackle on the hearth, words spoken to an audience thrilled by the inward excitement of the speaker, and again words to be read only at the foot of ancient monuments, on the steps of a campanile or the slope of a mountain, words to teach the truth, words to evoke the past,—words to charm the fancy, words to touch the heart and hold it spell-bound beneath a dome which but veils infinity, or by a tomb which hides but nothingness. . . . If we analyse some of these words we may perhaps come to understand why so many have listened to the voice.

CHAPTER I

ANALYSIS

THERE is a story that in 1851 some Scotch farmers, seeing in the windows of a bookshop a pamphlet entitled *Notes on the Construction of Sheepfolds*, by John Ruskin, and thinking to find some useful advice in the matter of herding sheep, expended two shillings and carried off the pamphlet. They found that they had purchased instead a theological thesis which inculcated the doctrine of "One Flock One Shepherd," and ended by expressing the hope that England might become a New Jerusalem.

Thus the very title of a work by Ruskin challenges attention and sets logic in disarray. The banner that he displays is equally splendid and incomprehensible. What more beautiful ensign than *Deucalion*, a title so concise that it serves as a telegraphic address for his publisher, what more beautiful than *Queen of the Air*, *Munera Pulveris*, *Love's Meinie*, the *Crown of Wild Olive*, *Sesame and Lilies*, *Aratra Pentelici*, *Ariadne Florentina*, *On the Old Road*, and *Our Fathers have told us*? But what less informing? Who can guess what will be found under these many-coloured flags that flutter in the wind? And if we pass to the descriptive sub-titles, what enlightenment shall we gain from those of *Sesame and Lilies*—I. "King's Treasuries," II. "Queen's Gardens," III. "The Mystery of Life and its Arts?" or from that of *Hortus Inclusus*—"The Message from the Wood to the Garden"? But because the human mind is averse to leaving a fact or a strange word unexplained, the key is sought and not infrequently found. Sometimes the significance of the title is vouchsafed by the preface, as in *Unto this Last;* sometimes we must wait till the last page, as in *Munera Pulveris;* here it is taken from an Ode of Horace and there from a Gospel parable. *S. Mark's Rest* is an allusion to the relics in the church at Venice, and *Love's Meinie*, an essay in ornithology, is owed to a verse of the *Roman de la Rose* where it is said of Love *il était tout couvert d'oisiaulx*. At other times the title is borrowed from an old Florentine engraving of the Labyrinth (*Ariadne Florentina*) and sometimes from a poem of Keats (*A Joy for Ever*). Ruskin himself felt how baffling some of his titles were, and tried to put his readers on the track. In *Fors Clavigera*—a series of monthly letters addressed to workmen from 1871 to 1884—there are three pages devoted to this thankless task, at the end of which one begins to realise that *Fors*, the root word of "Fortune," means "Destiny," that *Clavi-* means the *key* needed to open the door of Truth (*clavis*), as well as the *club* of Hercules needed to war against evil (*clava*) and the *helm* which keeps us in the course of life (*clavus*);

I. ANALYSIS

finally the *-gera* from *Gero* means "that which carries." But what is the use of all these etymologies? The titles of the works of a writer who is for ever championing Art against the modern social state are battle-cries. As long as they make themselves heard it does not signify what they mean. How many of those who rushed to the assault crying "Montjoie et Saint Denis!" knew the meaning of their cry?

If after scrutinising the flag we pass to the goods which it covers, we are not less outraged by their disorder than attracted by their riches. No coherent scheme, no consistent arrangement, at the utmost—"a tendency like the law of form in crystal."

"The subject which I want to bring before you is now branched and worse than branched, reticulated in so many directions that I hardly know which shoot of it to trace or which knot to lay hold of first." So Ruskin lays hold of everything at once, and at a bound you are in the heart of the subject. Stunned however by the shock, you do not exactly see what that subject is. Pitchforked into the midst of this vast display of ideas, you branch off in all directions, fearing to lose yourself and yet charmed to be rambling. There is no lack of guides or of labels. Ruskin uses these more than any other writer; each phrase is numbered, and Ruskinians say among themselves, "Do you remember Paragraph 25 of the 6th chapter, Volume II., *Stones of Venice?*" or perhaps, "Let us think over Paragraph 213 of *Aratra Pentelici.*" Everywhere there are partitions, divisions, compartments, which

would appear to divide the subjects one from another.
But put no faith in them. Some chapters are reprinted in several different volumes: there are others
which, anticipating those that follow or going back
on those that have preceded them, upset the whole
economy of the volume. "This," he acknowledges from
time to time, "belongs to another part of my subject."
His books are as entangled as our Budgets, and their
composition as perplexing as those time-tables which
forlorn travellers strive to unravel in the railway
stations.

"A friend in whose judgment I greatly trust, remon-
strated scornfully with me, the other day, on the de-
sultory character of Fors; and pleaded with me for the
writing of an arranged book instead. But he might as
well plead with a birch tree growing out of a crag, to
arrange its boughs beforehand. The winds and floods
will arrange them according to their wild liking; and
all that the tree has to do, or can do, is to grow gaily,
if it may be; sadly, if gaiety be impossible; and let the
black jags and scars rend the rose-white of its trunk
where Fors shall choose."

Certainly in his early works, *Modern Painters*,
Seven Lamps of Architecture, and *Stones of Venice*,
there is some perceptible attempt at composition even
if it is unskilful, and his materials are classified, if not
in order, at any rate with some kind of symmetry.
But after he has laid these mighty foundations of his
life's work all plan vanishes and his composition becomes wholly amorphous. At all seasons Ruskin will

I. ANALYSIS

speak to you of all subjects, "Of Many Things" indeed, as says the sub-title of a volume of *Modern Painters*, a title which excited no little amusement, but yet is the only one at all exact that he has assigned. If you expect a book of his to give any single connected thesis on a definite subject, if you have not made up your mind, ere opening it, to abandon all desire of logic and all instinct of classification, you had best not venture into the marvellous maze. *Sesame* would not serve to open the door, nor would *Ariadne* supply a guiding thread.

Within the maze we adventure ourselves nevertheless, because although the whole is confused, each particular idea to be distinguished therein shows clearer and sharper cut than in any ordinary treatise on Æsthetic. We are not invited to consider such axioms as the following: "The object of Art is to discover the Me in external objects," or Art is "the interpretation of the beauty of nature and the beauty of force by means of their most expressive signs;" nor are we asked to draw long deductions from the thought, "The Beautiful is the splendour of the True"—propositions which the reader is the more careful not to contest in that he does not in the least understand them. No. A simple and concrete thesis is advanced, for example this:—

"The art of Bellini is centrally represented by two pictures of Venice; one, the Madonna in the Sacristy of the Frari with two saints beside her, and two angels at her feet; the second, the Madonna with four saints, over the second altar of San Zaccaria.

"Observe respecting them—

"First, they are both wrought in entirely consistent and permanent material. The gold in them is represented by painting, not laid on with real gold. And the painting is so secure, that four hundred years have produced on it, so far as I can see, no harmful change whatever, of any kind.

"Secondly, the figures in both are in perfect peace. No action takes place except that the little angels are playing on musical instruments, but with uninterrupted and effortless gesture, as in a dream. A choir of singing angels by La Robbia or Donatello would be intent on their music, or eagerly rapturous in it, as in temporary exertion: in the little choirs of cherubs by Luini in the Adoration of the Shepherds, in the Cathedral of Como, we even feel by their dutiful anxiety that there might be danger of a false note if they were less attentive. But Bellini's angels, even the youngest, sing as calmly as the Fates weave.

"Let me at once point out to you that this calmness is the attribute of the entirely highest class of art: the introduction of strong or violently emotional incident is at once a confession of inferiority.

"Those are the two first attributes of the best art. Faultless workmanship, and perfect serenity; a continuous not momentary action. You are to be interested in the living creatures; not in what is happening to them.

"Then the third attribute of the best art is that it compels you to think of the spirit of the creature, and therefore of its face, more than of its body.

"And the fourth is that in the face, you shall be led to see only beauty or joy;—never vileness, vice, or pain.

"Those are the four essentials of the greatest art. I repeat them, they are easily learned.

" 1. Faultless and permanent workmanship.
" 2. Serenity in state, or action.
" 3. The Face principal, not the body.
" 4. And the Face free from either vice or pain."

We have here a clear thesis. Every reader knows what position he has to meet, what plastic practical results and what modifications of his judgment and future work the side he takes will entail. He foresees that Michael Angelo with his studies of outline, Raphael who sets on bodies so eloquent, heads so indifferent and so mute, Ribera with his anguished faces,—all these will be proscribed by this definition of great art; while on the contrary the primitives and certain artists of the earlier Renaissance will be ordained as models. And if so be he cares first and foremost for the movement of limbs displayed, for the human figure hurtling through space, for the telling effect of wrinkles, and the contraction of facial muscles, he will range himself against the æstheticist. But in so ranging himself against the latter's thesis he at any rate pays homage to his lucidity. For he can only dissent in that he has understood.

Having so understood he will follow easily when the professor of Fine Art, in order to defend his thesis, would take him still deeper into the subject, and, to make his own æsthetical impressions clear, shall disentangle them by analysis. For example the thesis in one of Ruskin's books is this, that the worst form of deceptive architecture is deception of handiwork, that is to say the substitution of castings fashioned by machinery for hand-made work. This deception is dishonest, he says. But why? Demand of yourself how it first impressed you—and you will learn.

"Ornament has two entirely distinct sources of agreeableness: one, that of the abstract beauty of its forms, which, for the present, we will suppose to be the same whether they come from the hand or the machine; the other, the sense of human labour and care spent upon it. How great this latter influence we may perhaps judge, by considering that there is not a cluster of weeds growing in any cranny of ruin, which has not a beauty in all respects *nearly* equal, and, in some, immeasurably superior, to that of the most elaborate sculpture of its stones: and that all our interest in the carved work, our sense of its richness, though it is tenfold less rich than the knots of grass beside it; of its delicacy, though it is a thousandfold less delicate; of its admirableness, though a millionfold less admirable; results from our consciousness of its being the work of poor, clumsy, toilsome man. Its true delightfulness depends on our discovering in it the record of thoughts, and intents, and trials, and heart-breakings—of recoveries and joyfulnesses of success; all this *can* be traced by a practised eye; but, granting it even obscure, it is presumed or understood; and in that is the worth of the thing, just as much as the worth of anything else we call precious. The worth of a diamond is simply the understanding of the time it must take to look for it before it is found; and the worth of an ornament is the time it must take before it can be cut. It has an intrinsic value besides, which the diamond has not; (for a diamond has no more real beauty than a piece of glass;) but I do not speak of that at present; I place the two on the same ground; and I suppose that the hand-wrought ornament can no more be generally known from machine work, than a diamond can be known from paste; nay, that the latter may deceive, for a moment, the mason's, as the other the jeweller's, eye; and that it can be detected only by the closest examination. Yet exactly as a woman of feeling would not wear false jewels, so would a builder of honour disdain false ornaments."

You will now understand how such and such a work appeals to you. But that is not enough. You must also understand the intention of him who created it. Not that you should assign to him ideas and feelings which in truth he had not—that Ruskin holds to be mere puerility though it was the outcome of all the energies of a whole school of criticism during fifty years. Rather you should seek by thorough study of the artist's works to determine simply to what end his effort was directed. In order that we may be convinced of the error of modern architects, who substitute machine work for the hand of man, Ruskin invites us to examine ourselves, and ourselves to give an exact account of our own feelings in presence of a work of art, in short, in a manner to make our æsthetical confession of faith. In order really to feel the greatness of the ancient artists—the Greek for instance—of their myths, and of their religious imaginings, there is something yet more difficult to be done—namely to reconstruct the psychology of their art. Ruskin compares the Greek to a child and asks himself what the child sees, what he seeks, what he desires, and of what he dreams.

"So far as I have myself observed, the distinctive character of a child is to live always in the tangible present, having little pleasure in memory, and being utterly impatient and tormented by anticipation: weak alike in reflection and forethought, but having an intense possession of the actual present, down to the shortest moments and least objects of it; possessing it, indeed, so intensely that the sweet childish days are as long as twenty days will be; and setting all the faculties of heart and imagination on little things, so as to be able to make anything out of them he chooses. Confined to a little garden, he does not imagine himself somewhere else, but makes a great garden out of that; possessed of an acorn-cup, he will not despise it and throw it away, and covet a golden one in its stead: it is the adult who does so. The child keeps his acorn-cup as a treasure, and makes a golden one out of it in his mind; so that the wondering grown-up person standing beside him is always tempted to ask concerning his treasures, not, 'What would you have more than these?' but 'What possibly can you see *in* these?' for, to the bystander, there is a ludicrous and incomprehensible inconsistency between the child's words and the reality. The little thing tells him gravely, holding up the acorn-cup, that 'this is a queen's crown,' or 'a fairy's boat,' and, with beautiful effrontery, expects him to believe the same. But observe — the acorn-cup must be *there*, and in his own hand. 'Give it me; then I will make more of it for myself.' That is the child's one word, always.

"It is also the one word of the Greek—'Give it me.' Give me *any* thing definite here in my sight, then I will make more of it."

The example is typical but it is as charming as it is clear; and these subtle psychological points, which the æstheticist raises to make himself better understood, greatly assist the reader to hear him to the end. Without wandering from his thesis, Ruskin has relieved its severity by introducing us to the simplest child's play and the most undogmatic talk. It no longer seems tiresome to delve deep into the underlying significance of the plastic product before us—on the contrary it amuses, the mind relieving the eye, and the understanding aiding the sensible impression. One wearies soon of seeing and admiring the purely external aspect of things without knowledge of their

F

structure, of their history, of their functions, or of their symbolism. If you have spent hours on the sea-shore and watched the coming and going of ships, yachts or merchant craft, fishing boats or coasters, admiring ignorantly these common things and involuntarily following them with your eyes, you will not reject the teacher who whispers in your ear the cause of all this unreasoned admiration and involuntary sympathy.

"The boat's bow is naïvely perfect: complete without an effort. The man who made it knew not he was making anything beautiful, as he bent its planks into those mysterious, ever-changing curves. It grows under his hand into the image of a sea-shell; the seal, as it were, of the flowing of the great tides and streams of ocean stamped on its delicate rounding. He leaves it when all is done, without a boast. It is simple work, but it will keep out water. And every plank thenceforward is a Fate, and has men's lives wreathed in the knots of it, as the cloth-yard shaft had their deaths in its plumes.

"Then, also, it is wonderful on account of the greatness of the thing accomplished. No other work of human hands ever gained so much. Steam-engines and telegraphs indeed help us to fetch, and carry, and talk; they lift weights for us, and bring messages, with less trouble than would have been needed otherwise; this saving of trouble, however, does not constitute a new faculty, it only enhances the powers we already possess. But in that bow of the boat is the gift of another world. Without it, what prison wall would be so strong as that 'white and wailing fringe' of sea. What maimed creatures were we all, chained to our rocks, Andromeda-like, or wandering by the endless shores, wasting our incommunicable strength, and pining in hopeless watch of unconquerable waves? The nails that fasten together the planks of the boat's bow are the rivets of the fellowship of the world. Their iron does more than draw lightning out of heaven, it leads love round the earth."

Should you be among mountains where the flora is rich and varied, and at each step, in retired nooks, on high uplands, in clefts of chalky rocks, in damp combes and in long water-courses, you come upon blossoms for which the dull labels of horticultural exhibitions have no name, you will wish not only to see, but also to know; and if to the pure artist there is indeed a charm in walking amongst plants and flowers, knowing only that they are lovely, just as one may pass through a reception-room full of unknown beauties, the average passer-by nevertheless likes to find out something about them. And amongst all these beauteous anonyms he will regret that there is no botanist at hand to give him the name of their outward aspects, and the ideas instinct in their forms. For the eye is already sated with pleasure long-drawn-out, and the flower will drop from the listless hand if there be nothing for the intelligence to work upon. But in the nick of time the historian appears from under the shadow of a rock and takes up his parable.

"No tribes of flowers have had so great, so varied,

or so healthy an influence on man as this great group of Drosidæ, depending not so much on the whiteness of some of their blossoms, or the radiance of others, as on the strength and delicacy of the substance of their petals; enabling them to take forms of faultless elastic curvature, either in cups, as the crocus, or expanding bells, as the true lily, or heath-like bells, as the hyacinth, or bright and perfect stars, like the star of Bethlehem, or, when they are affected by the strange reflex of the serpent nature which forms the labiate group of all flowers, closing into forms of exquisitely fantastic symmetry in the gladiolus. Put by their side their Nereid sisters, the water-lilies, and you have in them the origin of the loveliest forms of ornamental design, and the most powerful floral myths yet recognised among human spirits, born by the streams of Ganges, Nile, Arno, and Avon.

"For consider a little what each of those five tribes has been to the spirit of man. First, in their nobleness; the Lilies gave the lily of the Annunciation; the Asphodels, the flower of the Elysian fields; the Irids, the fleur-de-lys of chivalry; and the Amaryllids, Christ's lily of the field: while the rush, trodden always under foot, became the emblem of humility. Then take each of the tribes, and consider the extent of their lower influence. Perdita's 'The crown imperial, lilies of all kinds,' are the first tribe; which, giving the type of perfect purity in the Madonna's lily, have, by their lovely form, influenced the entire decorative design of Italian sacred art; while ornament of war was continually enriched by the curves of the triple petals of the Florentine 'giglio,' and French fleur-de-lys; so that it is impossible to count their influence for good in the middle ages, partly as a symbol of womanly character, and partly of the utmost brightness and refinement of chivalry in the city which was the flower of cities."

From the very fields you step into a museum; as in many a small Italian township, for example, on the flowery hill of Fiesole or in the deserted island of Torcello; and from the growing corn, glowing in the sun, you pass immediately to chill and ancient stones, upon which even the mosses will no longer grow. These also at first appeal only to the eye. You admire the modelling, the relief, and the play of shadow, perhaps the graceful movement of a simple gesture, or the noble lines of multiplex folds, but unless you be truly a craftsman your attention will wander if your intellectual appetite be not excited. Those relics resting on the black marble pavements of chill halls in the British Museum, or standing in the niches of the German galleries of sculpture are so far from life! So scarcely do they touch the economy of the great world as we know it, its passions or its sorrows as we feel them, its pleasures as we love them. . . . But indeed they do touch it, says the æstheticist, as dropping his flowers, he lays a finger on the dull, cold stone, on the fragment of sculptured drapery, and calls from its inert body the idea which stirred it at birth.

"All noble draperies, either in painting or sculpture (colour and texture being at present out of our consideration), have, so far as they are anything more than necessities, one of two great functions: they are the exponents of motion and of gravitation. They are the most valuable means of expressing past as well as present motion in the figure, and they are almost the only means of indicating to the eye the force of gravity which resists such motion. The Greeks used drapery in sculpture for the most part as an ugly necessity, but availed themselves of it gladly in all representation of action, exaggerating the arrangements of it which express lightness in the material, and follow gesture in the person. The Christian Sculptors, caring little for the body, or disliking it, and depending exclusively on the countenance, received drapery at first contentedly as a veil, but soon perceived a capacity of expression in it which the Greek had not seen or had despised. The principal element of this expression was the entire removal of agitation from what was so pre-eminently capable of being agitated. It fell from their human forms plumb down, sweeping the ground heavily, and concealing the feet; while the Greek drapery was often blown away from the thigh. The thick and coarse stuffs of the monkish dresses, so absolutely opposed to the thin and gauzy web of antique material, suggested simplicity of division as well as weight of fall. There was no crushing nor subdividing them. And thus the drapery gradually came to represent the spirit of repose as it before had of motion, repose saintly and severe. The wind had no power upon the garment, as the passion none upon the soul; and the motion of the figure only bent into a softer line the stillness of the falling veil, followed by it like a slow cloud by drooping rain: only in links of lighter undulation it followed the dances of the angels.

"Thus treated, drapery is indeed noble; but it is an exponent of other and higher things. As that of gravitation, it has especial majesty, being literally the only means we have of fully representing this mysterious natural force of earth (for falling water is less passive and less defined in its lines). So, again, in sails it is beautiful because it receives the forms of solid curved surface, and expresses the force of another invisible element."

Such words extend our field of thought and open our horizon. To further the comprehension of a work of art, to detain us an instant longer before a detail in sculpture, Ruskin lays the whole physical world under contribution, as elsewhere the world of morals. Here in the fold and fall of drapery he sees the mysterious law which governs the stars, and there in the curve of a petal the flower which foreshadows a God. All scientific or moral ideas, accumulated during centuries, group themselves naturally round the object which he examines with us. For him more than for any one else "The sound of the Ocean is prison'd in a shell," and every grain of dust is a magic Sesame for the palace of Knowledge. He seems to possess some circular receptive apparatus like that used to take panoramic photographs. Wherever he places himself he discerns as a whole the harmony of natural phenomena and human sympathies: and into whatever chalice he gazes it reflects a universe of things on high.

From these simple comparisons is born a poetry, healthy, scientific, instructive. Ruskin neither invents nor creates nor discovers nor imagines; he does but link ideas together, pass rapidly from one point of view to others hitherto unperceived, and synthetises unsuspected sympathies. Taking up a central position where the conclusions of science, of art, of religion and philosophy converge, he puts these ideas into sudden communication as an electric circuit is closed by a touch—and lo! a flash! . . . What new force is this? Here were two ideas dormant without energy, instinct with no poetry. There is nothing new: simply these ideas, charged as they were with infinity, kiss, and lo! life, where once was but inert matter of thought. Carlyle wrote of Ruskin on the 19th of April 1861:—

"Friday last I was persuaded—in fact had inwardly compelled myself as it were—to a lecture of Ruskin's at the Institution, Albemarle Street. Lecture on Tree Leaves as physiological, pictorial, moral, symbolical objects. A crammed house, but tolerable even to me in the gallery. The lecture was thought to 'break down,' and indeed it quite did *as a lecture*; but only did from *embarras de richesses*—a rare case. Ruskin did blow asunder as by gunpowder explosions his leaf notions, which were manifold, curious, genial; and in fact I do not recollect to have heard in that place any neatest thing I liked so well as this chaotic one."

The truth is that with such a method as this chaos cannot be avoided, and the attention is exhausted at last by the ceaseless display of incongruous treasure. Ruskin, with his mania for appropriating all things, comes in the end to resemble the child in St. Augustine's story, who would have the sea to stay in a hole he was digging on the sea-shore. We weary of passing from one idea to another. Bidden evoke all science and all dogma, our intelligence satisfied and our memory replete, we resent a longer tension. We are overfeasted with ideas.

CHAPTER II

IMAGERY

AND here thought blossoms into imagery. . . . Just as Ruskin makes the reader understand so he makes him see, and the moment that, weary and wandering, we would steal away from dialectic, we are captive again through the imagination. In what at first sight seems to appeal to sense only, the æstheticist shows the intellectual element, and that usually held to be purely intellectual is now to be made perceptible by sense. He has transformed the visible imagery of the painters into ideas; he is going to transform the ideas of philosophers into visible imagery. He will demonstrate by way of narration, and paint by way of proof. If he pleads in favour of simple composition in a historical landscape, he is not content with telling you that "the impression is destroyed by a multitude of contradictory facts, and the accumulation, which is not harmonious, is discordant," and that the painter "who endeavours to unite simplicity with magnificence, to guide from solitude to festivity, and to contrast melancholy with mirth, must end by the production of confused inanity," and that because "there is a peculiar spirit possessed by every kind of scene; and

II. IMAGERY

although a point of contrast may sometimes enhance and exhibit this particular feeling more intensely, it must be only a point, not an equalised opposition. Every introduction of new and different feeling weakens the force of what has already been impressed, and the mingling of all emotions must conclude in apathy, as the mingling of all colours in white,"—which would be an interesting but abstract view of the question. He tests his artistic thesis by a concrete example, by a landscape which he has seen; and his argument is shot through with that splendid fleeting vision well known to those who have followed the Appian Way at nightfall.

"Perhaps there is no more impressive scene on earth than the solitary extent of the Campagna of Rome under evening light. Let the reader imagine himself for a moment withdrawn from the sounds and motion of the living world, and sent forth alone into this wild and wasted plain. The earth yields and crumbles beneath his foot, tread he never so lightly, for its substance is white, hollow, and carious, like the dusty wreck of the bones of men. The long knotted grass waves and tosses feebly in the evening wind, and the shadows of its motion shake feverishly along the banks of ruin that lift themselves to the sunlight. Hillocks of mouldering earth heave around him as if the dead beneath were struggling in their sleep; scattered blocks of black stone, four-square, remnants of mighty edifices, not one left upon another, lie upon them to keep them down. A dull purple, poisonous haze stretches level along the desert, veiling its spectral wrecks of massy ruins, on whose rents the red light rests like dying fire on defiled altars. The blue ridge of the Alban mount lifts itself against a solemn space of green, clear, quiet, sky. Watch-towers of dark clouds stand steadfastly along the promontories of the Apennines. From the plain to the mountains, the shattered aqueducts, pier beyond pier, melt into the darkness, like shadowy and countless troops of funeral mourners, passing from a nation's grave." "Let us, with Claude, make a few 'ideal' alterations in the landscape," says Ruskin, and the dissertation continues. Thenceforth the author's thought and the reader's attention have a picture before them which soothes and assists concentration. Just as the mysterious laws of nature and the moral necessities of life were not lost sight of in gazing upon the falling folds of a Greek tunic or the delicate workmanship of a Gothic mullion, so the picturesque aspect of things is not neglected when we follow pure æsthetics, history, and natural or social science. We are not forced to quit the kingdom of form and colour because we would enter that of ideas. Art need not be deserted because one enters on the study of man. For it is not alone the life of a picture that Ruskin has delineated, it is also a picture of life.

Here is such a picture of Venetian life at the end of the fifteenth century, or rather a view of Venice as Turner or Ziem would have imagined it. It comes up suddenly in the course of a comparison between two colourists, Giorgione and Turner. Ruskin wishes to show what influence the first impressions of childhood, the rich surroundings in which he lived, would have upon the eye and soul of a painter, and to emphasise his point he recalls this scene to those who might have forgotten it:—

"A city of marble, did I say? nay, rather a golden city, paved with emerald. For truly, every pinnacle and turret glanced or glowed, overlaid with gold, or bossed with jasper. Beneath, the unsullied sea drew in deep breathing, to and fro, its eddies of green wave. Deep-hearted, majestic, terrible as the sea,—the men of Venice moved in sway of power and war; pure as her pillars of alabaster, stood her mothers and maidens; from foot to brow, all noble, walked her knights; the low bronzed gleaming of sea-rusted armour shot angrily under their blood-red mantle-folds. Fearless, faithful, patient, impenetrable, implacable, —every word a fate—sate her senate. In hope and honour, lulled by flowing of wave around their isles of sacred sand, each with his name written and the cross graved at his side, lay her dead. A wonderful piece of world. Rather, itself a world. It lay along the face of the waters, no larger, as its captains saw it from their masts at evening, than a bar of sunset that could not pass away; but for its power, it must have seemed to them as if they were sailing in the expanse of heaven, and this a great planet, whose orient edge widened through ether. A world from which all ignoble care and petty thoughts were banished, with all the common and poor elements of life. No foulness, nor tumult, in those tremulous streets, that filled or fell, beneath the moon; but rippled music of majestic change, or thrilling silence. No weak walls could rise above them; no low-roofed cottage, nor straw-built shed. Only the strength as of rock, and the finished setting of stones most precious. And around them, far as the eye could reach, still the soft moving of stainless waters, proudly pure; as not the flower, so neither the thorn nor the thistle, could grow in the glancing fields. Ethereal strength of Alps, dreamlike, vanishing in high procession beyond the Torcellan shore; blue islands of Paduan hills, poised in the golden west. Above, free winds and fiery clouds raging at their will:—brightness out of the north, and balm from the south, and the stars of the evening and morning clear in the limitless light of arched heaven and circling sea.

"Such was Giorgione's school—such Titian's home."

All things naturally strike Ruskin as in relief, in perspective, distinguished as light or shade. The most abstract problems of social economy always present themselves to him in plastic and picturesque guise. To his eyes there is no machinery of life which cannot be composed as a picture, nor any international problem which is not to be resolved into a living drama played by actors whom he himself creates, tricks out forthwith and produces in the theatre of his imagination. If he attacks the useless and costly system of armed peace which obtains with the Great Powers of Europe, it is in this highly coloured trope :—

"Friends, I know not whether this thing be the more ludicrous or the more melancholy. It is quite unspeakably both. Suppose, instead of being now sent for by you, I had been sent for by some private gentleman, living in a suburban house, with his garden separated only by a fruit wall from his next door neighbour's; and he had called me to consult with him on the furnishing of his drawing-room. I begin looking about me, and find the walls rather bare; I think such and such a paper might be desirable—perhaps a little fresco here and there on the ceiling—a damask curtain or so at the windows. 'Ah,' says my employer, 'damask curtains, indeed! That's all very fine, but you know I can't afford that kind of thing just now!' 'Yet the world credits you with a splendid income!' 'Ah, yes,' says my friend, 'but do you know, at present I am obliged to spend it nearly all in steel-traps?' 'Steel-traps! for whom?' 'Why, for that fellow on the other side the wall, you know: we're very good friends, capital friends; but we are obliged to keep our traps set on both sides of the wall; we could not possibly keep on friendly terms without them, and our spring guns. The worst of it is, we are both clever fellows enough; and there's never a day passes that we don't find out a new trap, or a new gun-barrel, or something; we spend about fifteen millions a year each in our traps, take it altogether; and I don't see how we're to do with less.' A highly comic state of life for two private gentlemen! but for two nations, it seems to me, not wholly comic. Bedlam would be comic, perhaps, if there were only one madman in it; and your Christmas pantomime is comic, when there is only one clown in it; but when the whole world turns clown, and paints itself red with its own heart's blood instead of vermilion, it is something else than comic, I think."

These last words are not proper to a writer developing an idea; they would be those of a lunatic were their speaker not a painter. Occupied always with visual sensations, Ruskin passes without transition from the red of vermilion to the red colour of blood—because in colour there is no transition. His images, as successively he calls them up, warp and destroy his argument. He might say, parodying a well-known aphorism, "Cogito ergo sum, video ergo sum!"—We must see in order to think. To praise the inward life—what does that amount to? or the teaching that man does not profit sufficiently by the experience of ancient leaders of men and by the thought of great philosophers? To most of us it is nothing but an idea, to Ruskin it is a picture, a landscape animated with figures: "It is a drawing of Kirkby Lonsdale churchyard, and of its brook, and valley, and hills, and folded morning sky beyond. And unmindful alike of these, and of the dead who have left these for other valleys and for other skies, a group of schoolboys have piled their little books upon a grave, to strike them off with stones. So, also, we play with the words of the dead that would teach us, and strike them far from us with our bitter, reckless will; little thinking that those leaves which the wind scatters had been piled, not only upon a gravestone, but upon the seal of an enchanted vault—nay, the gate of a great city of sleeping Kings, who would awake for us, and walk with us, if we knew but how to call them by their names."

And what is the external life—ambition and ostentation, sounding praise and vanity of vanities, which we seek even at the price of our peace? Again it is a picture, a canvas touched by the hand of a master, where Ribera's awful shadows alternate with the irony of a Holbein and the terror of a Schöngauer:—

"My friends, do you remember that old Scythian custom, when the head of a house died? How he was dressed in his finest dress, and set in his chariot, and carried about to his friends' houses; and each of them placed him at his table's head, and all feasted in his presence? Suppose it were offered to you in plain words, as it *is* offered to you in dire facts, that you should gain this Scythian honour, gradually, while you yet thought yourself alive. Suppose the offer were this: You shall die slowly; your blood shall daily grow cold, your flesh petrify, your heart beat at last only as a rusted group of iron valves. Your life shall fade from you, and sink through the earth into the ice of Caina; but, day by day, your body shall be dressed more gaily, and set in higher chariots, and have more orders on its breast—crowns on its head, if you will. Men shall bow before it,

G

stare and shout round it, crowd after it up and down the streets; build palaces for it, feast with it at their tables' heads all the night long; your soul shall stay enough within it to know what they do, and feel the weight of the golden dress on its shoulders, and the furrow of the crown-edge on the skull;—no more. Would you take the offer, verbally made by the death-angel? Would the meanest among us take it, think you? Yet practically and verily we grasp at it, every one of us, in a measure; many of us grasp at it in its fulness of horror. Every man accepts it, who desires to advance in life without knowing what life is; who means only that he is to get more horses, and more footmen, and more fortune, and more public honour, and—*not* more personal soul. He only is advancing in life, whose heart is getting softer, whose blood warmer, whose brain quicker, whose spirit is entering into Living [1] peace."

Let us turn several pages: the sombre vision has vanished. From the psychology of ambition we have passed to the psychology of the woman dear to Ruskin's heart, the intellectual and modest woman, to whom all knowledge should be given, not to "turn her into a dictionary," not "as if it were, or could be, for her an object to know; but only to feel and to judge."

And here again this penetrating analysis of feminine education is crowned by a portrait as full of play of light and shade as a canvas of Diaz:—

---

[1] "τὸ δὲ φρόνημα τοῦ πνεύματος ζωὴ καὶ εἰρήνη."

"Wherever a true wife comes, this home is always round her. The stars only may be over her head; the glowworm in the night-cold grass may be the only fire at her foot; but home is yet wherever she is; and for a noble woman it stretches far round her, better than ceiled with cedar, or painted with vermilion, shedding its quiet light far, for those who else were homeless."

"This, then, I believe to be,—will you not admit it to be,—the woman's true place and power? But do not you see that, to fulfil this, she must—as far as one can use such terms of a human creature—be incapable of error? So far as she rules, all must be right, or nothing is. She must be enduringly, incorruptibly good; instinctively, infallibly wise—wise, not for self-development, but for self-renunciation: wise, not that she may set herself above her husband, but that she may never fail from his side: wise, not with the narrowness of insolent and loveless pride, but with the passionate gentleness of an infinitely variable, because infinitely applicable, modesty of service—the true changefulness of woman. In that great sense—'La donna è mobile,' not 'Qual piúm' al vento'; no, nor yet 'Variable as the shade, by the light quivering aspen made'; but variable as the *light*, manifold in fair and serene division, that it may take the colour of all that it falls upon, and exalt it."

It is always with a painter's eye that the writer scrutinises dogmas and examines archives. For Ruskin history is as it were a perspective view of some great *piazza* by Canaletto, wherein are set figures by Guardi or Tiepolo, coming and going either splendidly or miserably attired, carrying banners which he joyfully describes, fashioning coat armour which he analyses with care, striking medals which with a prompt and subtle gesture he flashes before your eyes like the Piero de Medici's of the Uffizi. In a trefoil engraved under the feet of St. John, on a florin coined in the Val di Serchio, is expressed all the victory of the Florentines over the Pisans; and Ruskin follows the progress of the popular party at Florence by the development of the use of a certain colour in the arms of the town, as he might follow the march of the hours by some rising shadow on a wall.

When he speaks of lavas and siliceous rocks, of pudding-stones and limestones, of deposits in Cumberland, and the movement of glaciers in Switzerland, he is always an artist treating science like a landscape—a landscape, whose lines are modified insensibly by the pressure of elemental forces, here sinking there rising anew, the laws of change being expressed in forms of cloud and flower. All religions appear to Ruskin like the frescoes of the Primitive Master wherein cardinal virtues are expressed by grace of gesture, and dogmas are appraised by purity of colour. Paint-brush in hand he traverses the whole universe of ideas and things. The author thinks in images—which certain great painters of his country assuredly do not—and for that much more than for his drawings and water-colours he is really a *pictor* and one of the most truly *pictorial* of all that the United Kingdom has produced. This is so true that he cannot find words strongly coloured enough to translate his images. He is not satisfied with the general ideas which, formless and colourless from long use, his words present to the mind. Like a painter squeezing his tubes to force out more cobalt or vermilion, so Ruskin presses his words till he makes the original image which gave them birth emerge, and sparkle in their appeal to the eye.

"The 'Paese che Adice e Po riga' is of course Lombardy; and might have been enough distinguished by the name of its principal river. But Dante has an especial reason for naming the Adige. It is always by the valley of the Adige that the power of the German Cæsars descends on Italy; and that battlemented bridge which doubtless many of you remember, thrown over the Adige at Verona, was so built that the German riders might have secure and constant access to the city. In which city they had their first stronghold in Italy, aided therein by the great family of the Montecchi, Montacutes, Mont-aigu-s, or Montagues; lords, so called, of the mountain peaks; in feud with the family of the Cappelletti,—hatted, or more properly, scarlet-hatted, persons: And this accident of nomenclature, assisted by your present familiar knowledge of the real contests of the sharp mountains with the flat caps, or petasoi, of cloud (locally giving Mont Pilate its title, 'Pileatus,') may in many points curiously illustrate for you that contest of Frederick the Second with Innocent the Fourth, which in the good of it and the evil alike, represents to all time the war of the solid, rational, and earthly authority of the King and state, with the more or less spectral, hooded, imaginative, and nubiform authority of the Pope, and Church."

To excuse this mania for etymology, which at every moment draws him from his subject, in vain does he say that "philological and philosophical subtlety are one," for the end which he pursues is much less philosophical precision than brilliancy of tone.

But these are only images for the eye of the mind; Ruskin professes also to attract the physical eye of his reader. To that end he fills his volumes with graphic illustrations. Wherever he can, he gives the plastic instead of the literary example. No written page would avail to show the different manner in which Ghirlandajo and Claude Lorraine interpret the same landscape so well as the juxtaposition of two engravings which Ruskin displays in the fourth volume of *Modern Painters*. No poetry, however suggestive, could measure for us the remoteness of the bull of Indian art, conventional and cold, from the living bull of a Greek coin so well as the two engravings set side by side on p. 226 of *Aratra Pentelici*. And although it is more in fun than by way of demonstration that Ruskin gives together on the same page exquisite reproductions of god-man as he was formerly conceived—the Apollo of Syracuse—and the portrait of the London citizen,—the self-made man wearing a chimneypot hat, with spectacles astride on his nose, and whiskers brushed up, we have at once a more vivid presentment than we should gain from the longest report ever presented to a society by any anthropologist.

Ruskin's imagery pervades even the typing of his books, which is inspired by the same desire to fascinate the eye. The paragraphs are cleverly divided, the spacing is laboriously studied, italics and capital letters appear in great numbers, and words in old French or in Greek insinuate themselves gracefully into the monotony of the English paragraphs. More than that, where the author wishes to show that the nineteenth century has failed in its social duty, he is not content with reproducing as it stands a passage from the *Daily Telegraph* relating a drama of cruelty and misery which happened in the Spitalfields district. The words themselves might have seemed sufficiently pictorial, but the painter's instinct, which is in Ruskin, needs more colour, and so he prints them in red letters, alleging for reason that "the facts themselves are written in that colour, in a book which we shall all of us, literate or illiterate, have to read our page of, some day." Meanwhile, ere we come to that awful last Prelection, we may peruse in the volume of *Sesame* three blinding, bleeding pages which no one who has once read can ever forget—especially if he read them in the evening, by lamplight, for the utter weariness of his flesh!

Here Ruskin's passion for minuteness rages in all its intensity. Not but that it has a charm, when it succeeds to generalities. Etymology is a relief after vague eloquence, and it is refreshing to contemplate the colour of a single word after gazing on the tones washed so broadly over the frescoes of history. The images are in constantly varying dimension. From a comprehensive view of the Roman Campagna we pass to close study of details, of an individual, of an hour, of a blade of grass, of a syllable. If our eyes be tired with deciphering such puzzles as the letters of a missal, Ruskin directs them to distant plains spread out in the sunshine; the *l'Espace* of Chintreuil succeeds to the *Buisson* of Ruysdael. If on the other hand our sight be fatigued with wandering over expanses where it perceives nothing to analyse nor anything distinct to grasp, he recalls it to the beetle which crawls at our feet. Slingelandt after Turner. A panorama is a relief from the microscope, and the microscope from the panorama. At different stages of our journey it seems as if we took up sometimes an entomologist, sometimes a cosmographist. But whether entomologist, cosmographist, or poet, our companion always expresses himself as a painter; and as painter he does not invent or compose his pictures at his good pleasure out of scattered elements. When he describes a landscape it is not any landscape, but one which he has seen at a certain spot, in a certain season, at a certain time, in a certain light. Like Claude Monet painting his *Meules*, and like Achand working at a landscape, Ruskin would not add a blade of grass he had not seen, or before which he had not stood in rapture. He specifies: it is one hour he

II. IMAGERY

passed "near time of sunset, among the broken masses of pine forest which skirt the course of the Ain, above the village of Champagnole, in the Jura."

"It was spring time, too; and all were coming forth in clusters crowded for very love; there was room enough for all, but they crushed their leaves into all manner of strange shapes only to be nearer each other. There was the wood anemone, star after star, closing every now and then into nebulæ; and there was the oxalis, troop by troop, like virginal processions of the Mois de Marie, the dark vertical clefts in the limestone choked up with them as with heavy snow, and touched with ivy on the edges—ivy as light and lovely as the vine; and, ever and anon, a blue gush of violets, and cowslip bells in sunny places; and in the more open ground, the vetch, and comfrey, and mezereon, and the small sapphire buds of the Polygala Alpina, and the wild strawberry, just a blossom or two, all showered amidst the golden softness of deep, warm, amber-coloured moss. I came out presently on the edge of the ravine: the solemn murmur of its waters rose suddenly from beneath, mixed with the singing of the thrushes among the pine boughs; and, on the opposite side of the valley, walled all along as it was by grey cliffs of limestone, there was a hawk sailing slowly off their brow, touching them nearly with his wings, and with the shadows of the pines flickering upon his plumage from above; but with the fall of a hundred fathoms under his breast, and the curling pools of the green river gliding and glittering dizzily beneath him, their foam globes moving with him as he flew."

This has been actually *seen*—not laboriously translated into terms of imagery, but felt in a pictorial form. Here is no man of letters turning painter, but a painter turning writer. We have not a caligraphist labouring to introduce an image here and there into a Book of Hours he has copied: but an illuminator who, after long rubbing of his paint-brushes on the vellum, snatches up a pen wherewith to explain himself; and indeed it seems that some of the gold or ultramarine which he has handled so long still remains on the tips of his fingers. Pigments withal are needed in so hard a task, for he will presently undertake to paint the very air. But all the ideas, which he has discerned beneath the outward seeming of masterpieces of art and nature, come to his aid, till at last ideas and images mingled, coalescing and supporting each other, are so entirely fused that it is impossible to say whether the result is a lyric, a water-colour, or a page of natural history.

"The deep of air that surrounds the earth enters into union with the earth at its surface, and with its waters; so as to be the apparent cause of their ascending into life. First, it warms them, and shades, at once, staying the heat of the sun's rays in its own body, but warding their force with its clouds. It warms and cools at once, with traffic of balm and frost; so that the white wreaths are withdrawn from the field of the Swiss peasant by the glow of Libyan

II. IMAGERY

rock. It gives its own strength to the sea, forms and fills every cell of its foam; sustains the precipices, and designs the valleys of its waves; gives the gleam to their moving under the night, and the white fire to their plains under sunrise; lifts their voices along the rocks, bears above them the spray of birds, pencils through them the dimpling of unfooted sands. It gathers out of them a portion in the hollow of its hand: dyes, with that, the hills into dark blue, and their glaciers with dying rose; inlays with that, for sapphire, the dome in which it has to set the cloud; shapes out of that the heavenly flocks: divides them, numbers, cherishes, bears them on its bosom, calls them to their journeys, waits by their rest; feeds from them the brooks that cease not, and strews with them the dews that cease. It spins and weaves their fleece into wild tapestry, rends it, and renews; and flits and flames, and whispers, among the golden threads, thrilling them with a plectrum of strange fire that traverses them to and fro, and is enclosed in them like life.

"It enters into the surface of the earth, subdues it, and falls together with it into fruitful dust, from which can be moulded flesh; it joins itself, in dew, to the substance of adamant; and becomes the green leaf out of the dry ground; it enters into the separated shapes of the earth it has tempered, commands the ebb and flow of the current of their life, fills their limbs with its own lightness, measures their existence by its indwelling pulse, moulds upon their lips the words by which one soul can be known to another; is to them the hearing of the ear, and the beating of the heart; and, passing away, leaves them to the peace that hears and moves no more."

Something however would still be lacking if this confused mass of ideas and images contained the whole of Ruskin, and if, with our intelligence sated, and our imagination filled, he either left us there or else perpetually prepared the same feast for the imagination, the same repast for the intelligence. Others also in art criticism have known how to evolve the ideal from things of sense, and to make the one a relief to the other. Others have painted while thinking, and have thought while painting, have fed their poetry on the hidden meaning of nature and adorned science with the visible charms of her beauty. But a moment comes when the variety of all this cunning dilettantism, ceasing to refresh, becomes stale and tiresome. Passing hues, ideas flashing and reflecting, new points of view opening out, always the same landscape seen from different peaks, the relating of facts and the analysis of race—a spectacle so compounded does not suffice to call into play the whole of our being. Pleasures of imagination, pleasures of the intellect do not suffice alone for life. Our instinct seeks something more, something to enchain, to captivate, to animate these ideas and images, something which may not only attract our philosophic and artistic nature, but in addition may command all in us which is neither the one nor the other—something to touch the human soul more profoundly and more enduringly—a passion that will knit us yet closer to the religion of the Beautiful.

CHAPTER III

PASSION

AND this passion is that of love. All art critics have written, many have philosophised, few have loved. Too often we find the authenticity of a picture discussed, as though it were security on a mortgage, and the soul of the writer is as the soul of a commission agent, unmoved by its loveliness. The reader soon tires of seeing without understanding; he tires also of understanding without seeing; but he will weary alike of seeing and understanding if he may not love. With Ruskin we understand, we see, and we love; and by this last I mean that he invokes passion in favour of an epoch, a people, or the talent of an artist; and as soon as we perceive by what living fibres a statue or a portrait is chained to our own lives, their joys, their sufferings, their misfortunes, and their welfare, we become at once zealous partisans. Dilettantism, the disinterested curiosity of the æsthete, is not Ruskin's affair and he derides it. In Lessing we find arguments of the same order more logically connected, and with Michelet the same imagery better followed out. Stendhal gives us psychology, Topffer humour, Fromentin technique, Winckelmann dialectic,

Th. Gautier colour, Reynolds instruction, Taine generalisation, Charles Blanc selection; but Ruskin gives us love. Notes of enthusiasm or of anger sound throughout his books: the arguments to which we have alluded serve only as engines of propaganda, the images he has called up appear only as material evidence. If both the one and the other are chaotic, it is because the hand of the advocate trembled with emotion as he marshalled them under the eye of the judge, his reader. Taken one by one these passages are not superior to many others in our own literature, but taken together, and quickened by the passion of the fighter, they carry us off our feet. Here love is the cinematograph to give them back their life.

Love also, as it penetrates every detail with a tenderness we might call Virgilian, smoothes away the wrinkles of the pedant and corrects the poses of the virtuoso. Why have we those thirty pages on clouds, on their equilibrium, on the projection of their shadows, on their geometrical forms, their fleecy masses, their chariots? Because it must be shown that Turner, who has been a scoff and a mockery, "stands more absolutely alone in this gift of cloud-drawing, than in any other of his great powers . . . none but he ever drew them truly."

Why these sixteen pages on the branches of trees? Because against certain interpretations of Claude Lorraine must be vindicated the surpassing beauty of branches and their ramifications which that classic painter expresses, much as a knapsack would express human shoulders, "and if it be still alleged that such work is nevertheless enough to give any one an 'idea' of a tree, I answer that it never gave, nor ever will give, an idea of a tree *to any one who loves trees*."

Thus understood the description has nothing in it artificial or rhetorical. It is not an intellectual pastime; often it were truer to say it is a heartache. Read for instance the preface to *Queen of the Air*, written at Vevey amidst the smoke of factories and steamboats.

"This first day of May, 1869, I am writing where my work was begun thirty-five years ago, within sight of the snows of the higher Alps. In that half of the permitted life of man, I have seen strange evil brought upon every scene that I best loved, or tried to make beloved by others. The light which once flushed those pale summits with its rose at dawn, and purple at sunset, is now umbered and faint; the air which once inlaid the clefts of all their golden crags with azure is now defiled with languid coils of smoke, belched from worse than volcanic fires; their very glacier waves are ebbing, and their snows fading, as if Hell had breathed on them; the waters that once sank at their feet into crystalline rest are now dimmed and foul, from deep to deep, and shore to shore. These are no careless words—they are accurately—horribly—true. I know what the Swiss lakes were; no pool of Alpine fountain at its source was clearer. This morning, on the Lake of Geneva, at half a mile from the beach, I could scarcely see my oar-blade a fathom deep.

"The light, the air, the waters, all defiled! How of the earth itself? Take this one fact for type of honour done by the modern Swiss to the earth of his native land. There used to be a little rock at the end of the avenue by the port of Neuchâtel; there, the last marble of the foot of Jura, sloping to the blue water, and (at this time of year) covered with bright pink tufts of Saponaria. I went, three days since, to gather a blossom at the place. The goodly native rock and its flowers were covered with the dust and refuse of the town; but, in the middle of the avenue, was a newly-constructed artificial rockery, with a fountain twisted through a spinning spout, and an inscription on one of its loose-tumbled stones,—

"Aux Botanistes,
Le club Jurassique."

Ah, masters of modern science, give me back my Athena out of your vials, and seal, if it may be, once more, Asmodeus therein. You have divided the elements, and united them; enslaved them upon the earth, and discerned them in the stars. Teach us, now, but this of them, which is all that man need know,—that the Air is given to him for his life; and the Rain to his thirst, and for his baptism; and the Fire for warmth; and the Sun for sight; and the Earth for his meat—and his Rest."

Be not surprised at this cry of distress about smoke which passes away nor at these tears over a "tuft of saponaria" which has missed the call of spring. This

III. PASSION

passion is all of the virtuoso there is in Ruskin. He describes only because he loves. His affection is bestowed on everything which pleases the eye;—on the crystals of which he has celebrated the virtues, the caprices, the quarrels, the sorrows and the slumbers; on the mountains which he calls the muscles and the sinews of the body of the earth distended by furious and convulsive energy; on the plains and the low hills—its repose or ease while the muscles rest or sleep; on the snows and the glaciers whose journeys he has sung; and on the stones whose history he has told, "the iris of the earth," "the living waves," *bruma artifex* and the "schism of the mountains." He bestows it on all plants, on those which have their habitation on the soil, like the lilies, or on the surface of the rocks or the trunks of other plants, like the lichens and the mosses. Some remain a year, others many years, others an æon, but all when they perish pass as the Arab who folds his tent, "poor nomads of the vegetable life who leave no record of themselves." And also on the builder plants, which "raise a structure on the earth and thrust deep down their roots"— the architectural plants. It is given alike to the bud and to the stalk which carries the buds, sacrificing to each some of its diameter, like "the spire of Dijon or turretted fountain of Ulm or the columns of the Verona"; and also to the leaf, of which he says, "If you can paint a leaf you can paint the whole world"; and to the tree-trunk, which he calls "a messenger to the roots"; and to the roots themselves, who "have at heart the same desire;—which is, the one to grow as straight as he can towards bright heaven, the other as deep as he can into dark earth." And he has tears still for those of the buds which have never opened, sacrificed by an inflexible law to the beauty of the whole. And this tenderness, breathed forth with the soft voice of a Virgil, passes over the tops of forests waving in the wind, descends to the motionless leaves, touches the little recluses with the flowing brush of a Corot, and in touching them infuses that life which love gives to all that is beloved.

"We have found beauty in the tree yielding fruit, and in the herb yielding seed. How of the herb yielding *no* seed, the fruitless, flowerless lichen of the rock?

"Lichen, and mosses (though these last in their luxuriance are deep and rich as herbage, yet both for the most part humblest of the green things that live), —how of these? Meek creatures! the first mercy of the earth, veiling with hushed softness its dintless rocks; creatures full of pity, covering with strange and tender honour the scarred disgrace of ruin,—laying quiet finger on the trembling stones, to teach them rest. No words, that I know of, will say what these mosses are. None are delicate enough, none perfect enough, none rich enough. How is one to tell of the rounded bosses of furred and beaming green,—the starred divisions of rubied bloom, fine-filmed, as if the Rock Spirits could spin porphyry as we do glass,— the traceries of intricate silver, and fringes of amber,

III. PASSION

lustrous, arborescent, burnished through every fibre into fitful brightness and glossy traverses of silken change, yet all subdued and pensive, and framed for simplest, sweetest offices of grace? They will not be gathered like the flowers, for chaplet or love-token; but of these the wild bird will make its nest, and the wearied child his pillow.

"And, as the earth's first mercy, so they are its last gift to us. When all other service is vain, from plant and tree, the soft mosses and gray lichen take up their watch by the head-stone. The woods, the blossoms, the gift-bearing grasses, have done their parts for a time, but these do service for ever. Trees for the builder's yard, flowers for the bride's chamber, corn for the granary, moss for the grave."

The human note touched by Ruskin when he calls up the idea of man who suffers and remembers amid the joys of expanding nature which remembers not, allures those who would not have been persuaded by mere admiration for the beauty of plants themselves. For with Ruskin pity for humanity seldom fails to trouble his admiration for things. Flowers do not hide men from him as did the roses of Heliogabalus. Works, even works of art, do not make him forget the workers. In the silent museum, among the exquisite or the grandiose creations that past centuries have provided for our pleasure, Ruskin thinks of the present century, and when injustice triumphs and the wail of misery arises, he turns from the pictures and sends forth a cry of anger against the realities of things, which appeals to those who have been deaf to his cry of ecstasy. One day at Oxford, while he was conjuring up before his pupils' eyes two of the greatest pages of art in the whole world, the *Last Judgment* of Michael Angelo at the end of the Sistine, with its fall of the damned, and the *Paradise* of Tintoretto filling the end of the great hall of the Palace of the Doges with its souls in bliss rising to the ceiling, descending on to the plinths, overflowing the doors—at the moment that he was concluding his comparison between these two *chef-d'œuvres* by deploring that the *Paradise* should be doomed to destruction by the bad condition of the hall, all of a sudden he stopped, thinking of other misfortunes. . . . It was Paris which was besieged, Paris a prey to famine and fire, and he asked if justice could be claimed for works of art when there was no pity among men. . . . And the calm dissertation on chronology and dialectic was cut short by an excited harangue, which thrilled his auditors to the innermost fibre of their hearts.

"The years of that time have perhaps come, when we are to be taught to look no more to the dreams of painters, either for knowledge of Judgment, or of Paradise. The anger of Heaven will not longer, I think, be mocked for our amusement; and perhaps its love may not always be despised by our pride. Believe me, all the arts, and all the treasures of men, are fulfilled and preserved to them only, so far as they have chosen first, with their hearts, not the curse of God, but His blessing. Our Earth is now encumbered

III. PASSION

with ruin, our Heaven is clouded by Death. May we not wisely judge ourselves in some things now, instead of amusing ourselves with the painting of judgments to come?"

Some months later the fusillades of Satory interrupted his dream and are echoed even in his descriptions. It is indeed a case of "the heart making big the words," according to the old writer's adage, causing the æstheticist, before the hackneyed picture of an illustrated journal, to burst forth into apostrophes, exasperated, confused, extravagant, but very human and very rarely found among the words of art critics or collectors of curios.

"Did you chance, my friends, any of you, to see, the other day, the 83rd number of the *Graphic*, with the picture of the Queen's concert in it? All the fine ladies sitting so trimly, and looking so sweet, and doing the whole duty of woman—wearing their fine clothes gracefully; and the pretty singer, white-throated, warbling 'Home, sweet home' to them, so morally, and melodiously! Here was yet to be our ideal of virtuous life, thought the *Graphic!* Surely, we are safe back with our virtues in satin slippers and lace veils;—and our Kingdom of Heaven is come again, *with* observation, and crown diamonds of the dazzlingest. Cherubim and Seraphim in toilettes de Paris,—(bleu-de-ciel—vert d'olivier-de—Noé—mauve de colombe-fusillée,) dancing to Coote and Tinney's band; and vulgar Hell reserved for the canaille, as heretofore! Vulgar Hell shall be didactically pourtrayed, accordingly; (see page 17,) —Wickedness going its ways to *its* poor Home— bitter-sweet. Ouvrier and pétroleuse—prisoners at last—glaring wild on their way to die.

"Alas! of these divided races, of whom one was appointed to teach and guide the other, which has indeed sinned deepest—the unteaching, or the untaught?—which now are guiltless—these, who perish, or those—who forget?

"Ouvrier and pétroleuse; they are gone their way —to their death. But for these, the Virgin of France shall yet unfold the oriflamme above their graves, and lay her blanched lilies on their smirched dust. Yes, and for these, great Charles shall rouse his Roland, and bid him put ghostly trump to lip, and breathe a point of war; and the helmed Pucelle shall answer with a wood-note of Domrémy; yes, and for these the Louis they mocked, like his master, shall raise his holy hands, and pray God's peace."

Concluded after this fashion, the analysis of a work of art does not dry up the heart. The study of impressions experienced, the culture of the *Ego*, has only rendered it more kindly to human sorrow, just as a tree is pruned to make it yield more fruit. Ruskin warms with a ray of love his analysis of the human mind, as well as his analysis of nature and his analysis of art. When in his lectures at Woolwich he probed the soul of the young soldier, his tenderness was the same that he lavished on the mosses of the forest or the Paradise of Tintoretto.

"To be heroic in danger," cries he, in appealing to the wives of the English officers, "is little; you are Englishwomen. To be heroic in change and sway of fortune is little;—for do you not love? To be patient through the great chasm and pause of loss is little;—for do you not still love in heaven? But to be heroic in happiness; to bear yourselves gravely and righteously in the dazzling of the sunshine of morning; not to forget the God in whom you trust, when He gives you most; not to fail those who trust you, when they seem to need you least; this is the difficult fortitude. It is not in the pining of absence, not in the peril of battle, not in the wasting of sickness, that your prayer should be most passionate, or your guardianship most tender. Pray, mothers and maidens, for your young soldiers in the bloom of their pride; pray for them, while the only dangers round them are in their own wayward wills; watch you, and pray, when they have to face, not death, but temptation."

So Love it is which, having veiled whatever is too minute in the analysis, mitigates whatever is too paradoxical in the irony of the master. But the impulse of his thoughts proceeds quite as often from humour. His persiflage disconcerts those whom his lyrical outbursts exalt. He scatters his hearers, and gathers them to him again; shocks them and charms them in a breath. He will not lull you to sleep as a poet with the rhythmic flowing of a tender and noble song; but at his most lyric moment will rudely wake you with a violent paradox propounded in a manner familiar and slightly oratorical, and indeed qualified by himself as too antithetic.

"The only absolutely and unapproachably heroic element in the soldier's work seems to be—that he is paid little for it—and regularly: while you traffickers, and exchangers, and others occupied in presumably benevolent business, like to be paid much for it—and by chance. I never can make out how it is that a *knight*-errant does not expect to be paid for his trouble, but a *pedlar*-errant always does;—that people are willing to take hard knocks for nothing, but never to sell ribands cheap; that they are ready to go on fervent crusades, to recover the tomb of a buried God, but never on any travels to fulfil the orders of a living one;—that they will go anywhere barefoot to preach their faith, but must be well bribed to practise it, and are perfectly ready to give the Gospel gratis, but never the loaves and fishes."

Enough, you cry. . . . But the author has tired even more quickly than we. His irony takes no delight in itself or in cold and fruitless play. For it does not proceed from want of fellow-feeling or contempt of mankind, but from indignation against evil and hypocrisy,—that is to say from love,—not from a heart which does not beat, but from a heart which beats too quickly.

Even his habit of paradox is but a means to vary effects and another form of passion; and it leads always to charity. Ruskin tells us that we should take for a device of noble life, "Let us eat and drink,

III. PASSION

for to-morrow we die." Is this a paradox? No; listen to what follows: ". . . but let us *all* eat and drink. And not a few only, enjoining fast to the rest." "Dress yourselves nicely and dress everybody else nicely. Lead the fashions for the poor first, make them look well first, and you yourselves will look—in ways of which you have now no conception—all the better," says he to women, and he goes on to develop his thought with an irony so keen that it would be unbearable, did not his sarcasm melt into a love-song as legendary sword-points of old blossomed into flowers.

"Let those arches and pillars . . . alone, young ladies: it is you whom God likes to see well decorated, not them. Keep your roses for your hair—your embroidery for your petticoats. You are yourselves the church, dears; and see that you be finally adorned, as women professing godliness with the precious stone of good works, which may be quite briefly defined for the present, as 'decorating the entire tabernacle'; and clothing your poor sisters with yourselves. Put roses also in *their* hair, put precious stones also on *their* breasts; see that they also are clothed in your purple and scarlet, with other delights; that they also learn to read the gilded heraldry of the sky; and, upon the earth, be taught, not only the labours of it, but the loveliness. For them, also, let the hereditary jewel recall their father's pride, their mother's beauty."

When it has attained these heights of charity, Love

can only rise higher by coming to Christ. Is it to be led to Him by a theological dissertation? by a pious biography? No, but by one of the most secular things in the world—a lyric which the æstheticist recites smiling at the end of a lecture on the education of women, entitled "Queens' Gardens," in *Sesame and Lilies*. For all Ruskin's æsthetical passion is saturated with the poetry which the Gospel holds in store for all, even for singers and romanticists who repudiate its teaching but echo its charm. And just when the last words seem to have been said—at the moment when he has made the figures in the frescoes and the leaves of the trees speak their human utmost, there by a movement of infinite adroitness he sets them vibrating to the harmonies of Heaven. And those fervent or mystic souls who have been already guided by the dignity of charity to the æsthetic of apparel and adornment, attain now to the true æsthetic of the plants and flowers, which rise like Christ in the spring-time and are adorned with fair colours by the subtle perception of the Divine Gardener:—

> "'Come into the garden, Maud,
> For the black bat, night, has flown,
> And the woodbine spices are wafted abroad,
> And the musk of the roses blown?'

"Will you not go down among them?—among those sweet living things, whose new courage, sprung from the earth with the deep colour of heaven upon it, is starting up in strength of goodly spire; and whose purity, washed from the dust, is opening, bud by bud, into the flower of promise;—and still they turn to you, and for you, 'The Larkspur listens—I hear, I hear! And the Lily whispers—I wait.'

"Did you notice that I missed two lines when I read you that first stanza; and think that I had forgotten them? Hear them now:—

> "'Come into the garden, Maud,
> For the black bat, night, has flown,
> Come into the garden, Maud,
> I am here at the gate, alone.'

"Who is it, think you, who stands at the gate of this sweeter garden alone, waiting for you? Did you ever hear, not of a Maud, but a Madeleine, who went down to her garden in the dawn, and found One waiting at the gate, whom she supposed to be the gardener? Have you not sought Him often;—sought Him in vain, all through the night;—sought him in vain, at the gate of that old garden where the fiery sword is set? He is never there; but at the gate of *this* garden He is waiting always—waiting to take your hand—ready to go down to see the fruits of the valley, to see whether the vine has flourished, and the pomegranate budded. There you shall see with Him the little tendrils of the vines that His hand is guiding —there you shall see the pomegranate springing where His hand cast the sanguine seed;—more: you shall see the troops of the angel keepers that, with their wings, wave away the hungry birds from the path-sides where He has sown, and call to each other between the vineyard rows, 'Take us the foxes, the little foxes, that spoil the vines, for our vines have tender grapes.' Oh—you queens—you queens! among the hills and happy greenwood of this land of yours, shall the foxes have holes, and the birds of the air have nests; and in your cities, shall the stones cry out against you, that they are the only pillows where the Son of Man can lay His head?"

If this ecstatic tone were prolonged it would quickly exhaust all that can vibrate in us. But Ruskin presently lowers it to the pitch of conversation, and behold the prophet, who was crying upon the mountain, now seated in a rocking chair, and crossing his legs to read the newspaper!

While enthusiasm and irony contest his thought, the period and the brilliant touch fight for mastery in his style, the one by its masterful continuity, to sweep the reader away; the other by its fanciful mobility, to save him from exhaustion. It is the first of these two forms of style, which predominates in the earlier half of Ruskin's life-work from 1843 to 1860, when Hooker's *Ecclesiastical Polity*, George Herbert, Johnson, and Gibbon seem to have been his models. His great phrases with their facile cadences and their sonorous periods, containing as many as 619 words and 80 intermediate signs of punctuation, unroll themselves slowly, like those long waves that are of no moment to a swimmer, but in succession curve and swell one after the other until the last breaks, and all the tossing foam, and all the noisy tumult leave scarcely so much as a trace of brine on the shore. And all this hubbub is pervaded by a science of melody, of rhythm, which, if we are to believe Mr. Frederick Harrison, is "without rival in English literature." But after 1860 everything is changed. No longer have we that passion for theory of a young man who with all life before him fights deliberately and studies his attitudes. We become conscious of a combatant who means once for all to strike home. Those long waves are no more; the sea is short and rude. A hail-storm of crisp apt phrases falls upon the reader, and yet for all their brevity these reflect what there is of blessedness in earth and heaven. Here is a very armoury of sunrays. We walk no longer by the dim light of the *Seven Lamps of Architecture* but in the clear Attic sunshine of the *Queen of the Air*. Ruskin has washed the bitumen from his canvases, and even repudiates half-tones, not graduating the passage from style to style any more than the painters of his country graduate the intervals of their discordant tints. He will not gloss his surface over. There is no padding. Everything is ideas. And as if to compress a greater number of ideas into the space—like those flowers "which press one on the other in love"—not only his phrases but his words are cut short. The end of the preface to *Queen of the Air* is almost entirely composed of monosyllables. It seems as if the splendours of style embarrass him as he rises into the pure region of philosophy, and like an aeronaut who in order to mount higher throws out his superfluous gear, Ruskin makes jetsam of the "long periods," and the "bombastic phrases," the "quaintnesses" of the time of Elizabeth, "the inversions, the long exegetic sentences," and the *purpurei panni* and the *cascade fashions* and the alliterations,—all the superfluities of *Seven Lamps* and of *Modern Painters*,—and his style, thereby lightened, makes direct, precise and prompt, for its goal.

And now we have the real Ruskin, and may gather here the ripest though not the most brilliant fruits of his mind: intellectual images flowering into ideas, ideas transformed into images, reveries developed into polemics, analyses completed by acts of worship. Ruskin still keeps enough antithesis to give him distinctness, sufficient erudition to give him balance, too much poetry to let him grovel, too much science to let him soar, and to save him from being quite the dupe of his heart, he retains withal a certain humour, and to save him from being at all the dupe of his intellect, a great store of love.

In illustration of this we may cite his "Letter to young girls" on the manner in which they should practice charity.

"If you can afford it, get your dresses made by a good dressmaker, with utmost attainable precision and perfection; but let this good dressmaker be a poor person, living in the country; not a rich person living in a large house in London. Devote a part of every day to thorough needlework, in making as pretty dresses as you can for poor people, who have not time nor taste to make them nicely for themselves.

"Never seek for amusement, but be always ready to be amused. The least thing has play in it,—the slightest word, wit,—when your hands are busy and your heart is free. But if you make the aim of life amusement, the day will come when all the agonies of a pantomime will not bring you an honest laugh.

"What of fine dress your people insist upon your wearing, take—and wear proudly and prettily, for their sakes; but so far as in you lies, be sure that every day you are labouring to clothe some poorer creatures. And if you cannot clothe, at least help with your own hands. You can make your own bed; wash your own plate; brighten your own furniture,—if nothing else.

"Don't fret nor tease yourself about questions of religion, far less other people. Don't wear white crosses, nor black dresses, nor caps with lappets. Nobody has a right to go about in an offensively celestial uniform, as if it were more *their* business, or privilege, than it is everybody's, to be God's servants.

"Help your companions, but don't talk religious sentiment to them; and serve the poor, but for your lives, you little monkeys, don't preach to them. They are probably without in the least knowing it, fifty times better Christians than you; and if anybody is to preach, let *them*. Make friends of them when they are nice, as you do of nice rich people; feel with them, work with them, and if you are not at last sure it is a pleasure to you both to see each other, keep out of their way. For material charity, let older and wiser people see to it; and be content, like Athenian maids in the procession of their home-goddess, with the honour of carrying the basket."

CHAPTER IV

THE MODERN SPIRIT

THE words we have cited are instinct with the spirit of our own day. They are full of analytical curiosity, cosmopolitan imagery, and human tenderness. No other epoch could have inspired or have understood them. Consider on the one hand what are the three great characteristics of our modern life. It is more analytical than that of our fathers, that is to say, it examines into the reason of its impressions; it is more cosmopolitan, that is to say, it is coloured by recollections gleaned from a larger field; and it is more socially conscious, that is to say, more conscious of the difficulties and more conscious of the strife of classes. If on the other hand one is to sum up the impressions which the Ruskinian criticism leaves with us as compared with ordinary criticism, we perceive that it embarks on a more detailed analysis of artistic work—that it draws its examples from a greater variety of countries and landscapes, and that it is more penetrated with the social significance of art and with its obscure relations to the life of the masses. And it is in these three most obvious aspects of his work that the man of

Brantwood is seen to be not an author of a past time, but an author of the time present or even to come. Each day which passes now, like a leaf which falls from a tree, reveals a little more of the heaven that he conceived. As our life becomes more and more analytic, more wandering and more restless, as we gain greater knowledge and more store of imagination and of human pity, so we feel more sympathy for Ruskin's science, his cosmopolitanism, and his social theory. Those who, deceived by the Tory and Lake-school phases of his mind, term him "antiquated" and out of date, have neither understood his work nor the life of our age.

In every age no doubt there have been analysts of nature and of art, but they have not always had at their disposal the material and the documents either of science or of contemporary historical criticism. In every age there have been artists, but these have not always been able to select examples from every museum in Europe, to study the hues of every glacier, or to dip their brushes in the water of every lake. In every age there have been apostles, and hearts full of sympathy for the misery of the poor, but the dominating idea of brotherhood with the needy has not always thus haunted the mind of the richer classes. Nor in bygone days has humanity lived continually in gloomy or feverish expectation of the inauguration of a new era. Ruskin therefore—like the nursling described by La Bruyère who, strengthened by her milk, turns to beat his nurse—is fighting his

IV. THE MODERN SPIRIT

own century, and the very words he uses do but reflect the force of what he execrates.

In listening a moment ago to his analytic discourse, we were reminded of Mazzini's words: "Ruskin's is the most analytic mind in Europe at this moment." He carries scientific investigation into the very heart of poetry—pulling the words to pieces to examine their structure, and the motive of their imagery or their song; resolving the massing of clouds into geometric figures the better to understand their perspective and their schemes of light and shade, making a study of the geology of Turner's mountains, of the botany of Claude Lorraine's trees, of the psychology of Della Robbia's angels, of the physiology of Pollajuolo's or Ghiberti's birds, of the pathology of the sculptured head of Santa Maria Formosa, of the dynamics of the bas-reliefs of John of Pisa,—searching all science to find scaffolding for his æsthetical structure. And in the process he has given rein to his feelings for or against many things—the arguments of Saussure, of Darwin, of Tyndall, of James Forbes, of Alphonse Fabre, of Heim; putting forward his own theories on the movement of serpents, the progression of glaciers; bethinking him as he faces a Greek or a Florentine sculpture of the "variability of species," ever anxious to give the appearance of scientific experiment to his systems. His books as we have seen are filled with examples disposed in the form of equations, with arguments *pro* and *con*, and sometimes accompanied by diagrams. As early as 1845 at Venice he was studying by means of the daguerreotype architectural details, which till then had escaped attention, and in 1849 he was photographing the Matterhorn — doubtless the first to do so. To turn over his books is to turn the pages of a Lionardo manuscript, pages closely packed, rich and sparkling—here the dimensions of a catapult following a treatise on the muscles, sketches overlapping mathematical calculations, caricatures insinuating themselves among notes on volitation, and mechanics side by side with landscapes. Ruskin, like Lionardo, felt in all things the beauty of science, and in every case endeavoured to formulate a science of beauty. As we read we may well doubt whether he is most at home in a museum or a laboratory; and the figure of him that suggests itself is such as that of Pasteur as once M. Edelfeldt represented him, eye and thought intent upon a jar which he handles in the brilliant light of a clinical laboratory. And it ceases to astonish us that Sir John Lubbock, when asked whether Ruskin or Goethe had done most for science, replied that Ruskin had "undoubtedly done very much more valuable work, and that without any pretensions to profound scientific knowledge, he had an extraordinary natural gift for observation and seemed to know by instinct what to observe, what was important amidst so much that was fanciful and poetical."

In our first glance at the main outlines of his opinions we noted that they were preoccupied with

IV. THE MODERN SPIRIT

social theories even more strongly than with science. In addition to those works which treat specially of political economy, such as *Unto this Last, Munera Pulveris, Time and Tide, Crown of Wild Olive, Fors Clavigera, A Joy for Ever*, there are many others that touch the same subject at some point. The æstheticist has rarely been able to write a whole chapter on Art without some recollection breaking in upon his serenity—of those human beings " who have a strong objection to hearing a disquisition on Michael Angelo when they are cold." Throughout his works Ruskin is the same man who from the Hotel Danieli at Venice wrote in *Fors Clavigera* :—

"Here is a little grey cockle-shell, lying beside me, which I gathered the other evening, out of the dust of the Island of St. Helena; and a brightly spotted snail-shell, from the thistly sands of Lido; and I want to set myself to draw these, and describe them in peace. 'Yes,' all my friends say, 'that is my business; why can't I mind it, and be happy?' But alas! my prudent friends, little enough of all that I have a mind to may be permitted me. For this green tide that eddies by my threshold is full of floating corpses, and I must leave my dinner to bury them, since I cannot save : and put my cockle-shell in cap, and take my staff in hand, to seek an unencumbered shore."

These words were written over twenty years ago. They might well have seemed incomprehensible to the dilettanti travelling that winter in Italy. But in these days they are understood, or at any rate there is some inkling abroad of their profound and sad significance. The world is no longer surprised if the tourist pays as much attention to the social problems of a country, in which he travels, as to its stones and monuments. And when Ruskin adds that: "It is the vainest of affectations to try and put beauty into shadows, while all real things which cast them are left in deformity and pain," and when he thereby makes a pretext in the middle of a dissertation on Art for talking to us of strikes, wages, and co-operation, we shall find his words even more applicable to industrial life to-day than they were yesterday.

At any rate they respond to the nomadic instinct in us and to our cosmopolitan curiosity. Ruskin is not content to teach at Oxford only; he follows his pupils on their journeys to Amiens, Florence, and Venice,—to save them from the heretical suggestions of Murray, Baedeker, Woerl, and such like. He follows them by means of little thin volumes of twenty pages for pocket use, bound in pliant covers, quickly read, and easy to manage, for they do not deprive the disciple of a hand or impede him in the purchase of an armful of almond blossom in the Lung' Arno on the road back from the Uffizi, nor in feeding the pigeons at S. Mark's on the way to the Palace of the Doges. These little books are *Mornings in Florence, S. Mark's Rest, Our Fathers have told us*, and *The Bible of Amiens*. When we reach the chapel or the museum out comes the book, and this little whispering demon in red, all promises, and surprises, pierces the old walls and the old canvases, and through them opens out to us horizons of ideas, valleys of dreams, and centuries of history. It is as though one of the window-holes in that interminable corridor of the Ponte Vecchio, connecting the Uffizi and the Pitti Palaces, were thrown open, and we turned from the innumerable dingy portraits of Grand Dukes to the flowing Arno and to Florence, and to the marble mountains and the gardens and the snowy summits, to the villas of the Decameroni, and the monasteries of saints and the loggias and the porticos. A whole vision of living nature, bright and gay, speaking straight to the heart, bursts in among the dead things, saying to the wanderer: Weary one! Be not sad! All that thou seest is living yet. In the pictures the trees have faded and the flowers are brown, but outside there are green forests, and perfumed flowers, running rivers, smiling women, fighting warriors, mobs to curse or applaud,—and the breezes which sweep through the tops of the cypresses of San Miniato, or raise the lily heads at Fiesole, are as strong and as sweet as when they garnered perfume of white lilies for Fra Angelico, or blew away over the blue sky golden lilies on the banners of Charles the Eighth.

By thus infusing new life into faded works of art and cities grown cold with age, and by mingling with his criticism the unfailing charm of nature and melancholy born of thought, Ruskin endows us with a new sense to wait upon our travels. Without him we had a great deal—express trains enabling us to rush from one monument to another and to compare the portal of Amiens immediately with the bronze gates of Ghiberti; sleeping-cars allowing us to arrive among these masterpieces with heads clear and minds attuned, prompt to receive the most delicate messages of art. We had hotels and the almost magical apparatus of modern comfort wherein a finger on one button annihilates distance, on another produces light, on a third heat; where a polyglot and provident establishment spares us even the fatigue of giving an order, where everything tacitly conspires to leave the mind its penetrative power unimpaired between one museum and another, and the soul all its strength to summon up the ghosts of past ages in the intervals of a historian's lectures. In a manner, then, we had all that was needful for seeing the world; only we needed an excuse for so seeing it and for enjoying it when we saw. Ruskin has supplied all this. We were walking forward on our own way; he came and opened a new horizon. We had eyes and saw not; Ruskin gave us eyes to see. And withal he gave us plausible reasons for our wandering habit, and noble pretexts for our amusements, and he told us where we were going and why. Chiefly he has addressed his own compatriots, and because they believe him they are now infinitely more observant of all things of art in their path, and study these with an ecstatic air to be sought in vain among such as do not belong to what the sacristans in Italy already term "the Ruskin Brotherhood."

But do they really understand these things the better? I dare not wager so, but at least they know that an Englishman has understood them. Have they a greater enjoyment of them? At least they know that one of their own race and faith has enjoyed them, and that for scientific reasons and with moral motives, which it is honourable to share. He it is who by his sense of history, and the raising of dead men to life, has made them realise that countless generations have paused in front of these monuments "with admiration, joy, and love." Therefore we also now admire, enjoy, and love. And by this continuity of worship, we seem to be linked with the great world-soul which has vibrated and will ever vibrate in contemplation of the same horizons. On the balcony of the Palace of the Doges, or at the windows of the Campanile of Santa Maria del Fiore, or again on the highest turret of the Cathedral of Milan, whence may be espied the fleecy blue of the distant Alps, should you cast a glance at the stones on which you lean you will see them scrawled and hacked with inscribed names and dates—names of inhabitants of every village in Europe, and dates of every year, good or bad, in the latter half of this century. All these folk of humble condition—mainly German or English, who occupy most of the time they spend there in writing their unknown names on these illustrious marbles, in attaching something of their ephemeral life to these all but eternal monuments — these folk are feeling some instinctive desire to join in admiration with the rest of humanity. Assuredly they acquire a sense of increased nobility by contact with these monuments, the goal of so many pilgrimages; and they imagine they are honouring themselves, while in fact they dishonour the monument by their shameless scrawls. This rare visit is a gleam of poetry, in their existence, to be recalled again and again, while they sew by the hearth at home or smoke in the halls of the "Bierbrauerei,"—nameless travellers, swift-flowing ripples of the river, chasing each other past a town, and reflecting for an instant the palaces, the cathedrals, the mountains, the forests, and all the transient and diverse colours of the banks, and thence returning to the ocean whence they came—to the crowd and routine of every day, and the grey monotonous life, with no light to cast a shade. . . . But if at the moment that these rays darted upon the wayfarers they were asked, "What is it you think? What is it you feel?" they would not be able to say. They who have read Ruskin would know—for what they have not seen in the heavens they find in his diagrams, what they have not divined in the stones they discover in his antitheses, what they have forgotten to love among tangible and living realities, they adore in the images which a great poet has painted in tones of love.

Ruskin may be said then to speak to us as a

cicerone more than as a professor or a theorist on society. He magnifies his functions into a divine mission and turns the inn, wherein he preaches, to a temple, which need not be the less sacred to us because it happens to be provided with lifts and electric light. We can be thrilled in a castle by the recollection of the sojourn of a king, or in a monastery which shows us the dwelling of a saint. For the castle was formerly the outward sign of power; the monastery that of zeal and devotion. Both stood on mountains or plains as abiding-places for those who sought to know the world in its grandeur or in its charity. In these days when kings alight at hotels, and when wandering saints neither wear peculiar garb nor dwell amid ideal architecture, the inn has inherited the poetry of the ancient manorial or monastic building. It may be an ancient palace, as at Venice; or it may be the precincts of a chapel, as on the shores of the Mediterranean. So an apostle may well teach there, and his eloquence may be displayed without let or hindrance. Ruskin is just such an apostle of cosmopolitan caravansaries. He is like an archangel to Cook's tourists, or a railway-station prophet, and the locomotive gives him night and day his column both of fire and smoke. In the days gone by, the days of undisturbed lives and rooted existences, this function of an æstheticist, and teacher of the people, would not have been understood. But now that restless humanity upsets its household gods, extinguishes the fire on its hearth, and goes forth to visit every shrine, to the foot of every mountain, to cities long dead but still cherished as reliquaries of the past—to gather knowledge concerning this earth which we find too small and that past which we find too short—now that doubtful of the future we seek rather to prolong our existence in this world, to live through past centuries by identifying ourselves with lives pictured only in museums, or to get experience of the complex life and aspirations of the crowds about our path—surely for such an age this æsthetical guide becomes like the priest—a minister of the Infinite. . . . He brings back for us the life of buried ages and unknown peoples. His words endow us with life; they are the life we lead and still more they are the life we desire to lead —analytic like our scientific life, suggestive like our cosmopolitan life, unquiet like our social life. These words share all the vivacity of life, because they touch on all subjects, and guide towards all lands; share all its contradictions, because they reflect all impressions and all systems; share all its subtlety, because they mingle enthusiasm with irony and humour with love. And if here and there they seem to hold something of mystery, may it not be because life with its ever recurring problems and infinity is scarcely less mysterious than death itself. . . .

PART III

HIS ÆSTHETIC AND SOCIAL THOUGHT

PART III

HIS ÆSTHETIC AND SOCIAL THOUGHT

ANCIENT wisdom has said that it is impossible to plunge twice into a river and find it the same flood. As we close the varied volumes filled with striking pages of analysis, imagery, and passion, we feel inclined to echo, It is impossible to plunge twice and find the same Ruskin. His contradictions are the joy of his adversaries, and furrow as with a plough the foreheads of his disciples. M. Augustin Filon once stated that he would undertake to extract from the works of Ruskin the most contradictory doctrines, and Mr. Whistler amused himself by collecting into a large volume aphorisms which may be said to rival in distinctness that renowned artist's *Symphony in Black*. After reading one page of the Master we think we have grasped his idea; after reading ten we feel doubtful; after twenty we are lost. With all the subtleties, all the waverings, all the convolutions of his various æsthetical, religious, and social systems, he is ever an ethereal and elusive magician. If we try to imprison him in a logical formula, he escapes in smoke like the genius of the *Thousand and one*

Nights, and we seem to have before us a host of little things, precious and varied, glittering and attractive, but fitful and changeful as the flame or the wave.

And yet the river remains the same, and flows in the same place, and is called by the same name as when our grandfather took us by the hand to show it us for the first time. This leaping flame which peoples with strange figures the great hall of the old family mansion recalls in its general aspect the flame that warmed our childish fingers, and gave us the beautiful dreams now vanished up the chimney. No wave is precisely the wave of yesterday, but the river is unchanged. No flame reproduces photographically the arabesques of years gone by, but the hearth is unchanged. Ruskin is like a river and like a flame. He never resembles himself, he renews himself unceasingly, and yet he is always the same. His thoughts spring ever from the same lofty region. They go ever to swell the same far-distant ocean. What is this source? Where is this ocean?

Let us go in search of it. If in the search we disturb some established prejudice founded on some isolated text of Ruskin's, our excuse must be the fact that this is not an analysis of one or other of his works, but a general view of his thought from 1843 up to 1888,—his thoughts on Nature, his thoughts on Art, his thoughts on Life. And if perchance disciples more ardent than clear-sighted, or adversaries more ingenious than honest, have even in England adopted some false

HIS ÆSTHETIC AND SOCIAL THOUGHT

ideas of the Ruskinian doctrine, this proves nothing against the accuracy of the synthesis which follows, but pleads only for its necessity. Texts of the Master which seem to contradict us may indeed be easy to find, and as these texts are always aphoristic and absolute in form, they seem to exclude any other opinion. This is not, however, really the case. They are back-waters of the stream, eddies which momentarily and locally run counter to the current, but they do not change it. And even their violence does not affect the trend we believe we discern and wish to determine in his thought.

That thought—let there be no mistake—is Ruskin's not ours. If we propound it in all its native force, it is a proof not of our adherence but of our loyalty. We deem it neither useful nor opportune to delay the statement and complicate our scrutiny by personal remarks and reservations. To be discussed a doctrine must be known. We give that of Ruskin. Once completely realised, whoever will can contest it.

CHAPTER I

"NATURE"

§ 1

ARE there not more things æsthetic in heaven and earth than are dreamt of in our philosophy? Are not men more often guided by sight than by reason? Is it only children who look through the pages of picture-books, and who forget as they look the realities of life? Of this life we assuredly know already many things. The chemist takes a plant, carries it into his laboratory, analyses it, submits it to a multiplicity of tests, and tells us of how many elements it is composed, how much nitrogen, how much lime, how it grows and why it is developed. Be it so; it is very interesting. The economist scans balance sheets and market reports, follows the zig-zags of diagrams, deciphers ledgers and statistics, shakes the dust out of charters and deeds, and teaches us how the wealth of a country is developed by exchange, how the value of a commodity is fixed by its utility, and how a monetary crisis is brought about. Very well; that is all true, but is that all? Why, we may say to the chemist, do we on this winter's evening find the solitude less dull and the cold less rigorous because a bunch of roses is on the chimneypiece? They neither speak nor warm us. . . . Why, we may say to the economist, has this excrescence of a shell with no useful purpose a market value much greater than a sack of corn which would sustain a man for a given time? . . . And why, we should say to the man of science, are we saddened by the sound of a minor scale, and why are we cheered by a ray of sun? Why does not this fire which burns on the hearth gladden us like the sun which blazes in at the window? Nay more, why in this artificial fireplace, where a regulated jet of gas sets light to stationary blocks of asbestos, is there heat for the thermometer and so little warmth for the heart?

Let us leave this city where the sky is hidden by smoke and the earth is paved with wood, where fire burns only supplied by gasometers and water is such that one dares not drink it, and let us go forth to contemplate Nature where she yet abides undisfigured by man. Why should the same sky discourage us when it is grey and kindle hope when it is blue? Here among the fields look at this green, even turf trimmed as with a line, and then turn to that undulating ground full of wild herbs subtly interlaced. We find the same chemical composition, the same power of production, the same value. The two fields are exactly similar in the eyes of the agriculturist, the economist, the philosopher, and the tax-gatherer. Yet the one with its monotonous lines would not stay our steps or our cares. The other would attract us, would distract us, perhaps would charm us, and thanks to its thousand fantastic aspects and outlines we might for an instant forget the world and return home soothed, calmer, and morally refreshed. Why?

And why should Nature be full of colour as a picture instead of grey like an engraving? Why does she paint with most brilliant colours the most useless as well as the most inoffensive creatures? Assuredly there are poisonous toadstools which might have been washed in colour by Delacroix, and carrion-flies which might have been touched by the brush of Fra Angelico; but are not the gentlest birds usually the most beautiful? Bend over these rocks broken in their fall. "Pure earths are white when in powder; and the same earths which are the constituents of clay and sand, form, when crystallised, the emerald, ruby, sapphire, amethyst and opal. . . . It is a universal law that according to the purity of any substance, and according to the energy of its crystallisation, is its beauty of brightness. . . . The Spirit in the plant . . . is of course strongest at the moment of its flowering. . . . And where this Life is at its full power, its form becomes invested with aspects that are chiefly delightful to our own human passions; namely, first, with the loveliest outlines of shape; and secondly, with the most brilliant phases of the primary colours, blue, yellow, and red or white, the unison of all; and, to make it all more strange, this time of peculiar and perfect glory is associated with relations of the plants or blossoms to each other, correspondent to the joy

I. NATURE 149

of love in human creatures." . . . Why? Go higher up in the scale of life. What is this twisted brilliant object which slides on the pathway—"a rivulet of smooth silver which slips between the grass," a little "ridged" form "which rows on the earth with every scale for an oar. A wave, but without wind! a current, but with no fall! Why that horror? There is more poison in an ill-kept drain,—in a pool of dish-washings at a cottage-door, than in the deadliest asp of Nile." Or perhaps there is hidden in our heart some obscure relation between the form of the serpent and the idea of evil? . . . Why on the contrary is there pleasure in the "rapid and radiant passage of purpled wings" of no utility to man, while the grey, dull flesh of fowls is far more serviceable to him? Why this thrill of joy quick and instinctive in the free supple movement of a horse's limbs. The motor-car has none and yet carries us faster whither we would go. . . .

It may be objected that these things do not attract attention or give pleasure equally to all creatures. This is true, and is yet another mystery in them and in ourselves. Can it be that these impressions and their consequences on the actions of creatures are not truly existent? Is it not rather that having more or less existence they constitute between these beings a hierarchy, or if need be a classification not yet determined? Whence comes it that one man pauses and is impressed by the blue mountains on the horizon standing like waves made stationary by the wand of a magician, and that another creature proceeds on his way indifferent? Should not all who have eyes see alike? Are there differences between species other than those of which the biologists are aware? "How many manner of eyes are there? You physical-science students should be able to tell us painters that." "We see, as we try to draw the endlessly-grotesque creatures about us, what infinite variety of instruments they have; but you know, far better than we do, how those instruments are constructed and directed. You know how some play in their sockets with independent revolution,—project into near-sightedness on pyramids of bone,—are brandished at the points of horns,—studded over backs and shoulders,—thrust at the ends of antennæ to pioneer for the head, or pinched up into tubercles at the corners of the lips. But how do the creatures see out of all these eyes?" When you look at a serpent coming out of his hiding-place or resting on a branch like a coil of rope, or flattening against the glass of his cage the round curves of his clammy coils, have you ever asked whether the serpent is looking at you and what he sees of you? "It will keep its eyes fixed on you for an hour together, a vertical slit in each admitting such image of you as is possible to the rattlesnake retina, and to the rattle-snake mind. How much of a man can a snake see? What sort of image of him is received through that deadly vertical cleft in the iris;—through the glazed blue of the ghastly lens? . . . A cat may look at a king;—yes; but can it *see* a king when it looks at him? When a cat caresses you, it never looks at you. Its heart seems to be in its back and paws, not its eyes." The fawn, the horse, appear more susceptible to differences of aspect, the dog yet more, and man more than all beasts together. Man looks and considers; man enjoys and suffers through his sight; he is enraptured by things which have no function in his life:— before reflections which he cannot grasp, before rocks which he cannot cultivate, before the colours of that ether whither he cannot ascend. Why?

And why did the greatest of men—the saints whose histories are shown on banners or in the glories of old gilded panels—love to fortify their souls by the sight of mountains, wings, water, and flowers, "whenever they had any task or trial laid upon them needing more than their usual strength of spirit?" And finally, why are these brilliant and disinterested impressions more acute and more profound in the same man when his heart is free from low passion or mean envy? Why is the joy of colour deeper in his soul when his constitution is sound, and in his spirit when it is calm, and in his senses when they are at rest? Why in this case does the joy of colour and its recollection stay by him for the rest of his life on earth? "Let the eye but rest on a rough piece of branch of curious form during a conversation with a friend, rest, however, unconsciously, and though the conversation be forgotten, though every circumstance connected with it be as utterly lost to the memory as though it had not been, yet the eye will, through the whole life after, take a certain pleasure in such boughs which it had not before, a pleasure so slight, a trace of feeling so delicate as to leave us utterly unconscious of its peculiar power, but undestroyable by any reasoning, a part thenceforward of our constitution." Why? Many things indeed are explained in our schools, but who can explain the part that form and colour play in our lives? The properties of bodies are analysed,—but has any one ever sought to understand that quality of qualities which mingles and combines all things in this world — the power of attraction and sympathy? The arguments of our physiologists and psychologists are ingenious enough, but would they not apply equally well to all our surroundings, irrespective of curve of line or charm of colour? Would the teaching of philosophers who describe this world in terms so abstruse, so grey, and so cold, ever lead us to imagine it to be such shimmer of foliage, such a flood of sunshine, such pulsation of life, such a tremor of eyelids and fire of glances, as indeed constitute all its value? Philosophers construct systems which explain everything in the world except its charm. They analyse all the secret forces of the soul except its power of admiration. They dissolve all our relations with Nature, so-called inanimate, except its power of love. . . .

All these things, our professor may reply, come into the province of diverse sciences, which to some extent take note of them, or perhaps they come into no province at all, because being only variable impressions in each individual they are not capable of scientific analysis, and can in every case be resolved into mere appearances or *effects of perception.* Effects of perception? Granted. But is it likely that because they are so labelled they will lose their power over man and his existence? Do you doubt that to perception, that is, the perception of glory and the perception of love, we owe most of our resolutions and most of our weaknesses—and in consequence, most of our misery and most of our happiness? Is it not to the presentment of ancient heroism that we owe our true modern heroes; and from the illusion of the oasis, the mirage itself, that we derive sufficient consolation to pursue our path towards the reality? Are legends true? and assuming the contrary, have they exercised less influence than history on the facts of life? Waiving all proof of religion, is it not to the phantoms of the sky that we owe most of the things which have transformed the earth? Can we say the radiance of the sun is not needful to our lives so long as it gives us light, or the harmony of the flowers, so long as they give us healing? Should we not rather say that the relation of these things to man, of these ideas to our intelligence, of these phenomena to our acts and sentiments, that all these mighty yet imperceptible fibres,

"These mysterious fibres by which our hearts are bound,"

are too subtle or too personal to be disentangled without damage by the rude scalpel of science as at present organised, and organised to meet quite other needs.

Any science of nature to accomplish this end must give heed not only to her chemical or physical composition, her truth, her utility, her riches, her evolution, even her fecundity, but to that also which we worship in life and despise in argument, which is graven in facts and proscribed by systems, which we seek in silence and dream of with awe—the Beautiful. The only psychology capable of explaining the phenomena just described and a thousand others foreseen or divined, is one which would treat the qualities of form and colour as part of the primary and dominant qualities of natural objects exercising their action not only on the sense of touch but on that nobler sense of sight, and not so much on our sentiment of desire or possession as on the most unselfish of sentiments, that of admiration. The only complete philosophy would be one which would not only ask the cause of *forces* but also of *forms*. It should ascertain not only the *laws* but *also and above all* the *joys* of creation, and should classify human beings not alone according to their aspects and mechanical functions—as engines are classed in an exhibition of machinery—but chiefly according to their artistic attributes and their evidence or expression of Beauty—just as pictures or statues are classified in a Gallery.

We shall be told that this science or this philosophy would not be strictly speaking either a science or a philosophy at all. Perhaps so; we will not dispute

I. NATURE

about words. Between the two methods of research, there is truly a profound difference. "Science deals exclusively with things as they are in themselves; and art exclusively with things as they affect the human senses and human soul. "Her work is to portray the appearance of things, and to deepen the natural impressions which they produce upon living creatures. The work of science is to substitute facts for appearances, and demonstrations for impressions. Both, observe, are equally concerned with truth; the one with truth of aspect, the other with truth of essence. Art does not represent things falsely, but truly as they appear to mankind. "Science studies the relations of things to each other; but art studies only their relations to man; and it requires of everything which is submitted to it imperatively this, and only this,—what that thing is to the human eyes and human heart."

§ 2

There is a difference greater still between the diverse faculties called into play by these two investigations. For although our present inquiry is to be scientific, that is to say experimental, in one direction it will be chiefly artistic and intuitive. It is the function of the artist to interpret the effect of Nature on the eyes and on the heart, and to this end clear vision is more important than much knowledge. His faculty of perception penetrates far deeper than the instruments of the student. "The labour of the whole Geological Society, for the last fifty years, has but now arrived at the ascertainment of those truths respecting mountain-form which Turner saw and expressed with a few strokes of a camel's hair pencil fifty years ago, when he was a boy. "The knowledge of all the laws of the planetary system, and of all the curves of the motion of projectiles, would never enable a man of science to draw a waterfall or a wave; and all the members of the College of Surgeons helping each other could not at this moment see, or represent, the natural movement of a human body in vigorous action, as a poor dyer's son [Tintoret] did two hundred years ago." And in order to feel all the power of Nature upon the heart as well as upon the eye, it is needful not only to see her well but also to love her well. "We cannot fathom the mystery of a single flower, nor is it intended that we should; but that the pursuit of science should constantly be stayed by the love of beauty, and accuracy of knowledge by tenderness of emotion."

What then is this inward faculty which enables us to see and to study man as something more than a marvellous automaton, plants as something more than alembics, flowers as something more than remedies? And how shall we designate it? Clearly it is not the intellect, for ideas of beauty are instinctive, and the most we can say for the intellect when it deals with them is that it is useless. Any doubt as to this

I. NATURE

may be removed by reading M. Thiers where he treats of art criticism. "If ever a critic tells you two colours do not go together make a note of it, so as to put them as often as possible side by side." Should we call it sensibility? If we must lean to one or other side it is to this that we should incline, for sensibility is what is both most powerful and most noble in us. "Men are for ever vulgar, precisely in proportion as they are incapable of sympathy — of quick understanding, — of all that, in deep insistence on the common, but most accurate term, may be called the 'tact' or 'touch-faculty,' of body and soul: that tact which the Mimosa has in trees, which the pure woman has above all creatures; —fineness and fulness of sensation, beyond reason; —the guide and sanctifier of reason itself. Reason can but determine what is true:—it is the God-given passion of humanity which can alone recognise what God has made good."

But does sensation suffice? All created things have sensation. Even the plant feels—does it therefore perceive Beauty? Are not the sensations of men so diverse that they seem to differ not only in degree but also in kind? Is the sense of charm as we watch a sunbeam skim along the distant waters of a lake at all akin to the sense of pleasure given by the savour of roast beef? This latter sensation is much the most useful—but it is precisely in the former that the relation between Nature and the soul is to be discerned. Further, it is these so-called useless sensations which are the most powerful, the most exquisite, and the most indefinitely enduring. "The pleasures of touch and taste are given to us as subservient to life, as instruments of our preservation —compelling us to seek the things necessary to our being, and that, therefore, when this their function is fully performed, they ought to have an end; and can only be artificially, and under high penalty prolonged." Although it is very necessary to eat in order to live, it becomes destructive to live in order to eat. "But the pleasures of sight and hearing are given as gifts. They answer not any purposes of mere existence, for the distinction of all that is useful or dangerous to us might be made, and often is made, by the eye without its receiving the slightest pleasure of sight. We might have learned to distinguish fruits and grain from flowers, without having any superior pleasure in the aspect of the latter. And the ear might have learned to distinguish the sounds that communicate ideas, or to recognise intimations of elemental danger without perceiving either music in the voice, or majesty in the thunder. And as these pleasures have no function to perform, so there is no limit to their continuance in the accomplishment of their end, for they are an end in themselves, and so may be perpetual with all of us—being in no way destructive, but rather increasing in exquisiteness by repetition. Herein then we find very sufficient ground for the higher estimation of these delights, first in their being eternal and inexhaustible, and secondly, in their being evidently no means or instrument of life, but an object of life. Now in whatever is an object of life, in whatever may be infinitely and for itself desired, we may be sure there is something of divine."

The faculty therefore which apprehends the beautiful is not "a mere operation of sense." Something else is interwoven to preserve it from the material and to prolong the passing element. Something is mingled which combines the serene peace of contemplation and the formless force of the senses. If we need to be convinced of this let us recall the feelings which assert themselves in the presence of the horizon we love best, at the magical moments of special inspiration. Let us recall what every one must have experienced as he passed in a carriage some lovely spot, where he felt "I must come back, I must pass my life here," yet he has never returned. It is primarily a sensuous pleasure, but it is accompanied with joy, with love for the object, with a kind of veneration for its unknown cause, "with a perception of kindness in a superior intelligence," with gratitude towards Beauty for itself and for its gift to us who alone have eyes to perceive it—perchance also the same feeling as in some pictures of the early masters where the Virgin and flowers are contemplated by knights and donors here below, while from the clouds they are watched over by the Eternal Father and His angels. . . . "No idea can be at all considered as in any way an idea of beauty, until it be made up of these emotions, any more than we can be said to have an idea of a letter of which we perceive the perfume and the fair writing, without understanding the contents of it, or intent of it; and as these emotions are in no way resultant from, nor obtainable by, any operation of the intellect, it is evident that the sensation of beauty is not sensual on the one hand, nor is it intellectual on the other, but is dependent on a pure right and open state of the heart, both for its truth and for its intensity, insomuch that even the right after-action of the intellect upon facts of beauty so apprehended, is dependent on the acuteness of the heart feeling about them." The heart is the source of high and serene emotion in the presence of the large expanse of Nature. And the response is a faculty of the heart—a sentiment.

This is the "æsthetical sentiment," or as Ruskin terms it the "theoretic faculty." It is this sentiment which thrills us in the most exquisite hours of life, those hours alone worthy of being lived. It is this sentiment which establishes that mysterious harmony between Nature and man, which we ask science in vain to analyse. We must not confound it with any other faculty either higher or lower. We must hold fast to its autonomy. We shall have against us the pure Hedonists and the pure Rationalists. We shall have to fight against those who see in this sentiment a physiological instinct, as well as against those who treat it as a process of reason. It is neither the one nor the other. This æsthetical sentiment ("theoretic faculty ") is not the far-off echo of a physical instinct ; it is an intuition differing from all other instinct, and physiology has nothing to do with it. "A girl is praised because she is like a rose, not a rose because it is like a girl." Neither is it love in the higher sense of sacrifice of self; such love is self-surrender, and in the pleasure we receive from plants and water and light, we take everything and we surrender nothing. Still less is it the product of reasoning: the impression disappears directly we begin to reason. For example: " All these sensations of beauty in the plant arise from our unselfish sympathy with its happiness, and not from any view of the qualities in it which may bring good to us, nor even from our acknowledgment in it of any moral condition beyond that of mere felicity; . . . the moment we begin to look upon any creature as subordinate to some purpose out of itself, some of the sense of organic beauty is lost. Thus, when we are told that the leaves of a plant are occupied in decomposing carbonic acid, and preparing oxygen for us, we begin to look upon it with some such indifference as upon a gasometer. It has become a machine; some of our sense of its happiness is gone." —" It is true that reflection will show us that the plant is not living for itself alone, that its life is one of benefaction, that it gives as well as receives, but no sense of this whatsoever mingles with our perception of physical beauty in its forms. These forms appear to be necessary to its health; the symmetry of its leaflets, the vivid green of its shoots, are looked upon by us as signs of the plant's own happiness and perfection; they are useless to us, except as they give us pleasure in our sympathising with that of the plant."—"Both the Book of Job and the Sermon on the Mount give precisely the view of nature which is taken by the uninvestigating affection of a humble, but powerful mind. There is no dissection of muscles or counting of elements, but the boldest and broadest glance at the apparent facts, and the most magnificent metaphor in expressing them. 'His eyes are like the eyelids of the morning. In his neck remaineth strength, and sorrow is turned into joy before him.' And in the often repeated, never obeyed, command, 'Consider the lilies of the field,' observe there is precisely the delicate attribution of life which we have seen to be the characteristic of the modern view of landscape. . . . There is no science, or hint of science; no counting of petals, nor display of provisions for sustenance: nothing but the expression of sympathy, at once the most childish, and the most profound." It is the "æsthetical sentiment" or "theoretic faculty."[1]

[1] In these pages and those which follow an effort has been made to give a faithful rendering not of the words of Ruskin but of his thought. It has been sometimes necessary to transpose the words so as to give the idea more accurately. For instance, here the phrase "æsthetic sentiment" has been used in every case where Ruskin would use the phrase "theoretic faculty." The word "æsthetic" has been proscribed by Ruskin in English as meaning something other than this "energy of contemplation" which he is considering. But in French the word "æsthetic" has quite the same sense that Ruskin gives to "theoretic." It is the sense that has been given to it by all æstheticists, especially

I. NATURE

It is this faculty that apprehends better than Reason or the Senses, "the claim of all lower nature on the hearts of men; of the rock, and wave, and herb as a part of their necessary spirit life." We have found the instrument of our study as well as our goal, and its reward as well as its instrument. Enthusiasm alone can analyse enthusiasm. Admiration alone can deal with the phenomena of admiration. The accusation of *Schwärmerei*, Enthusiasm, will not deter us, and we leave the scoffers to their barren task. When with their cold critical minds they attempt to analyse impressions of beauty, they might as well gravely set about lowering the temperature of those objects upon which they propose to study the action of heat. Far from enlightening and sharpening the faculty of the æstheticist, the critical spirit falsifies it, experience blunts it, science destroys it. "If it were possible for us to recollect all the unaccountable and happy instincts of the careless time, and to reason upon them with the maturer judgment, we might

---

M. Charles Lévêque in his *Science du Beau*. And when Töpffer speaks in his *Menus Propos* of the "æsthetic faculty," or when more recently M. Cherbuliez in his book *L'Art et la Nature* analyses the *plaisir esthétique*, they express the same idea in the same manner as Ruskin, though they use another phrase.

Translator's note.—To meet the difficulty of translating the phrase *sentiment esthétique*, I shall in future use Mr. Ruskin's own words, "theoretic faculty," although perhaps the difference might be rendered by the phrase "æsthetical sentiment" which I have used hitherto. Also, as Mr. Ruskin proscribes the use of the words æsthetic and æsthete, I have used *æsthetical* and *æstheticist* to render the French *esthétique* and *esthéticien*.

arrive at more rapid and right results than either the philosophy or the sophisticated practice of art have yet attained." Only those who have preserved the purity of their impressions can fathom the purity of crystalline colours. The world of beauty is like the beryl in Rossetti's ballad:

"None sees here but the pure alone,"

and, in truth, "ye must be as little children or ye will not enter into the kingdom" of art.

Because it belongs to the simple-minded and does not depend upon active reason, this faculty is not to be ignored, still less is it to be disdained. For this were to despise the most precious of the gifts distributed by those good fairies who stood by the cradle of humanity. The theoretic or æsthetical faculty belongs to man alone. Whether an animal is affected by the Utility of things, we cannot assert or deny, but before Beauty man alone is moved and trembles. "So much as there is in you of ox or swine perceives no beauty and creates none. What is human in you, in exact proportion to the perfectness of its humanity, can create it and receive." That the animal sees is indisputable, and up to a certain point he reasons: but man contemplates. Paul Potter's *Vache qui se mire* looks at her own reflection: but man marvels at the likeness of God. "It is the human faculty, entirely human, which makes us love rocks not for ourselves but for themselves," — for their outline against the blue sky. We need look no further for

I. NATURE

the fundamental difference between man and all that is said to resemble him. For instance: Here is a beautiful and slender plant with infinitely changing curves and harmoniously assorted tints: some creature on all fours rushes towards it, seizes it, and devours it. What was that creature? I do not know. It was a sudden impulse. But it tore up the plant in order to hide it and find it again. What creature was that? I do not know. There are many animals that hide their prey or their food. It is an act which borders on the reasoning power.—But yet another creature paused before the plant for a long time to admire it. What was this creature? I know that well: it was a man. The *theoretic* faculty was there.

Whereas this faculty is distinctive of the nature of man, nothing human should escape from its grasp. Every true philosopher furnished with this instrument of study must take into consideration the part which nature and beauty play in every action or idea brought to his notice. He must seek in the soul for the lines of the landscapes upon which the eye gazed. He must seek in the heart for the resolves left there by the "grandeur or expression of the hills." While searching out final causes in the presence of "frowning rocks," he will not say in the words of a past thinker, wondering in himself for whom their creator could have made them, "They are inhabited by the beasts"; but he will study whether they "seem to have been built for the human race as at once their schools and cathedrals, full of treasures of illuminated manuscript for the scholar, kindly in simple lessons to the worker, quiet in pale cloisters for the thinker, glorious in holiness for the worshipper." He will inquire whether "the occult influence of mountains has been both constant and essential to the progress of the race," and whether he can "justly refuse to mountain scenery some share in giving the Greeks and the Italians their intellectual lead among the nations of Europe." He must consider for example that "there is not a single spot of land in either of these countries from which mountains are not discernible; almost always they form the principal feature of the scenery. The mountain outlines seen from Sparta, Corinth, Athens, Rome, Florence, Pisa, Verona, are of consummate beauty; and whatever dislike or contempt may be traceable in the mind of the Greeks for mountain raggedness, their placing the shrine of Apollo under the cliffs of Delphi, and his throne upon Parnassus, was a testimony to all succeeding time that they themselves attributed the best part of their intellectual inspiration to the power of the hills."

Perhaps too the source of many great ideas which govern the world might be traced to the contemplation of certain familiar horizons: for instance the source of patriotism. The country is in fact the beloved face of this mother—$T\grave{\eta}\nu\ \mu\eta\tau\rho\iota\delta a$—which else would be represented by a cold abstraction only, or by a heavy female statue like those in the Place de la Concorde. We do not associate our country with an assembly of bald and black men, gesticulating in the light of parliamentary gas, or writing within the precincts of municipal offices: no, but rather it is the fringe of mountains, the flowing water of rivers, the blue curves of limpid bays, the undulating valleys scored, like engraved plates, with fields and furrows, the villages scattered by the roadside, the smoke of cities rising in the azure sky of evening. . . . And the more beautiful the vision so much the greater will be the love its image will inspire. The Scot for example adores his country. For "it is the peculiar character of Scottish as distinct from all other scenery on a small scale in North Europe, to have these distinctively 'mindable' features. One range of coteaux by a French river is exactly like another; one turn of glen in the Black Forest is only the last turn returned; one sweep of Jura pasture and crag, the mere echo of the fields and crags of ten miles away. But in the whole course of Tweed, Teviot, Gala, Tay, Forth, and Clyde, there is perhaps scarcely a bend of ravine, or nook of valley, which would not be recognisable by its inhabitants from any other. And there is no other country in which the roots of memory are so entwined with the beauty of nature, instead of the pride of men."

Hence it follows that this Beauty ought to be the chief preoccupation of the patriot, inasmuch as she has been his chief instructress. For it boots little what we do to perpetuate the idea of our country if we do not also preserve her beloved face with solicitude. It is not by scattering statues broadcast that we shall reap a harvest of great men, but by respecting the unhewn stones throughout the land. "A nation is only worthy of the soil and the scenes that it has inherited, when, by all its acts and arts, it is making them more lovely for its children."

§ 3

Finally, when the effects of Nature and Beauty on the human soul have been fully studied, and we enter upon a survey of the causes of Nature and Beauty, the "theoretic faculty" is again called upon to intervene. Of the great problems belonging to the soul nothing should be decided without reference to that science whose domain is a part of the soul, nor until it is measured and gauged by this superior instinct. Ruskin teaches us that to propound any theory of the law, origin, and destiny of the universe is useless if, while satisfying our reason, it jars with our feeling; if all the enthusiasm of our nature protests against its conclusions. Whenever the theory of "Progress by Evolution" is advanced, we should seek the presence of the Theseus of the Parthenon to explain why that glorious and immortal relic bears witness to what Taine once termed "a more complete humanity than our own." And likewise in the British Museum in front of an "Etruscan Demeter riding on a car, whose wheels are of wild roses," we have to learn wherein — setting aside their perfume — these

I. NATURE

roses differ from those growing wild on the hillside at Brantwood. Trifling problems indeed. Has a student leisure to look up to the eyes of statues or to lower his own to the roses? No! but those who have the leisure should be satisfied with this sort of curiosity. "To a painter the essential character of anything is the form of it; and the philosophers cannot touch that. They come and tell you, for instance, that there is as much heat, or motion, or calorific energy, (or whatever else they like to call it) in a tea-kettle as in a Gier-eagle. Very good; that is so; and it is very interesting. It requires just as much heat as will boil the kettle, to take the Gier-eagle up to his nest; and as much more to bring him down again on a hare or a partridge. But we painters, acknowledging the equality and similarity of the kettle and the bird in all scientific respects attach, for our part, our principal interest in the difference in their forms. For us, the primarily cognisable facts, in the two things, are, that the kettle has a spout, and the eagle a beak; the one a lid on its back, the other a pair of wings."

Further, "when we examine these wings and find in all birds such divers types of beauty," or when "we study the varied colours which correspond to our innermost sensations of joy or melancholy, awaking them at the sight of a passing redbreast, or again lulling them to rest," let us beware of explanations, which account for everything except that beauty, and thereby destroy the very charm we desire to preserve. Darwin was a great man, and we owe him many true ideas concerning what he saw, but did he see everything? "We might even sufficiently represent the general manner of conclusion in the Darwinian system by the statement that if you fasten a hairbrush to a millwheel, with the handle forward, so as to develop itself into a neck by moving always in the same direction, and within continual hearing of a steam-whistle, after a certain number of revolutions the hairbrush will fall in love with the whistle; they will marry, lay an egg, and the produce will be a nightingale." Although perhaps somewhat extravagant, this interpretation of the origins of beauty does not differ very largely from statements propounded with great gravity by learned men. "The Theorists of development say, I suppose, that partridges get brown by looking at stubble, seagulls white by looking at foam, and jackdaws black by looking at clergymen." After these hypotheses we may perhaps be permitted to remark that the feathers of birds are usually "reserved and quiet in colour" when they are "feathers of force" and brilliant when they are intended for "decoration or expression."— "There is no iridescent eagle, no purple and golden seagull; while a large mass of coloured birds—parrots, pheasants, humming birds—seem meant for human amusement. Seem meant—dispute it if you will: no matter what they seem, they are the most amusing and infinitely delicious toys, lessons, comforts, amazements, of human existence."

Thus when an explanation is offered of the creation of birds or any other organised creatures, its artistic side must not be overlooked. "Hold fast to the form and defend that first as distinguished from the mere transition of forces. Discern the moulding hand of the potter commanding the clay from his merely beating foot as it turns the wheel. It is curious how far mere form will carry you ahead of the philosophers." For the æsthetic instinct proceeds by synthesis, and "a modern philosopher is a great separator: it is little more than the expansion of Molière's great sentence: 'It follows from this that all that is beautiful is to be found in dictionaries, it is only the words which are transposed.'" But "there is beyond the merely formative and sustaining power another which we painters call 'passion.'" "I don't know what the philosophers call it; we know it makes people red or white; and therefore it must be something itself: and perhaps it is the most truly 'poetic' or 'making' force of all, creating a world of its own out of a glance, or a sigh: and the want of passion is perhaps the truest death, or 'unmaking' of everything;—even of stones."

Now this power is that of the artist; and it is unmistakable. "I can very positively assure you that in my poor domain of imitative art, not all the mechanical or gaseous forces of the world, nor all the laws of the universe, will enable you either to see a colour, or draw a line, without that singular force anciently called the soul." The power of chance is very great but it is not artistic, and though if forced to it we might imagine "a clock without a clockmaker," it is very difficult to study a masterpiece and forthwith deny the master. The learned are quite at their ease over this problem. They do not see the picture! The more they reason about the æsthetical side of nature, the more they prove by their arguments that they do not perceive it. When they pretend to explain the Beautiful by the Useful, "they can be compared to nothing so accurately as to the woodworms in the panel of a picture by some great painter, if we may conceive them as tasting with discrimination of the wood, and with repugnance of the colour, and declaring that even this unlooked-for and undesirable combination is a normal result of the action of molecular Forces."

For those who have seen the picture, for those who have found the happiness of their lives in its varied and delicate colour, its hues spiritual, harmonious, and powerful, who have loved it with the passion of youth and sought to produce unworthy though faithful imitations, who have suffered when anything came to tarnish it and wept for joy when it was restored to them in its primitive purity, for such as these the problems of creation cannot be altogether solved by "variations of species," and the last word is not said though men have thought for six thousand years.

"The æsthetic relations of species are independent of their origin. The flower is the end or proper object of the seed, not the seed of the flower. The reason for seeds is that flowers may be; not the reason of flowers that seeds may be. The flower itself is the creature which the spirit makes; only, in connection with its perfectness, is placed the giving birth to its successor. The main fact then about a flower is that it is the part of the plant's form developed at the moment of its intensest life: and this inner rapture is usually marked externally for us by the flush of one or more of the primary colours. What the character of the flower shall be, depends entirely upon the portion of the plant into which this rapture of spirit has been put. Sometimes the life is put into its outer sheath, and then the outer sheath becomes white and pure, and full of strength and grace; sometimes the life is put into the common leaves, just under the blossom, and they become scarlet or purple; sometimes the life is put into the stalks of the flower, and they flush blue; sometimes into its outer enclosure or calyx; mostly into its inner cup; but, in all cases, the presence of the strongest life is asserted by characters in which the human sight takes pleasure, and which seem prepared with distinct reference to us, or rather, bear, in being delightful, evidence of having been produced by the power of the same spirit as our own. . . . And observe, again and again, with respect to all these divisions and powers of plants, it does not matter in the least by what concurrences of circumstance or necessity they may gradually have been developed: the concurrence of circumstance is itself the supreme and inexplicable fact. We always come at last to a formative cause, which directs the circumstance and mode of meeting it. If you ask an ordinary botanist the reason of the form of a leaf, he will tell you it is a 'developed tubercle,' and that its ultimate form 'is owing to the directions of its vascular threads.' But what directs its vascular threads? 'They are seeking for something they want,' he will probably answer. What made them want that? What made them seek for it thus? Seek for it, in five fibres or in three? Seek for it, in serration, or in sweeping curves? Seek for it, in servile tendrils, or impetuous spray? Seek for it, in woollen wrinkles rough with stings, or in glossy surfaces, green with pure strength, and winterless delight? There is no answer. But the sum of all is, that over the entire surface of the earth and its waters, as influenced by the power of the air under solar light, there is developed a series of changing forms, in clouds, plants, and animals, all of which have reference in their action or nature to the human intelligence that perceives them; and on which, in their aspects of horror and beauty, and their qualities of good and evil, there is engraved a series of myths, or words of the forming power, which, according to the true passion and energy of the human race, they have been enabled to read into religion. And this forming power has been by all nations partly confused with the breath or air through which it acts, and partly understood as a creative wisdom; proceeding from the Supreme Deity; but entering into and inspiring all intelligences that work in harmony with Him. And whatever intellectual results may be in modern days obtained by regarding this effluence only as a motion or vibration,

I. NATURE 175

every formative human art hitherto, and the best states of human happiness and order, have depended on the apprehension of its mystery (which is certain) and of its personality (which is probable)."

At this point the Prophet of the Beautiful stops. He has said enough for those who love Nature, and too much for those who do not love her. Yet he cannot be reproached either with prejudice or dogmatism. He affirms only what his eyes have seen: he repeats only what his ears have heard. The faith that cradled his childhood is long since vanished under the stress of doubt. From the professorial chair at Oxford, to the scandal of the old university, he attacked with righteous indignation the tyranny of dogma and "the insolence of faith." He denounced the pride of that church which "imagines that myriads of the inhabitants of the world for four thousand years have been left to wander and perish, many of them everlastingly, in order that, in fulness of time, divine truth might be preached sufficiently to ourselves," and derided those mystics "who are withdrawn from all such true service of man, that they may pass the best part of their lives in what they are told is the service of God; namely, desiring what they cannot obtain, lamenting what they cannot avoid, and reflecting on what they cannot understand." Yet he renounced not at the behest of materialism the free discussion of his perceptions, nor bowed the knee before "the insolence of science." He maintained at the doors of laboratories the same earnest scepticism he dared to advocate in the precincts of cathedrals. He would not by denying or belittling the problems before him accept the solutions of either reason or faith. In the fulness of his strength and fame, in all sanity of thought, and before the evening of life, Ruskin turned again to Nature and found her still unexplained, if not in her forces at least in her beauty. The Beauty of Nature, he always insisted, is the mainspring of men's actions, the supreme joy and the law for ever. Therefore it demands explanation, or, if it cannot be explained, the mystery which hangs about our most intense life, the life of "admiration," must be acknowledged. The gate of the Unknown, that science would fain close, he opens quietly but firmly, showing that there is no one science, but simply divers sciences, and among them one so little advanced as to be hardly recognised or definable, but which must exist since its object plays so important a part among those things which make us what we are, as well as among those which we ourselves create. It seems clear to him that the question he asked remains unanswered, and that there is truly "more Æsthetic in heaven and earth," than is taught in our schools of philosophy. . . .

Thus he returns to the God of his youth, not so much because He is Truth as because He is the revelation of Beauty, and the philosophers explain only Ugliness. Throughout the range of legend he yields to the spell that mars no beauty and casts no gloom, and that accords best with his own "theoretic faculty." Christ becomes for him the supreme and benign Artist Who works with His hands to adorn

I. NATURE

the dwelling-place of man; He is the Gardener met by the Magdalen, Who watches over new-born flowers; He is the unknown Painter Who gives to the edge of the gentian the touch that beautifies; He is the subtle Weaver Who arrays the lily in glory greater than that of Solomon; He is the Labourer in the vineyard, admitted to the feast of Cana, Who in every cluster of grapes changes the water of earth and heaven into wine. In the awakening of Spring, in the light that shines on the hills, in the refreshing stream from the mountain,—Christ is all in all. He is Nature, He is Beauty, He is Love. We cannot then wonder that the disciple of Beauty is the disciple of Christ; nor yet that, towards the evening of his life in September 1888, when making his intellectual testament and garnering into a sheaf all the radiance of his thought —as the sun at the moment of setting seems to gather up every beam it scattered during the day, Ruskin says: "And now, in writing beneath the cloudless peace of the snows of Chamouni, what must be really the final words of the book which their beauty inspired and their strength guided, I am able, with yet happier and calmer heart than heretofore, to enforce its simplest assurance of Faith, that the knowledge of what is beautiful leads on, and is the first step to the knowledge of the things which are lovely and of good report; and that the laws, the life, and the joy of Beauty, in the material world of God, are as eternal and sacred parts of His creation as, in the world of spirits, virtue; and in the world of angels, praise."

CHAPTER II

"ART"

§ 1

IF this be Nature, what must be demanded of Art? Verily something exceeding great, and at the same time exceeding humble; great compared with ourselves, humble compared with Nature. For if "the life, the joys, and the laws of Beauty in God's material world are as sacred a part of His creation as" virtue in the world of spirits, the man who investigates those laws recalls those joys, and prolongs that life, the artist, accomplishes one of the highest tasks of humanity. He stands between us and nature. He is the decipherer, the singer, the recorder. All others have their divers pursuits, their writing, their cricket, their business. His mission is to arrest and say to us: "Look at this pebble and its veins. Look at this blade of grass and learn its lesson. Look at this muscle. Look at this sky. . . . Do you think this is purposeless?"

"Who, among the whole chattering crowd, can tell me of the forms and the precipices of the chain of tall white mountains that girded the horizon at noon yesterday?"—"One says, it has been wet; and another, it has been windy; and another, it has been warm."—"Who saw the narrow sunbeam that came out of the south, and smote upon their summits until they melted and mouldered away in a dust of blue rain?" The artist sees it all. He makes us pause with him, or at any rate he makes it pause for us. For this man performs miracles. "He may at last literally command the rainbow to stay and forbid the sun to set ... he incorporates the things which have no measure and immortalises the things that have no duration." He watches Nature like a sentry. He awakens our admiration. He grasps elusive laws; he gives us living joys; it is he who unfolds the æsthetical mysteries that bind us to things on high and to things on earth. Further, it is he who shows us how his age and his country understood these things, and who bequeathes to us the truest testimony. "Great nations write their autobiographies in three manuscripts: the book of their deeds, the book of their words, and the book of their art. Not one of these books can be understood unless we read the two others; but of the three, the only quite trustworthy one is the last. The acts of a nation may be triumphant by its good fortune; and its words mighty by the genius of a few of its children; but its art, only by the general gifts and common sympathies of the race." Thus towards ourselves "all art is teaching."

But at the same time and in the same way that

the function of Art is very great as regards ourselves, it is very humble as regards Nature. With regard to her "all art is Praise." For if the material world has been specially organised with artistic design—if the clouds are painted *al fresco* each evening to delight our eyes as we look up, and the blossoms washed with colour each morning to delight them when they look down—it is in Nature that we must seek for all Beauty. She is the supreme type and the eternal model. Beauty is not found in dreams of the imagination, or in some ideal imposed by tradition. "It is to be found in the leaf that fades and falls to the passing wind, in the smallest pebble which rolls down from the mountain, in the frailest reed which bends over the water. . . . In each of these things the eye of an artist discerns the signature of the Supreme Artist. Nowhere has He forgotten to impress the Seal of Beauty."

What matter if a passer by, absent and preoccupied, observed not the beauty of a dead leaf touched by the sun at the door of a picture-gallery, and when within the gallery admired the picture of some such leaf touched by the far weaker paint-brush of a Venetian. What matter that when he reflected on it, he was surprised and scandalised that Art should have caused him to admire the image of something when he did not admire the reality. Finally, what matter that this man was Pascal, and that his observation is a postulate of the strangest controversies on Nature and Art. It merely proves that he may be a great

II. ART

logician and a poor artist. No artist would have passed with indifference a leaf touched by the sun; he would see it, would look at it, would love it for its golden browns, for its decay, for its touch of light, and for its effect as background; if he had his paint-box perhaps he would have copied it, and thus diverted by this little object despised of Pascal, he would forget to visit the collection of pictures which Pascal felt it his duty to admire. For "a true artist always prefers those reflections which quiver in the Grand Canal to those which sleep in a Canaletto, and the bronzed beggars who bask in the sun at Seville to the mellow flesh tones on the canvases of Murillo." "What healthy art is possible to you must be the expression of your true delight in a real thing, better than the art. . . . You may think, perhaps, that a bird's nest by William Hunt is better than a real bird's nest. We indeed pay a large sum for the one, and scarcely care to look for, or save, the other. But it would be better for us that all the pictures in the world perished, than that the birds should cease to build nests." Yes, leaf or nest, branch or pebble, pearl or wave, in Nature all is Beauty.

It is useless to seek for it on rare occasions or in passing effects. It is useless to lie in wait for marvellous sunsets or to hunt on high plateaux for a flower whose species is almost extinct. "On the shapes which in the everyday world are familiar to the eyes of men, God has stamped those characters of beauty, which He has made it man's nature to love. . . . Yes. . . . Only a coteau, scarce a hundred feet above the rivers, nothing like so high as the Thames banks between here and Reading,—only a coteau, and a recess of calm water, and a breath of mist, and a ray of sunset. The simplest things, the frequentest, the dearest; things that you may see any summer evening, by a thousand streams among the low hills of old familiar lands. Love them, and see them rightly,—Andes and Caucasus, Amazon and Indus, can give you no more."

Idealists deceive themselves when they seek far and high the mysterious formula which is graven on every leaflet like the fortune to be told in every open hand. The classical school sought for it in the impossible; the romantic school sought for it in the exceptional. It is in the familiar and the frequent, and we may boldly assume "that which is most (visibly) frequent to be most beautiful."

Mark, not in the things of man but in the things of Nature, the most ordinary things ordained by her, not the extraordinary things of the gardeners; the commonest realities of the mountain not the most ingenious artifices of the mason; the rocks not the rockeries; the lakes not the reservoirs; the clouds not the smoke; the mosses not the carpets. There will indeed be relics of nature and in consequence relics of beauty in a plant trained on a wall, in a tree pruned for its crop of fruit or leaves, in a field saturated with superphosphates, in a canal made with concrete for irrigation. But these are only relics, poor recollections of the great one we have defaced. We can still love them as we love the features, however withered and seamed and scarred, of a face that was dear to us. We can no longer see their prototype and the criterion of beauty. Only in nature, and in virgin nature, is it present, because nature is only truly herself when nothing has been done to travesty or deface her. "Note that there is this great peculiarity about sky subjects, as distinguished from earth subjects;—that the clouds, not being much liable to man's interference, are always beautifully arranged. You cannot be sure of this in any other feature of landscape. The rock on which the effect of a mountain scene especially depends is always precisely that which the roadmaker blasts or the landlord quarries; and the spot of green which Nature left with a special purpose by her dark forest sides, and finished with her most delicate grasses, is always that which the farmer ploughs or builds upon. But the clouds, though we can hide them with smoke, and mix them with poison, cannot be quarried nor built over, and they are always therefore gloriously arranged."

It is in the presence of the free unbridled waves, in the deep valleys, where the water, the herbs, the lights, the shadows, and all living growths have full play that the artist finds the keenest enjoyments of his life. "The pure love of nature in myself has always been quite exclusively confined to wild, that is to say, wholly natural places, and especially to scenery animated by streams, or by the sea. The sense of the freedom, the spontaneous, unpolluted power of nature was essential in it." All that leads back to Nature makes for Beauty. All that departs from her walks in the way of ugliness.[1]

This conception of Beauty determines the attitude the artist adopts towards Nature, and the attitude he adopts towards Nature is the only question in art.

All the technical experiments of a painter among his colours or pounded bones, or of the sculptor kneading his clay, all the philosophical comments of æstheticists haranguing in their lectures, lead back at last to this question: What attitude to adopt towards Nature? From the answers given, all the schools, cliques, sects, and studios derive their differences. Divested of the verbiage and ambiguities which encumber it, the question propounds itself to these witnesses to the splendour of nature under heaven, in just the same form that it is put to witnesses of the crimes of men in a court of justice. Shall I speak the truth? Shall I speak the whole truth? Shall I speak nothing but the truth? asks the landscape painter under his tent, the sculptor with his chisel, the portrait painter walking round

[1] On this point as on all others the statement that we make of Ruskin's thought is not based on an isolated text nor on a passing opinion of the Master, but on the general scope of his teaching. So that the thesis here expounded is taken from the works belonging to all the periods of his life, from *Modern Painters*, published 1843-1860, from *Seven Lamps*, 1849, from *Elements of Drawing*, 1857, from *The Art of England*, 1883, and from *Præterita*, 1883-1889.

his model. Shall I draw the oak as it appears to me in its entirety, without adding anything to it, without falsifying its appearance, but massing the foliage and overlooking certain branches seemingly unnecessary to its beauty? or in other terms, shall I tell the truth? Shall I draw the smallest details? Shall I mark out with equal distinctness even the accidents and the appearances which please me least —in other words, shall I tell the whole truth? Shall I not add to the theme suggested by this oak, the improvements, the embellishments, all the other ideas of oaks that I may have—in a word, shall I say nothing but the truth? According to his decision the artist will be classed as an eclectic, a realist, or an idealist. He will follow one of the three great theories whence all the theories of art proceed; the theory of choice, the theory of literal imitation, the theory of idealisation.

We have defined Beauty to be "the signature of God upon His works," and even in the very least of His works, if we have affirmed that all Nature is Beauty, we do not therefore accept the theory of choice, still less that of idealisation. Choice! Who would dare make it?

"Let therefore the young artist beware of the spirit of Choice; it is an insolent spirit at the best, and commonly a base and blind one too, checking all progress and blasting all power, encouraging weaknesses, pampering partialities. . . ." "He draws nothing well who thirsts not to draw everything;

when a good painter shrinks, it is because he is humbled, not fastidious; when he stops, it is because he is surfeited, and not because he thinks Nature has given him unkindly food. . . . I have seen a man of true taste pause for a quarter of an hour to look at the channelings that recent rain had traced in a heap of cinders. . . . Perfect art perceives and reflects the whole of nature; imperfect art is fastidious, and impertinently prefers and rejects."

Therefore it follows according to the saying which created Pre-Raphaelitism, that the artist "should go to nature in all singleness of heart, rejecting nothing, selecting nothing, and scorning nothing."

Is it necessary to add also idealising nothing? To choose is insolence, but to idealise is sacrilege. It is the paradoxical, absurd pretension of a narrow mind which, unable to penetrate the beauty scattered throughout Nature, undertakes to create beauty according to its own wretched imagination. Imagination must create nothing; its function is to "penetrate truth, to associate truth, to contemplate truth." It is not to substitute or add anything to truth. "The error respecting this faculty is, in considering that its function is one of falsehood, and that its operation is to exhibit things as they are not." Why falsify when the reality is so beautiful? What "moulding and melting of individual beauties together," what academic outline, what marble statues, could ever have the value of living children of men with "their colour heightened by the sun," and "their hair drifted by the breeze"?

II. ART 187

"No Greek goddess was ever half so pretty as an English girl of pure clay and temper." The greatest of the Old Masters introduced into all their works claiming imagination, their Paradises and Resurrections, the true portraits of their patrons, of their servants, of their mistresses, of their creditors; and this was "not an error in them, but the very source and root of their superiority in all things; for they were too great and too humble not to see in every face about them that which was above them, and which no fancies of theirs could match or take place of."

What need have we to paint those regions of dreams to which we have never attained, those creatures of faith which we have never seen? When the masters have attempted it they have always fallen therein below their accustomed level. "Whatever is truly great in either Greek or Christian art is also restrictedly human, and even the raptures of the redeemed soul who enters 'celestemente ballands' the Gate of Angelico's Paradise were seen first in the terrestrial yet most pure mirth of Florentine maidens." "Of that which is more than creature no creature ever conceived," and it is neither useful nor proper to attempt it. Not to see beauty in a swallow and to fancy we can depict it in a seraph, what madness! "If you are not inclined to look at the wings of birds which God has given you to handle and to see, much less are you to contemplate or draw imaginations of the wings of angels which you can't see. Know your own world first—not denying any other—

but being quite sure that the place in which you are now put is the place with which you are now concerned." And above all do not dare under the pretence of idealism or of mysticism to teach nature or "to improve the works of God."

Realism then is all that is left for us, and we should approve of it if Realism, as the modern studios understand it, were truly the imitation and worship of nature. But far from admiring and seeking nature, there is perhaps no school extant that has more deliberately proscribed it and more insolently traduced it than the Realistic. Far from attempting to reproduce what is natural and original in the world, it has set itself to depict the artificial and the accidental. The sophism of this school must be unmasked. Starting from a true principle, namely that Nature far surpasses human imagination, it has by a strange abuse of words arrived at the extravagant conclusion that everything due to man's handiwork—factories, pavements, locomotives, cabs, bicycles, tea-gardens, and railway banks, may be classed as nature, and under this title must compel our admiration. These whimsical lovers of reality who begin by fabricating according to their own ideas some ugly object opposed to all natural laws, and then assert that the object is beautiful simply because it is real, show both a lack of precision in their argument (because in this manner the real cannot be contrasted with the artificial) and of love for the reality, which they disfigure before reproducing.

They invent a tall hat, a chimney-pot *à huit reflets*, and immediately reproduce it on canvas or in bronze, saying it is beautiful because it is nature. They go into a bar, catalogue its collection of many-coloured bottles, study the dimmed and many-spotted mirrors, steep themselves in its smoky atmosphere, and then paint the barmaid in the midst of this grim circumstance of false civilisation, and say to us it is beautiful because it is nature. They go into a hospital and taking a face under chloroform, anæsthetised, and insensible, turn *rhéophores* on to it, to galvanise smiles from a suffering man, obtain angry grimaces where all was at rest, study thus each movement of the muscles, and then tell us that they have found "Nature and the man that has lived," when they should say that they have taken pains to find artifice and the man that is dead. Even worse, they go and look for nature in the theatre with the light not of the sun but of the gas, lighting no living flesh but "the gauze transparencies of creatures," skimming not the ground but boards, breathing not beneath the clouds but "chemical illuminations," treading not with bare lithe feet but pirouetting, their toes deformed by dancing—and dancing to some *pizzicato* mode, not to a measure of flutes in an ancestral barn. Here is Nature, they say, taken in the act, and here also is Beauty. But if this is Nature, what is artifice? If this be the earth, where then is the soil and the nourishing corn and the consoling flowers? If this be sky, where then is the firmament, whence come

the rain which fructifies and the rays which ripen,
—to find them again, rather let us open our windows;
no, let us leave the theatre where the realists seek
models for their faces; let us pass the suburbs where
they seek the models for their landscapes; and let
us go forth where electricity does not meander along
the ground, where the air is not imprisoned or compressed to carry telegrams but free to form clouds;
where "the play shall be wholesome play, not in
theatrical gardens with tin flowers and gas sunshine,
and girls dancing because of their misery; but in
true gardens, with real flowers and real sunshine, and
children dancing because of their gladness." There
is nature and there also is beauty.

The plastic beauty in form as well as the picturesque in landscape—that is plain enough, for if we
maintain that it is to be found in the human body
as created by nature, we do not say that the types
ordinarily chosen by the realists represent nature or
correspond to beauty. Let us take an elector or a
petty official sitting outside a café, who with a suitable
gesture drinks a good *bock*, or tastes an absinthe.
He is stooping under the weight of inherited ill, deformed by the accessories of modern costume, soured
by the passions and vices of our time, his muscles
atrophied by want of use, his skin white and discoloured from useless clothing, his hand trembling
with drink. . . . Is this the natural man, and if ever
there was an artificial being in the world is it not
he? Is the *morphomaniac* or the *chlorotic* woman

as Nature made her, or the powdered and enamelled lady with hair interwoven with threads of gold? Is it Nature who formed the hands of modern workmen, who has put these weals on the leather-dresser, those blisters on the workers in metal? Is the complexion of a face under an electric lamp natural? According to this, which would be the true light, which the artificial? Doubtless that of the sun. . . . Under what pretext do the realists proscribe the lights of the romanticists or of M. Hébert as false, as gleams filtered into cellars, when they admit in their own pictures the lights of theatres and factories, when all the artificial effects of M. Hébert or of M. Henner can be obtained if necessary by the well-combined play of gas and electricity? When they show us, in those hospital scenes which they so much affect, the electrical treatment on the muscles and the skin, or when they whiten the face of a clown and transfer him to their canvases, informing us that these are all realities, have they truly any realism, and have they any real respect for that nature whose name they inscribe on their banner? No, the man of nature, the true creature supremely beautiful, is such a form as arises lithe and joyous from the strong hand of the Potter Who moulds the human clay, not such as the needs, true or false, of civilisation have caricatured it. It is the man of the early ages, straight as a lath, not the man of the age of steam, distorted by a false education. It is the Apollo of Syracuse, not Mr. Gladstone's elector. It is the man made by nature, not the "self-made man."

The beautiful is not then to be found in an ideal on the one hand, nor is it on the other hand in nature deformed as copied by the realists, but in natural Nature, and if in the present day we do not easily find this nature, if all the human figures around us are blurred by "the visible and instant operation of unconquered Sin," then let us go back not to a dream but to a reality,—a reality which has passed away, to a memory of the happy time when man, strong, pure, radiant and confident, stepped free in the splendid landscapes, not yet destroyed or polluted. Plato possibly was not very far wrong. The ideal of to-day is perhaps merely a memory of the realities gone by. . . . Let us piously keep the recollection of this brilliant vision not the less real because it has passed away. Let us respect the monuments which have been left to us. "A beautiful thing may exist but for a moment as a reality;—it exists for ever as a testimony. To the law and to the witness of it the nations must appeal *in sæcula sæculorum;* and in very deed and very truth a thing of beauty is a *law* for ever."

The reply then to the question: What is the aim of art, and what should it show us? is simply: Nature as it is, Man as he has been. The road to virgin nature is easy to find; it leads us to the valleys that factories have respected and to the seas they cannot pollute. For the painter of figures and for the sculptor, it is perhaps a difficult enterprise to reconstitute man not yet debased by vice or deformed by mechanical labour, but at any rate we must press towards the attainment of this reality, and not in the direction of anything but reality. We must have no abstractions, additions, or embellishments, but we may banish from the face the signs of degradation that the artificial life of our day has stamped upon him. We must not invent anything outside reality, but we may efface the accretions that civilisation and misfortune have added to reality. Thus we shall not be effacing natural truths but on the contrary reconstituting the true text by getting rid of interpolation. "Now, first of all, this work, be it observed, is in no respect a work of imagination. Wrecked we are, and nearly all to pieces; but that little good by which we are to redeem ourselves is to be got out of the old wreck, beaten about and full of sand though it be; and not out of that desert island of pride on which the devils split first, and we after them. . . . We lay it down for a first principle that our graphic art, whether painting or sculpture, is to produce something which shall look as like Nature as possible."

§ 2

But Nature how looked at? With the eyes or with the Röntgen rays? Nature how touched? With the hand or with the scalpel? Nature how observed? Contemplatively during years as by the recluse of Mount Athos or of the Alps, or *chronophotographically* in the two-thousandth of a second by a disciple of Mr. Muybridge or of Mr. Marey, who arrives, photographs, and departs by the next express? We must distinguish, for in Æsthetics words are so accommodating, and the vocabulary so ill defined, that in saying we ought to keep close to Nature we may be taken for a photographer, for an anatomist, for a geologist, for a scavenger. None of these men see, or come near to seeing, Nature æsthetically, any more than the fireman standing behind the scenes has any idea of the effect of an opera. He is opposite to the things he ought only to see in profile, and deafened by a single part, he cannot seize the whole. He will only see something the day the theatre takes fire. We shall need him then, and he will know better than we do why it burns, the causes thereof, and—speaking of the student's view of Nature—the mighty convulsions of the human machine which holds our soul, of the earth and the sea around us; but in that day there will be no more art, and the spectacle will be at an end. . . . As long as it lasts it is not as a student, but as a *seer* that we must look at Nature —simply with the eyes of a man "in health," and with the heart of a lover who seeks only to admire. "Turner, in his early life, was sometimes good-natured, and would show people what he was about. He was one day making a drawing of Plymouth harbour, with some ships at a distance of a mile or two, seen against the light. Having shown this drawing to a naval officer, the naval officer observed

II. ART

with surprise, and objected with very justifiable indignation, that the ships of the line had no port-holes. 'No,' said Turner, 'certainly not. If you will walk up to Mount Edgecumbe, and look at the ships against the sunset, you will find that you can't see the port-holes.' 'Well, but,' said the naval officer, still indignant, 'you know the port-holes are there.' 'Yes,' said Turner, 'I know that well enough; but my business is to draw what I see, and not what I know is there.'"

What we see, what we know, what we feel, not what we understand,—this is æsthetical truth as opposed to scientific truth, and this is the truth which Art should as closely as possible express, and should penetrate in order to express. Do those learned men who maintain that they show things as they are adhere to the plan of Nature? No, they violate it, for her plan is often to show us the things as they are not. And to reproduce the keels hidden under the dark water, the bones hidden under opaque flesh, movements disguised by the rapidity with which they are executed,—in a word, to show in everything the "appearances" she hides from our eyes is not to follow Nature, nor to be faithful to her,—it is to betray her. All treachery is punished, and Nature does not give her full beauty to the artist who has questioned her without reverence and despoiled her without love. She bestows her treasure on those who love her. She yielded herself to the Greeks who beheld her in her plastic purity, living, moving, blushing, fading, trembling before them. . . . The Greeks went in quest of her in full light of day, in the free air, under the blue sky of Attica, following her design and the way she wishes to be seen—and they captured her beauty. The study of the nude is the science of the living.

The learned men of the Renaissance looked at her otherwise, with inquisitorial and indiscreet eyes. They exposed the muscle and studied the anatomy of the human frame by torchlight, in its darkest recesses. It is the science of the tomb. What has come of it? Muscles swollen and stiffened, figures as if flayed in the pictures of Mantegna, iron-bound outlines as in the engravings of Dürer, bundles of ropes for tendons and knots for muscles. "Look at Mantegna's magnificent *Mythology of the Vices* in the Louvre for instance, the anatomy is entirely revolting to all women and children. . . . In the middle of the gallery of the Brera at Milan there is an elaborate study of a dead Christ entirely characteristic of early fifteenth-century Italian madman's work. It is only an anatomical study of a vulgar and ghastly dead body, with the soles of the feet set straight at the spectator and the rest foreshortened. It is exactly characteristic of this madness in all of them—Pollajuolo, Castagno, Mantegna, Vinci, Michael Angelo—these great artists who polluted all their work with the science of the sepulchre."

The great crime of the Renaissance was not, as the Mystics have supposed, indolence and pleasure, but knowledge. The Renaissance did not sin by too much exuberance of life, and of love, but by too much ambition, deadness, and horror. Where love dwells there can be no scientific inquiry, no learned display of discoveries. We shall not vivisect what we love. Elsa asked his name of Lohengrin, but not the number of the muscles of his skin nor the form of his spinal apophyses, and even she asked too much. Lohengrin disappeared. . . . It is the eternal punishment of the scientific spirit taking the place of love. This punishment awaits all our investigators, our anatomists, our radiographists, our chemists, our electro-biologists, our chronophotographers, and our mathematicians. The scientist thinks to discover movement; he stops it. He thinks to command light; he destroys it. He thinks to seize the life of the muscle; he kills it.

It is the letter of Science which killeth, the spirit of Art which maketh alive; the spirit of Art is nothing but Love, simple, passionate admiration, satisfied with what the eyes see, seeking neither to fathom its mystery nor to improve it outwardly. In saying that "all great Art is Praise," Ruskin means that the artist must not only seek Nature with Love but come to her with reverence, that he must reverence not only her forms and colours but also her whole plan and her design, even in all the details and forms of art. He will not permit the artist to arrange or order her otherwise than she arranges or orders herself. He will be careful how he uses the word "daring nobility" in composition. He abominates generalisation, he distrusts all synthesis. If he admits that a picture should have a guiding line, a principal mass of light, a dominant figure, he adds immediately, "it is in the bad pictures that you would see this law most rigorously manifested." When he speaks of harmony it is as if he were writing a treatise on poison. When he permits the grouping of figures he derives its laws from the attentive examination of the grouping of plants. He only tolerates the subordination of one thing to another because he observes that whenever a leaf is composite—that is to say divided into other leaflets which imitate and repeat it—these leaflets are not symmetrical like the principal leaf, but always smaller in some part, so that one of the elements of subordinate beauty in every tree consists in the confession of its own humility and subjection. The laws of landscape control him equally in sculpture, and prompt those of "glyptic" engraving. He insists above all that the sculptured mass should present from a distance a pure and simple outline and an imperceptibly modelled surface, a "magnificent attribute of reciprocal interference," the planes melting softly one into the other —as in Nature hills are seen at a distance through the rays of the sloping sun, or like waving leaves or rounded fruits with no single flat spot, and no indentations or deep grooves such as Bernini and other artists of the decadence so much affect. The modelling of statues should follow the lines not of drapery but of the human flesh, and not the flat surfaces designed by men, but the rounded spaces decreed by God.

Even in architecture this "thread of Ariadne" is to guide us, because architecture is the art next to landscape which most recalls nature. Ruskin likes architecture better than statues, better than portraits, better than anything which deals with man alone. Because the Gothic style of architecture reproduces most fully and most faithfully the sinuosities of branches, of streams, of leaves, and of flowers, he has greatly preferred that style to the Roman, or Byzantine, or Arab, or Renaissance. In dark and deep recesses of cathedrals his predilections are still those of the landscape painter fascinated by the rocks and the meadows, the rivers and the sunshine. Among the Baptisteries he thinks of the rocky beds whence flow the rivers, and in view of the cupola he thinks of the rounded form of the granite mass. The mountains teach him the construction of churches. In a basilica he would have the stones placed as they lay embedded in the quarry, and not "set up on end." The blocks of marble must lie in accordance with quasi horizontal lines because the masses of the Matterhorn appear to lie thus. He looks askance at the straight line, for it is rarely to be seen in Nature herself, and he would have been ready to attack the cathedrals of Pisa, Florence, Lucca, and Pistoja, for their geometrical ornaments had he not recollected just in time that he has seen the same in crystals.

But as crystals are not often to be met with in the visible aspects of nature, he will not sanction the frequent recurrence of their forms in decoration.

Thus he is irritated by the architect who rounds the curves of the trefoils according to the most exact law of science. In studying the Romanesque and the Byzantine he awaits with impatience the moment when the arch takes the shape of a leaf, the ogive. He watches the length of the smooth and rounded pillars with the anxiety of a Tannhäuser, waiting till his staff bursts into blossom.... In proportion as the leaf of the Greek acanthus expands, subsides, "rolls hither and thither, as if just fresh gathered out of the dew" in the ravine, in proportion as he perceives the winding tracery of the stem rising into "wreaths of flowers on the capitals," he becomes agitated, he recognises a memory of nature, and cries: Here it is! He shares the Byzantine mind, delighting in "the delicacy of subdivision which Nature shows in the fernleaf or parsleyleaf, and so also often the Gothic mind, much enjoying the oak, thorn, and thistle." He praises "the builder of the Ducal Palace" for "using great breadth in his foliage, in order to harmonize with the broad surface of his mighty wall, as Nature delights in the sweeping freshness of the dockleaf or waterlily." In fact he demands that architecture should place "her most exuberant vegetable ornament just where Nature would have placed it."—"Thus the Corinthian capital is beautiful, because it expands under the abacus just as nature would have expanded it; and because it looks as if the leaves had one root, though the root is unseen."

And as in nature nothing is colourless or monotonous, this landscape-architect will have his buildings coloured from top to bottom. Not with red or blue lines marking out the blocks of stone or the fluting of the columns as the braided stripes of uniforms reproduce the ribs of the human skeleton, but on the contrary in varied tones, brilliant and interlaced, overlapping each other like the colours of a shield, playing on the surface of the building as they play in nature, softly veiling without hiding the interior structure of the great architectural building of stone.

Even the simplest houses were painted thus in old days. At Venice "the arms of the family were of course blazoned in their own proper colours, but I think generally on a pure azure ground; the blue colour is still left behind the shields in the Casa Priuli and one or two more of the palaces which are unrestored, and the blue ground was used also to relieve the sculptures of religious subjects. Finally, all the mouldings, capitals, cornices, cusps, and traceries, were either entirely gilded or profusely touched with gold."

Nature ordains it. And beyond ordaining she offers us the necessary materials for the beautifying of our towns. "This rock, then, is prepared by Nature for the sculptor and architect, just as paper is prepared by the manufacturer for the artist. The colours of marble are mingled for us just as if on a prepared palette. They are of all shades and hues (except bad ones), some being united and even, some broken, mixed and interrupted, in order to supply, as far as possible, the want of the painter's power of breaking and mingling the colour with the brush. But there is more in the colours than this delicacy of adaptation. There is history in them. By the manner in which they are arranged in every piece of marble, they record the means by which that marble has been produced, and the successive changes through which it has passed. And in all their veins and zones, and flame-like stainings or broken and disconnected lines, they write various legends, never untrue, of the former political state of the mountain kingdom to which they belonged, of its infirmities and fortitudes, convulsions and consolidations, from the beginning of time."

Let us take these materials and cover our dwellings with them. When this is achieved we have the *chefs-d'œuvre* of architecture,—the achievement of Gothic cathedrals, painted doorways, carved and coloured woods, panels gilded like the sunset. In the Venetian, where all was natural and covered with paintings as rich as the leaves of autumn, we find the apogee. The Renaissance with its grey palaces, its geometric panels, its precise, pompous, cold science, is the winter,—"the winter which succeeded was colourless as it was cold." The day the architect forgot Nature in all her variety of form and colour, that day he lost sight of Beauty. "The degradation of the cinque cento manner of decoration was not owing to its naturalism, to its faithfulness of imitation, but to its imitation of ugly, *i.e.* unnatural things. So long as it restrained itself to sculpture of animals and flowers, it remained noble. But the moment that unnatural objects were associated with these, and armour, and musical instruments, and wild meaningless scrolls and curled shields, and other such fancies," from the day when the landscapists gave place to the archæologists, we feel the chill of reopened sarcophagi, the deadly prick of the compasses, we feel the formalism of the classical and pedantic spirit permeating our dwellings and freezing them. The ribbon without beginning or end replaces the living grass, the senseless streamer knots together the scattered flowers, the sumptuous folds of draperies blown out by imaginary storms disguise the human form. "It is as if the soul of man, itself severed from the root of its health, and about to fall into corruption, lost the perception of life in all things around it; and could no more distinguish the wave of the strong branches, full of muscular strength and sanguine circulation, from the lax bending of a broken cord. "At that moment the doom of Naturalism was sealed, and with it that of the architecture of the world."

We are to follow then in all forms of art, painting, sculpture, architecture, the path Nature traces for us when we behold her with love, and we must seek after her teaching even in the smallest technical detail. Her first teaching is that of repose — repose in colour, repose above all in movement. Her transformations are not rapid, her gestures are not vehement. The tree slowly extends itself towards the sun; the sun sinks by degrees behind the mountain; the mountain stands immovable for centuries. Natural phenomena rarely exhibit those rapid changes of scene which are the joy of children in fairyland. Fullgrown men will marvel more at the slow miracles of germination or at the gradual growth of islands emerging from the sea, the product of myriads of tiny insects during myriads of years. In art we must then deprive ourselves of all representation of tumultuous events, of violent scenes, of figures which run, dance, fall, struggle, or wound; pictures of battles, of the Last Judgment, of Bacchanalian feasts, of martyrs in great contortions of pain, victims nailed to doors, and Christs dying on the Cross. We must condemn naturalism in death in the name of Nature's life, and also dying Christs in the name of her serenity. Simple shepherds kneeling around a cradle, the play of a fountain under the sky, the touch of a bow on a string, a procession of knights to a church, the slow march of ambassadors along a canal, the depression of Melancholy amid the tools of science, the fall of roses from the finger-tips of an angel one by one on to the soft form of the infant Christ playing below,—these are the movements which we may reproduce, because they do not shock our instinct of "permanence." The shepherds of Lorenzo di Credi may retain for any length of time their caressing posture; the monks of Mont Salvat and the great nobles of Carpaccio may pass eternally before our eyes without fatigue, Dürer's figure may remain leaning perpetually on her hand as motionless as a caryatid, and the angel of Botticelli shall strew his flowers everlastingly.

In the lines of these scarce visible gestures or of these pensive attitudes care must be taken to avoid the restlessness which has been excluded from the composition. We must not contort the limbs or twist the draperies of these tranquil personages after the manner of Bernini or Gustave Doré. "The great and temperate designer does not allow himself any violent curves; he works much with lines in which the curvature, though always existing, is long before it is perceived." It is quite the same when he takes the paint-brush. As Nature teaches us repose of line, she teaches us repose of light and shade; and not the chiaroscuro of Salvator Rosa, of Rembrandt, or of Ribera. She does not allow herself great divisions of light and shade, she repudiates illuminated dungeons, the play of dark lanterns and pistol shots in caverns, she abhors contrasts, or tolerates them only well disguised, only allowing "the opposition to tell upon the mind as a surprise but not as a shock." Our interest in the work of art must be awakened in the same manner by the truth of colours and not by their contrasts, by the force of the limbs and not by their efforts, by their forms and not by their deformities. The scene portrayed must attract us not by the strangeness of the situation, but by the reality of the characters. No matter that there is no action amongst the figures, if the outline is so pure and the life so intense that we are in love with this outline and this life for their own sake. No matter that their feet carry them nowhere if they are beautiful in repose; that their hands do not work if they hold in their idle fingers "imprisoned destinies." This is a proof of the greatest art:—The figures in our picture are to be so beautiful that we are moved to love them, and then all action, all gesture, all incident, all movement, become immaterial. "To be with those we love is enough," says La Bruyère; "dreaming, speaking, or not speaking, thinking of them, or thinking of indifferent things, it is all the same to us if only we are near them."

Because we regard her with love Nature must be reproduced with all her minutiæ. The smallest details about those we love are interesting to us, the fleeting expression of the countenance, the veriest detail of the features, the shadow of an eyelid on the cheek, the setting of a nail on the finger, the line, ever deepening, alas, which an invisible hand draws along the forehead. . . . Thus Nature must be rendered with "an eagle's keenness of eye, fineness of finger like a trained violinist, and patience and love like Griselda's." The modern engraver is "presumptuous who covers his plate with intersecting lines sketched at random in shadow with no effort to express a simple leaf or a clod of earth," and draws with flat vague outlines a nameless landscape which we may see anywhere from the window of a railway carriage travelling at sixty miles an hour. "The more cautious he is in assigning the right species of moss to its favourite trunk, and the right kind of weed to its necessary stone, in marking the definite and characteristic leaf, blossom, seed, fracture, colour, and inward anatomy of everything, the more truly ideal his work becomes. All confusion of species, all careless rendering of character, all unnatural and arbitrary association, is vulgar and unideal in proportion to its degree."

But from the very beginning this absolutely correct and precise line must be obtained "with the point, not of pen or crayon, but of the brush, as Apelles did, and as all coloured lines are drawn on Greek vases." Accustomed to draw with the brush, the artist will have much greater facility in the execution of his picture, for he can at any moment rectify by a stroke of his brush any line that a preceding touch had obliterated. The painter who cannot outline with his brush has not mastered the art of drawing. "By the greatest men—by Titian, Velasquez, or Veronese —you will hardly find an authentic drawing at all. For the fact is, that while we moderns have always learned, or tried to learn, to paint by drawing, the ancients learned to draw by painting—or by engraving, more difficult still. The brush was put into their hands when they were children, and they were forced to draw with that, until, if they used the pen or crayon, they used it either with the lightness of a brush or the decision of a graver."

To judge is to choose. Because in the recesses of a thicket the "veins and lines wind and cross by millions, the leaflets make apertures, the angles of the stipules and spines intrude, the circles of the sporangia, the ellipses of the tendrils roll up," because in nature everything is beautiful, must her design be effaced in the drawing and her beauty lost in her luxuriance? No. Nature has its characteristic features and Art should express them. "It may be with lines as with soldiers: three hundred, knowing their work thoroughly, may be stronger than three thousand less sure of their aim." Moreover this is exactly the meaning of the word drawing or designing in things, these qualities that Taine has defined as the "essential qualities of the object." But Taine like all philosophers maintains that the artist should and can make use of this character of Designer according to his particular fancy, his special human inclinations, and his individual temperament. He admits that in so doing the artist becomes superior to his model, and that according to the vigorous and adequate expression of Cherbuliez, "he disentangles Nature." Ruskin never admits even for an instant the superiority of Art over Nature. The artist is not free to choose as he will this or that line in Nature; the conditions of his sight are imperative. Practically in

a thicket we do not see all; we cannot see all. . . .
Now "the really scientific artist is he who not only
asserts bravely what he does see, but confesses
honestly what he does not. You must not draw all
the hairs in an eyelash; not because it is sublime to
generalise them but because it is impossible to see
them. How many hairs there are, a sign painter or
anatomist may count; but how few of them you
can see, it is only the utmost masters, Carpaccio,
Tintoret, Reynolds, and Velasquez, who count and
know." Does the chiromancer regard all the cross-
ings in the open hand that you present to him? No.
There are some lines which alone determine the
Fortune—the master lines. "It is by seizing these
leading lines, when we cannot seize all, that likeness
and expression are given to a portrait, and grace and
a kind of vital truth to the rendering of every natural
form. I call it vital truth, because these chief lines
are always expressive of the past history and present
action of the thing. They show in a mountain, first,
how it was built or heaped up; and secondly how it is
now being worn away, and from what quarter the
wildest storms strike it. In a tree, they show what
kind of fortune it has had to endure from its childhood:
how troublesome trees have come in its way, and
pushed it aside, and tried to strangle or starve it;
where and when kind trees have sheltered it, and
grown up lovingly together with it, bending as it bent;
what winds torment it most; what boughs of it behave
best, and bear most fruit, and so on. In a wave or

cloud, these leading lines show the run of the tide and of the wind, and the sort of change which the water or vapour is at any moment enduring in its form, as it meets shore, or counter-wave, or melting sunshine. Now remember, nothing distinguishes great men from inferior men more than their always, whether in life or in art, *knowing the way things are going.* Try always, whenever you look at a form, to see the lines in it which have had power over its past fate and will have power over its futurity. Those are its *awful* lines; see that you seize on those, whatever else miss."

§ 3

Finally Nature teaches us the worship of colour. We mean colour and not chiaroscuro, which is quite different: "Here is an Arabian vase, in which the pleasure given to the eye is only by lines;—no effect of light, or of colour is attempted. Here is a moonlight by Turner, in which there are no lines at all, and no colours at all. The pleasure given to the eye is only by modes of light and shade, or effects of light. Finally, here is an early Florentine painting, in which there are no lines of importance, and no effect of light whatever; but all the pleasure given to the eye is in gaiety and variety of colour.

"In preparing to draw *any* object, you will find that, practically, you have to ask yourself, Shall I aim at the colour of it, the light of it, or the lines of it? You

II. ART

can't have all three; you can't even have any two out of the three in equal strength.

"And though much of the two subordinate qualities may in each school be consistent with the leading one, yet the schools are evermore separate: as for instance, in other matters, one man says, I will have my fee, and as much honesty as is consistent with it; another, I will have my honesty, and as much fee as is consistent with it. Though the man who will have his fee be subordinately honest, though the man who will have his honour, subordinately rich, are they not evermore of diverse schools?

"So you have, in art, the utterly separate provinces, though in contact at their borders, of

> The Delineators;
> The Chiaroscurists; and
> The Colourists;"

or, to give them their right names, the schools of Raphael, Rembrandt, and Fra Angelico; the laws of Rome, the laws of Amsterdam, and the *Laws of Fésole.*

It is Nature herself who teaches us the *Laws of Fésole.* There have been great masters in the three schools, just as in the dissensions of the Church there have been saints in every order. But the true draughtsman is to look at things in the light of the sun which shimmers, trembles, and blurs the lines. The chiaroscurists have looked at them in the half light and in the mystery of the studio, the walls of which they have sometimes painted in black, so as to concentrate all the strength of light into a focus which kindles the flesh tints, which flashes on armour, or lights the points of spears like tapers. Whoever looks at things in the full light and full air, simply, truthfully, joyously, as Nature herself shows them, will see them not in black and white squares, but in a conglomeration of coloured points. "It is better to consider all Nature merely as a mosaic of different colours, to be imitated one by one in simplicity," and take no count of the supposed laws of chiaroscuro or of shade. We must follow Angelico and Perugino, who are without shade, without sadness, without evil, and not Caravaggio or Spagnoletto, these black slaves of painting. In ourselves there is no shade any more than light; there are only degrees of colour stronger, deeper, thicker. Away then with the grey, the black, the brown, all the tar-brush of the French landscapists of the middle of the century, who seemed to look at "Nature carelessly in the dark mirror." We must darken each tint not with a mixture of dark colour but with its own tint strengthened. Neither must we speak of weakening anything under the pretext of "aërial perspective." There is no special colour which expresses distance. It is false that because our object is far away it has less colour than if it were near. "Vivid orange in an orange is a sign of nearness, for if you put the orange a great way off, its colour will not look so bright; but vivid orange in sky is a sign of distance, because you cannot get the

II. ART

colour of orange in a cloud near you. The green of a Swiss lake is pale in the clear waves on the beach, but intense as an emerald in the sunstreak six miles from shore. It is absurd to expect any help from laws of 'aërial perspective.' Look for the natural effects, and set them down as fully as you can, and as faithfully, and *never* alter a colour because it won't look in its right place. . . . Why should you suppose that Nature always means you to know exactly how far one thing is from another? She certainly intends you always to enjoy her colouring, but she does not wish you always to measure her space. You would be hard put to it, every time you painted the sun setting, if you had to express his 95,000,000 miles of distance in 'aërial perspective.'"

But it would be a mistake to imagine that Ruskin, this Guèbres in love with colour, did not appreciate both its delicacies and its harmonies. And as he knew his fellow-countrymen's taste for loud colours, he boldly warns them not to trust in them. "If colours were twenty times as costly as they are, we should have many more good painters. If I were Chancellor of the Exchequer I would lay a tax of twenty shillings a cake on all colours, and I believe such a tax would do more to advance real art than a great many schools of design." Look at Nature. "She is economical of her fine colours. . . . You would think by the way she paints, that her colours cost her something enormous; she will only give you a single pure touch, just where the petal turns into light; but down in the bell all is subdued, and under the petal all is subdued, even in the showiest flower. . . . Sometimes I have really thought her miserliness intolerable; in a gentian, for instance, the way she economises her ultramarine down in the bell is a little too bad." Like her, we must be lovingly sparing of our colours. " A bad colourist does not *love* beautiful colour better than the best colourist does, nor half so much. But he indulges in it to excess; he uses it in large masses, and unsubdued; and then it is a law of Nature, a law as universal as that of gravitation, that he shall not be able to enjoy it so much as if he had used it in less quantity. His eye is jaded and satiated, and the blue and red have life in them no more. He tries to paint them bluer and redder, in vain: all the blue has become grey, and gets greyer the more he adds to it; all his crimson has become brown, and gets more sere and autumnal the more he deepens it. But the great painter is sternly temperate in his work; he loves the vivid colour with all his heart; but for a long time he does not allow himself anything like it, nothing but sober browns and dull greys, and colours that have no conceivable beauty in them; but these by his government become lovely: and after bringing out of them all the life and power they possess, and enjoying them to the uttermost,—cautiously, and as the crown of his work, and the consummation of its music, he permits the momentary crimson and azure, and the whole canvas is in a flame."

The plan of Nature must be imitated not only in colour but also in composition. "There are all kinds of harmonies in a picture, according to its mode of production. There is even a harmony of touch. If you paint one part of it very rapidly and forcibly, and another part slowly and delicately, each division of the picture may be right separately, but they will not agree together. . . . Similarly, if you paint one part of it by a yellow light in a warm day, and another by a grey light in a cold day, though both may have been sunlight, and both may be well toned, and have their relative shadows truly cast, neither will look like light; they will destroy each other's power." This clearness, this precision of effect, must govern all the details of the composition. No more retouches, no more daubs, no more blotchy lines, no more dragged paint-brushes, no more slips, no more spreading of colour with the palette knife. Our colours are to be kept dry and our palette clean, so that we can clearly see the pure tint, and may not be tempted to mix. Turner did quite the contrary, it is true, and his palette kept in the National Gallery is an eloquent witness of it; but on this point Ruskin disavows him. By the same rule he forbids all medium, varnish, bitumen, and even water. Thus in water-colour he forbids great washes and wetted surfaces. He speaks of the sponge as of a monster. The wet blot is his nightmare. He condemns coarse paper because it holds the water. He is a water-colourist with a horror of water. If we ask how we are to weaken the colour he teaches us to use white. His fear of a daub leads him to body-colour. For he is not one of those who say with admiration: This is done with nothing at all. He likes what is done with something. He has no care for transparency. "I am now entirely convinced that the greatest things that are to be done in art must be done in dead colour. The habit of depending on varnish or on lucid tints for transparency, makes the painter comparatively lose sight of the nobler translucence which is obtained by breaking various colours amidst each other. All the degradation of art which was brought about after the rise of the Dutch school, by asphaltum, yellow varnish, and brown trees would have been prevented, if only painters had been forced to work in dead colour. Any colour will do for some people, if it is browned and shining; but fallacy in dead colour is detected on the instant. I even believe that whenever a painter begins to *wish* that he could touch any portion of his work with gum, he is going wrong. "Whatever may be the pride of a young beauty in the knowledge that her eyes shine (though perhaps even eyes are most beautiful in dimness), she would be sorry if her cheeks did; and which of us would wish to polish a rose?"

Then we must make frescoes? Yes, and better still mosaics. "In drawing the trunk of a birch tree, there will be probably white high lights, then a pale rosy grey round them on the light side, then a (probably greenish) deeper grey on the dark side, varied by reflected colours, and, over all, rich black strips of bark and brown spots of moss. Lay first the rosy grey, leaving white for the high lights *and for the spots of moss*, and not touching the dark side. Then lay the grey for the dark side, fitting it well up to the rosy grey of the light, leaving also in this darker grey the white places in the paper for the black and brown moss; then prepare the moss colours separately for each spot, and lay each in the white place left for it."

This system of marking out applied to oil-painting leads the artist to superpose the leaves of a tree into the sky, or to cut out pieces of the sky in the interstices already made without repainting these on those or those on these. This is a condemnation of Corot and of nearly all our great landscapists.[1]

In fact Ruskin would not have mixed colour on his palette any more than on his canvas. We may mix two colours together if we will, but not more. "If you have laid a red colour, and you want a purple one above, do not mix the purple on your palette and lay it on so thick as to overpower the

---

[1] It is perhaps necessary to repeat here where the Ruskinian theory most shocks our French ideas on colour and composition, that the author of these pages intends in no way to state the truth on this question but only Ruskin's opinion, and even if this opinion seems worthy of investigation, it does not follow that it should be adopted.

red, but take a little thin blue from your palette and lay it lightly over the red, so as to let the red be seen through, and thus produce the required purple." Better still, place the bright colours in little spots on or in the interstices of the others and "carry out the principle of separate colours to the utmost possible refinement; using atoms of colour in juxtaposition, instead of large spaces." Finally he says, "If you have time, be careful to get the gradated distribution of the spots well followed in the calceolarias, foxgloves, and the like. "Practise the production of mixed tints by interlaced touches of the pure colours out of which they are formed."

Is not this *pointillisme*, prophesied here as early as 1856? It certainly is, and although we understand why some good critics attack Ruskin, we do not understand why they attack him as "obsolete." They would be right if they meant by this that he has sometimes defended certain eternal principles which were true before we were born, and which will remain true when we are no more. But those who have insinuated that he has neither admitted nor understood, nor foreseen the new schools, make acknowledgment that they have not read his works. For the man who in 1843 wrote that we must go to Nature, despise nothing, reject nothing, and thus foretold what realism was to be; he who in 1846 laid down the rule that extreme tints and pure colour might only exist on points, and in 1853 that the landscape must be painted from Nature in the open air up to the very last touch, and thus foretold the school of impressionists, is for all times not only a pioneer but the one pioneer amongst critics of art, who are wont generally " to fly to the help of victory" rather than take sides before the battle and lead a doubtful attack.

In this system, however, of minute drawing conscientious accentuated lines, and dull colours put on disconnectedly and laboriously, point by point, of hard, dry, and honest stippling, what scope is left for breadth of composition, flowing softness of touch, talent of hand, freedom of brush? None whatever, because there should be none. Freedom is a vice, virtuosity is ridiculous. The virtuoso is a Pharisee who takes pleasure in himself and not in beauty. Having entered into the temple he does not kneel down before the supreme God of Beauty beating his breast and saying, "I am a deformity." No, he struts about and congratulates himself for having so little imitated the saintliness of the model, and he holds to it. He is a juggler who juggles with his ochres, with his ultramarines, and his vermilion, instead of bringing them as tribute to priceless nature and illimitable sky. He says: "Look at my cleverness, look at my dexterity, look at the work of my hands." But he does not say: "See here, how beautiful she is! how far above our poor human artifice!" He says: "See how with the single stroke of the brush I flashed the light on to this crystal!" but he does not say: "See how a hundred strokes of the brush can never give the infinite softness of this curve, the radiant colour of this light composed of snow, of silver, of azure, and of night." The virtuoso delays with his trills and his wire-drawn notes. Why? Is it to extol the deep voices of nature? No, it is to extol his own little larynx. He makes Art for Art's sake. The true artist takes up his tools not to shine himself, but to make others admire the loveliness of nature; he expresses himself not in liberty of success, but in constraint of adoration; and not in order that men should say: "How clever he is!" but that they should say: "How beautiful she is!" He does not make Art for Art's sake: he makes Art for Nature and for Beauty.

Perfection in composition, skill, and success matter but little, for it is the effort which we should recognise. Unfortunate efforts! What matter, provided they are heroic? Painful efforts! What matter, provided they are passionate? The true lover is always awkward. Falls, errors, new beginnings, agonies, before this supreme model. . . . What matter, if everything combines to show how far this model is above our attainment? "The glory of a great picture is in its shame; and the charm of it, in speaking the pleasure of a great heart, that there is something better than picture." So long as you do not recognise this, the achievement is mediocre, "you have never sufficiently admired the work of a great workman if you have not begun by despising it." "The demand for perfection is always a sign of a misunderstanding of the ends of art. This for two reasons, both based upon everlasting laws. The first, that no great man ever stops working till he has reached his point of failure: The second reason is, that imperfection is in some sort essential to all that we know of life. It is the sign of life in a mortal body, that is to say, of a state of progress and change. Nothing that lives is, or can be, rigidly perfect; part of it is decaying, part nascent. The foxglove blossom,—a third part bud, a third part past, a third part in full bloom,—is a type of the life of this world. And in all things that live there are certain irregularities and deficiencies which are not only signs of life, but sources of beauty. No human face is exactly the same in its lines on each side, no leaf perfect in its lobes, no branch in its symmetry. All admit irregularity as they imply change; and to banish imperfection is to destroy expression, to check exertion, to paralyse vitality. All things are literally better, lovelier, and more beloved for the imperfections which have been divinely appointed, that the law of human life may be Effort, and the law of human judgment Mercy."

§ 4

Their exaggerations and paradox notwithstanding, no one can say that these are the ideas of a moralist. They are undoubtedly the sentiments of an artist, and he who has never experienced them is no artist, whatever his banner or his motto. To forget one's art for Nature, to forget oneself for art, is surely the express condition of all initiation into the mysteries of the Beautiful, and it is also the first condition of success from a practical point of view in monumental works of art. In saying that "all art is praise," humble and devoted, self-sacrifice and self-forgetfulness, the Master of the *Laws of Fésole* has expressed something more than a moral and sentimental aphorism. He has given a precise rule which can be applied every day to the most delicate æsthetical problems of our time. This enthusiast has seen clearly through these modern sophisms, and this prophet has discerned under the glosses of the critic and in spite of the interested theories of artists the true evil, the deep-seated evil, from which certain of our arts suffer—Vanity. He has noted and proclaimed that together with the material and technical qualities, without which there is no art,—"a *painter's* business is to *paint*, primarily," —a certain moral quality is also essential for the production of a great artistic creation. He has perceived that to science it is essential to add conscience, and to cleverness of hand simplicity of heart.

For if cleverness were sufficient, how is it that our age, so fruitful of clever men, can produce no monument to be compared to the Greek temples or the Gothic cathedrals? Were talent the only thing required of the artist, whence comes it that with so

II. ART

much talent, and the accumulated experience of so many schools, we can neither create nor perpetuate a style, nor accomplish the harmonious decoration of a work, nor compete with less educated and less skilful ages in the "worth and delightfulness of our implements of daily use and materials of dress, furniture, and lodging?" Do we not then lack something? This something may it not be moral qualities, and chiefly that quality which produces worship: Humility? Humility which does not seek rapid and noisy success, but follows slow and silent research; humility which does not confine itself exclusively to intellectual and aristocratic arts, nor recoil from any necessary task; humility which leads to the union of all artists, founded on the mutual esteem that each has for the work of all.

If nowadays we occasionally find beautiful easel pictures, pretty statues, good pieces in a building, but never an entirely beautiful decoration throughout the whole, it is not technique or talent which is lacking; it is that, in order to reach success and above all fortune more rapidly, the artist follows the artisan and specialises; he directs all his efforts towards attaining the highest virtuosity, and, in his works, the most lucrative subject. He avoids devoting himself to all the arts for fear he may not succeed in any. "Under the present system you keep your academician occupied only in producing tinted pieces of canvas to be shown in frames, and smooth pieces of marble to be placed in niches; while you expect your builder or constructor to design coloured patterns in stone and brick, and your chinaware merchant to keep a separate body of workwomen who can paint china, but nothing else." This subdivision of labour is, it seems, in industrial works most successful for rapidity and prompt return, but "it ruins all the arts at once." It separates them from their sources, and the greatest efforts cannot reunite them. It creates parts, nothing complete; collections, never an organic whole. To create true architecture demands the whole power and life, and that that life be given and always sustained by one creator or inspirer.

This is the law that created the great monuments that we admire in Italy. "Note this—that in the fourteenth-century group of great artists, Cimabue, Giovanni Pisano, Arnolfo, Andrea Pisano, Giotto, four out of the five men are architects as well as sculptors and painters. . . . And the meaning of that is that in this century the arts were all united and duly led by architecture . . . later, painting arrogated all and at last betrayed all. You may justly conclude therefore that the three arts ought to be practised together, and that no man could be a sculptor who was not an architect—that is to say who had not knowledge enough and pleasure enough in structural law to be able to build on occasion, better than a mere builder." And just as all the work can be done by the same hand, so every beauty should be gathered into the same work. "The junction of the three arts in men's minds, at the best time, is shortly signified in these words of Chaucer—

> " Everidele
> Enclosed was, and walled well
> With high walls, embatailled,
> Portrayed without, and well entayled
> With many rich portraitures."
> —*Love's Garden.*

We can perceive the proof of this unity of the arts at Florence in the campanile of Santa Maria del Fiore. "There are there two rows of hexagonal panels filled with bas-reliefs. Some are by unknown hands, some by Andrea di Pisa, some by Lucca della Robbia, two by Giotto himself, and one of these symbolic of the whole art of painting is represented by a painter in his *bottega*. This bas-relief is one of the foundation stones of the most perfectly built tower in Europe, and this stone was carved by the hand of the architect himself, and further this architect and sculptor, Giotto, was the greatest painter of his time, and the friend of the greatest poet."

The artist of our own day, far from being willing to finish for another the details of a great monument of art, despises even completing his own. "The modern system of modelling the work in clay, getting it into form by machinery, and by the hands of subordinates, and touching it at last, if indeed the (so called) sculptor touch it at all, only to correct their inefficiencies, renders the production of good work in marble a physical impossibility. The first result of

P

it is that the sculptor thinks in clay instead of marble, and loses his instinctive sense of the proper treatment of a brittle substance. The second is that neither he nor the public recognise the touch of the chisel as expressive of personal feeling or power, and that nothing is looked for except mechanical polish."

In engraving the same division of labour produces the same mediocrity of labour. "At the bottom of the pretty line engravings one saw always two inscriptions. At the left-hand corner, 'Drawn by so-and-so;' at the right-hand corner, 'Engraved by so-and-so.' And you will observe that the only engravings which bear imperishable value are engraved by the artist himself. It is true that, in wood cutting, both Dürer and Holbein have workmen under them who can do all they want. But in metal cutting it is not so. For, as I have told you, in metal cutting, ultimate perfection of Line has to be reached; and it can be reached by none but a master's hand; nor by his unless in the very moment and act of designing. Never, unless under the vivid first force of imagination and intellect, can the line have its full value." . . . "For it must be done throughout with the full fire of temper in it, visibly governing its lines, as the wind does the fibres of cloud."

But should the great painter condescend to plaster the walls, the sculptor to hew the marble himself, and the engraver to engrave his own design? Certainly, for there is no beautiful mural decoration, there is no beautiful engraving, there is no beautiful statue, but at that price. "Fine art is essentially athletic." It is precisely here we find what distinguishes it and puts it above all others. "Literature, while it gives play to intellectual and emotional faculties, does not require the physical organisation of the painter or sculptor," nor Music either. A dwarf can write and a cripple can make music, but for the severe labour of a Michael Angelo or a Tintoret we must have not only a strong soul but a vigorous body. The whole man must be given to his art. "The work of the limbs and the fingers aiding the soul." "All the great arts form one united system from which it is impossible to remove any part without harm to the rest. They are founded first in mastery, by strength of *arm* of the earth and sea, in agriculture and seamanship; then their inventive power begins, with the clay in the hand of the potter, whose art is the humblest but truest type of the forming of the human body and spirit; and in the carpenter's work, which probably was the early employment of the Founder of our religion."

"And man grows great by this labour. Nothing is more useful for developing the moral qualities of uprightness, patience, and simplicity, than the habit of struggling with difficult and stubborn matters. . . . All the great early Italian masters of painting or sculpture without exception began by being goldsmiths' apprentices. Francia was a goldsmith; Ghirlandajo was a goldsmith, and was the master of Michael Angelo; Verrochio was a goldsmith, and was the master of Leonardo da Vinci; Ghiberti was a goldsmith, and beat out the bronze gates which Michael Angelo said might serve for gates of Paradise. Several reasons may account for the fact that goldsmiths' work is so wholesome for young artists: first, that it gives great firmness of hand to deal for some time with a solid substance; again, that it induces caution and steadiness—a boy trusted with chalk and paper suffers an immediate temptation to scrawl upon it and play with it, but he dares not scrawl on gold, and he cannot play with it; and lastly, that it gives great delicacy and precision of touch to work upon minute forms." "All arts needing energy and physical application are equally good. Every artist should be a workman."

But at the same time to re-establish the equilibrium every workman should be an artist. It does not suffice for the thinker to work, the worker must also think. It matters little that, distracted sometimes by his thought, he forgets the mechanical regularity of his task, and that his fancy attempts to form an original but living work rather than a work slavishly following the given pattern. "I shall only give one example, which however will show the reader what I mean, from the manufacture already alluded to, that of glass. Our modern glass is exquisitely clear in its substance, true in its form, accurate in its cutting. We are proud of this. We ought to be ashamed of it. The old Venice glass was muddy, inaccurate in all its forms, and

II. ART

clumsily cut, if at all. And the old Venetian was justly proud of it. For there is this difference between the English and Venetian workman, that the former thinks only of accurately matching his patterns, and getting his curves perfectly true and his edges perfectly sharp, and becomes a mere machine for rounding curves and sharpening edges; while the old Venetian cared not a whit whether his edges were sharp or not, but he invented a new design for every glass that he made, and never moulded a handle or a lip without a new fancy in it. And therefore, though some Venetian glass is ugly and clumsy enough when made by clumsy and uninventive workmen, other Venetian glass is so lovely in its forms that no price is too great for it; and we never see the same form in it twice. Now you cannot have the finish and the varied form too. If the workman is thinking about his edges, he cannot be thinking of his design; if of his design, he cannot think of his edges. Choose whether you will pay for the lovely form or the perfect finish, and choose at the same moment whether you will make the worker a man or a grindstone. . . .

"Nay, but the reader interrupts me,—'If the workman can design beautifully, I would not have him kept at the furnace. Let him be taken away and made a gentleman, and have a studio, and design his glass there, and I will have it blown and cut for him by common workmen, and so I will have my design and my finish too.'

"All ideas of this kind are founded upon two mistaken suppositions: the first, that one man's thoughts can be, or ought to be, executed by another man's hands; the second, that manual labour is a degradation, when it is governed by intellect."

Rather it is a necessity. The artisan must have no ambition mechanically to perform an artistic trade, but artistically to follow his trade of artisan. Great decorative and great popular art can only be obtained at this price. And if nowadays we do not find among the cabinetmakers, masons, jewellers, blacksmiths, the marvellous craftsmen of the centuries of great art, it is not that the craftsmen do not exist, but that they have lost the sense of their true mission. They are no longer where they ought to be—the desire of raising themselves on the social ladder has made them leave the modest workshop where they would have created marvels, and has given them over to the plush and bric-à-brac of Kensington hotels, or to rows of villas where they only fabricate rubbish. Schools of painting and of sculpture without end have multiplied a hundredfold people making art into a profession. We shall no longer find in the pastures of Europe a Giotto taking care of sheep and goats, and it is hardly probable, with the fall in the price of paper, that any mute Miltons will lie inglorious in a village cemetery. But these schools of which we are so proud, while they give ambition do not give genius. They have only skimmed off, with no profit to painting or sculpture, the best artisans who might have intelligently decorated the base or carved the capital of a column. The cabinetmaker who with a sure hand might have composed and executed a reredos of beautiful design becomes an architect and constructs absurd exhibition buildings. The plasterer with the exact eye, who might have decorated ceilings and vaultings with right tones and harmonious decoration, becomes a painter, and exhausts himself fruitlessly in historical pictures. The whole democracy of working men aspire to become artists, till no artist is to be found among workmen; nothing but machines remain. It is a loss all round; great art is lowered; art in furniture does not improve, and the ambitious man who vegetates or dies of hunger among his unsold allegories and Venuses, with his divans and his marbles, would have been rich and prosperous as a cabinetmaker. Here too it is not intellectual power, it is not ambition or ideal that art demands, it is the solemn feeling produced by the unselfish admiration of Nature :—Humility.

The device of the artist then should be quite simple, and we find the whole of it in this saying that we cited at the beginning of our inquiry: "All great Art is Praise."

To seek Nature the true, not what we have made her, but what she is herself; to observe her with eyes that have been given us that we may see her, not with the instruments that have been made to betray her, and with the heart given us to feel her, not with the reason we have perfected in order to understand her; to observe her in the fields, and not in our workshops, with her own lights and not with our chiaroscuro; to follow her in the repose of her vigorous outline and not in our vain agitations, in her harmony and not in our adjustment, to love her for herself and not for ourselves, and if need be to set ourselves to the most humble manual toil to express her better or to make her more admired—all Art is in this. Therefore no more rules, no more receipts, entire freedom and God be with you.

"Go forth again to gaze upon the old cathedral front, where you have smiled so often at the fantastic ignorance of the old sculptors: examine once more those ugly goblins, and formless monsters, and stern statues, anatomiless and rigid; but do not mock at them, for they are signs of the life and liberty of every workman who struck the stone; a freedom of thought, and rank in scale of being, such as no laws, no charters, no charities can secure; but which it must be the first aim of all Europe at this day to regain for her children."

Art lives by praise of Nature but it dies of slavery to men. "The only doctrine or system peculiar to me," says Ruskin in *Saint Mark's Rest*, "is the abhorrence of all that is doctrinal instead of demonstrable, and of all that is systematic instead of useful: so that no true disciple of mine will ever be a 'Ruskinian'— he will follow, not me, but the instincts of his own soul, and the guidance of his Creator." "For, indeed,

II. ART

the arts, as regards teachableness, differ from the sciences also in this, that their power is founded not merely on facts which can be communicated, but on dispositions which require to be created. Art is neither to be achieved by effort of thinking, nor explained by accuracy of speaking." "No true painter ever speaks or ever has spoken much of his art. . . . The moment a man can really do his work he becomes speechless about it. All words become idle to him—all theories. . . . Does a bird need to theorise about building his nest—or boast of it when built?" Have the great artists ever had the occult or metaphysical motives, which their critics assign to them, at the moment they found the controlling line of a gesture, a happy harmony of tones, or the unexpected arrangement of a whole? No. A thousand times No. "They did it I think with the childlike unpretending simplicity of all earnest men: they did what they loved and felt." And it is precisely "because they did so that there is this marvellous life of changefulness and subtlety running through their every arrangement: and that we reason upon the lovely building as we should upon some fair growth of the trees of the earth that know not their own beauty."

Here then is the thought of the Master who has so often been accused of wishing to order painting by moral laws and of making verses of the Bible serve for the grammar of the art of drawing. And after the most minute researches that have ever been made into the mysteries of composition, after probings as profound as have ever been attempted by the Poussins, Reynolds, Gérard de Lairesse, Lessing, Stendhal, Topffer, Winckelmann, or Leonardo da Vinci, doubtless after many errors, as well as many penetrating observations, the great æstheticist owns with melancholy: "I have now stated to you all the laws of composition which occur to me as capable of being illustrated or defined; but there are multitudes of others which, in the present state of my knowledge, I cannot define, and others which I never hope to define; and these the most important, and connected with the deepest powers of the art. The best part of every great work is always inexplicable; it is good because it is good: and innocently gracious, opening as the green of the earth, or falling as the dew of heaven."

We may smile at this confession. We ought rather to admire it as we reflect how powerless reason is compared to our instinct. It may be said that it is superfluous to pile up so many books under our feet, only to raise our eyes to the edge of the wall which surrounds the *terra incognita* of the Beautiful. We ourselves would rather say this labour is necessary if we are to appreciate and affirm that there is in art a *terra incognita* where presumptuous geographists by means of ill-drawn maps may mislead and lose credulous travellers—and morever that man raises himself perhaps higher by the sentiment he has for what cannot be known than by the science he believes himself to have of the unknown. It might be said that here the failure of Æsthetic lies and also the condemnation of the philosopher who discussed it; but we would rather say it proves that this philosopher was an artist, and that he was greater as artist than as philosopher, since he grasped more things intuitively through enthusiasm than he was able to explain inductively by his science.

CHAPTER III

"LIFE"

§ I

"THE art is an exact exponent of the life." It is agreed that true art is to reproduce only beautiful bodies, and only beautiful landscapes, that is to say, such as are untouched by man. But if men and Nature are no longer beautiful? . . . And if it can be achieved only by simple, modest and devoted artists, and if simple, modest, devoted artists are no longer to be found? . . . Where are the models for such works, and above all where are the workmen? Where are the forms wherein Beauty dwells, and where are the souls who sacrifice themselves for her? Where is the great national idea, where the joyous ceremonies of public life, which supply the opportunity for achievements springing from the heart of the people like the cathedrals of olden days? Above all, where are the bonds of common æsthetical interest which should cause the multitude of artists and workmen to forget the differences in their stations and so to assist each other in realising the design? We see at once how Ruskin's æsthetical

III. LIFE

idea became a moral and social idea, and why since the middle of his career in 1860, he thinks it no longer possible to recover art-power without the reform and purification of social life.

Truly, however high a conception we may have of modern life, however high an idea we may have of its conquests and of its progress, on one point at any rate this progress is not easy to discover, for our country has not in any sense added to human patrimony in respect of Beauty. Day by day the picturesqueness of our houses, of our dress, of our festivals, of our fields, of our implements, even of our arms, disappears from life and is to be found only in the fictions of theatres or in the restorations of museums. The railways carry us quicker than formerly to favoured portions of the globe, but these are already disfigured by rails and tunnels before we arrive there. They convey us in a few hours to old and distant provinces that we may enjoy their kindly habits and traditional costumes, but they carry still more quickly newspapers to put these customs to flight, and Paris fashions to replace the national dress. The numerous hotels built upon "sites" whose charm lay in their wildness, enable us indeed to live comfortably among the rocks and the forests, but in order to erect them the rocks have been blasted, and in order to supply material the forests have been cleared. Each new line of railway worn like a wrinkle into the face of the country detracts something from its beauty. Old picturesque towns disappear stone by stone, rivers are dammed up and polluted wave by wave. Those among us who live by the pleasure of the eye, who derive their highest enjoyment from line and colour, are day by day deprived of the sights which delighted their fathers,—and are forced into exile hoping to find at a distance those rare cities and colonies not yet laid out in imitation boulevards, with the usual accompaniment of shops and black-coated uniformity. . . . Can Beauty exist in art when it no longer exists in life? . . .

Maybe so: the professors and the economists will say, but there is wealth. We must live before we philosophise. What matter that sundry effeminate dilettanti or certain idle dreamers regret these odd æsthetical pleasures which for our part we have never desired or experienced, if the well-being of the masses is increased and the people are happier for the industrial and economic régime which science has inaugurated?

The people? Let us look at this side of the subject. They are advancing with threats and grievances to the attack of modern society armed with heavier claims than were ever put forward in the ancient world. Day by day the tide-mark of crime rises like a flood of blood. Day by day the number of suicides grows in the columns of the newspapers and should be writ in letters of red, and—until now unheard of—even the suicide of children. . . . Day by day in some portion of the civilised globe we hear of workmen in revolt who destroy the wonderful and fragile machinery which science has invented for their happiness. "Our cities are a wilderness of spinning-wheels instead of palaces; yet the people have not clothes. We have blackened every leaf of English greenwood with ashes, and the people die of cold; our harbours are a forest of merchant ships, and the people die of hunger. . . ." The picturesque monuments of the Middle Ages are overthrown, even to the ramparts of the towns which until now formed a distant picture for the eye of the traveller, but has anything been given to the people in exchange? Have these stones been made bread? The trees of the forest have been cut to build workshops, and instead of the songs of birds the whistle and roar of the steam engine meet the ear. But are the workmen the happier? Do they sing the more? Alas, no. Formerly the poor in France were always singing: they sang at table, they sang at work. In these days France grown wealthy is like the rich cobbler of the fable—he sings no longer. The promises of the Manchester school then have deceived the world, or at least it thinks itself deceived, which is the same thing, for nothing is so subjective as the feeling of happiness. It is possible, nay probable, that all the socialistic theories which promise yet greater things will be followed by yet deeper and more bitter disenchantment, but this we need not consider. The professors and the economists, the men of progress, promised the masses when they deprived them of traditions, costumes, faith, and

Beauty, that they would give them happiness. Is this the result?

Reply is unnecessary. The cry of the rising generation replies for us. As soon as we grasp in the name of progress what the professors and the economists promised the people, we perceive that Happiness is not one of the things "*quæ numero, pondere, mensurave constant*"; but a divine coinage which we long ago dissipated, throwing the divine chimæræ to the winds. . . . Here is the cruel, evident, undeniable barrier; for though it may be demonstrated by the aid of ingenious and consoling statistics that the workman and the peasant of to-day are richer than the workman and the peasant of the good old times, can it be proved to him that he is happier when he feels the reverse?

In short, it is vain to hope that the murmurs of the artist against the devastation of modern progress can be drowned by the cheers of the artisan over its benefits. From below as from above the same reproach echoes. What have you done with Beauty? say the one side. And the other—What have you done with Happiness? Has this progress given a higher ideal? asks the first,—and the second: Has it lightened the burden of existence? Wonders indeed from graceless laboratories and factories have been exhibited in 1889 and will be exhibited again in 1900, and the envy of the poor who pass in front of these marvels will be excited;—but will their lot seem thereby more fortunate? It is announced that

III. LIFE

scenes of the French Revolution are to be represented in gigantic proportions among clouds. The clouds will be disfigured, but will the crowds below be more beautiful? We boast that rapidity of locomotion will be increased tenfold; the sorrows that we carry with us will only gallop the faster. It used to be said:—

> "Chagrin d'amour ne va pas en voyage,
> Chagrin d'amour ne va pas en bateau."

What are the sorrows which do not now go everywhere with man? And the more the difficulties of travel are minimised, the more the soul is left without resource to its private griefs. If every village on the globe were enclosed in a network of telephonic wire, would the news communicated be better news? If every road were furrowed by those horseless carriages still rare enough to attract people in the street, would that make them better worth looking at, or the landscape more beautiful for the passengers? However quickly they may go, will they ever reach another goal than that which all must reach one day, horsemen, pilgrims, monks, and cripples, that represented in the Campo Santo at Pisa? And is there any advantage in hurrying towards this end, inevitable alas, and common to all? . . .

But since in the same hour the happiness of man and the loveliness of nature are seen to vanish; since the same storm silences the singing of birds and men, does it not follow that from the same causes also arise the lack of social ease and æsthetic joys? Shall we then marvel greatly if Ruskin dreamed that in restoring Beauty to the world—Beauty in Nature—Beauty in the human form—Beauty in the human soul—he would by so doing restore Happiness?

§ 2

Now the leprosy which corrodes and destroys beauty in the landscape we love is due to machinery and speculation, in other words, simply to wealth. . . . A rich country is an ugly country. Ruskin relates that he once knew a small piece of land at the sources of the Wandle which he esteemed the most delicious landscape in the south of England. He tells us "that no clearer or diviner waters ever sang with constant lips," that "no pastures ever lightened in springtime with more passionate blossoming," that "no sweeter homes ever hallowed the heart of the passer-by with their pride of peaceful gladness—fain hidden, yet full confessed. . . ." Twenty years afterwards he returned to the sources of the Wandle. All was changed. . . . "Just where the welling of stainless water, trembling and pure, like a body of light, enters the pool of Carshalton, cutting itself a radiant channel down to the gravel, through warp of feathery weeds, all waving, which it traverses with its deep threads of clearness, like the chalcedony in moss-agate, starred here and there with the white grenouillette; just in the very rush and murmur of the first spreading currents, the human wretches of the place cast their street and house foulness; heaps of dust and slime, and broken shreds of old metal, and rags of putrid clothes; which, having neither energy to cart away, nor decency enough to dig into the ground, they thus shed into the stream, to diffuse what venom of it will float and melt, far away, in all places where God meant those waters to bring joy and health. Half-a-dozen men, with one day's work, could cleanse those pools, and trim the flowers about their banks, and make every breath of summer air above them rich with cool balm; and every glittering wave medicine, as if it ran, troubled only of angels, from the porch of Bethesda. But that day's work is never given, nor, I suppose, will be; nor will any joy be possible to heart of man, for evermore, about those wells of English waters."

Afterwards he walked slowly up through the village to the principal street, asking himself whether poverty was the cause of this culpable neglect of natural things. No. He found on the contrary signs of luxury everywhere, magnificent shop-windows, sumptuous public-houses, but neither greater happiness nor health among the inhabitants, only more pretension and useless parade of high iron railings everywhere. "Now, how did it come to pass that this work was done instead of the other: that the strength and life of the English operative were spent in defiling ground, instead of redeeming it: and in producing an entirely (in that place) valueless piece of metal, which can neither be eaten nor breathed, instead of medicinal fresh air and pure water? There is but one reason for it, and at present a conclusive one,—that the capitalist can charge percentage on the work in the one case, and cannot in the other."

If the economists deigned to make any reply they would certainly say that the capitalist system of the day, however despised by visionaries, is none the less the best hitherto discovered. They would admit that in developing industrial progress the principles of the Manchester school had not perhaps added much to the poetry of the world, but that was not the object in view, and assuredly they had added to its riches. They would maintain that to lead a crusade against capitalism because it entails factories, mines, and railroads does homage to it from the economic point of view, and that to demand its destruction is to demand at the same time the destruction of everything which makes the wealth of the proletariat as well as that of the capitalists, of nations as well as of individuals.

For that matter, given their conception of wealth, economists are right, but it never even occurs to them that this conception could be disputed. In an age when everything is doubted, they never for an instant suppose it could be questioned whether wealth were an essential, and whether accumulated money and nothing else were truly wealth. It is quite true that for making money the present economic system is the best. The colossal fortunes amassed in the present age prove it abundantly. It is even quite possible—whatever the socialists may say—that this system, in spite of its defects, is productive of the greatest pecuniary gain to the masses, and that precisely in those countries where the pinnacles of fortune have been lifted highest by speculation, the average of modest fortunes also rises. Granting all this, it remains to be proved whether the acquisition of wealth is a real gain in all circumstances—even when it involves the loss of life—and whether true wealth consists in the possession of gold, or can be procured by it. We should say so, looking at the business world, and the fever of speculation by which it is impelled, at the merchant in his office, and at the artisan on his way to the factory. He grudges nothing, care, fatigue, journeys, struggles, bad dreams, by day and night, all to gain one object — money. He does not think what he will do with this money, or he only thinks later on: his passion is to possess it, not necessarily as a mercenary man, but merely as a man of business according to the economical notions of our fathers. To make as much money as possible is in itself a final end, as admirable and as essential as it is in cricket to make runs. He does not read: he has no time, because he has to amass more money. He cannot see the blossoming flowers of spring in a landscape he loves: he must make yet more money. Later, much later, when he is very rich and very old, and when he has ruined ten rivals, and triumphed over ten strikes, these riches will procure him all that Nature can yield of flowers, all that Art can bestow of harmony, all that thought can grant of true joy,— were he still able to appreciate them. . . . But he will never reach this second stage: to procure every luxury of existence he ruins his health: to secure all the joys of the spirit he destroys his soul: and what this millionaire is pleased to call gaining his livelihood is in reality with great trouble and fatigue earning old age and death.

But this life, this health, these æsthetical pleasures, which he has sacrificed in pursuit of riches, are they not also wealth? And if money is an essential, is it not also needful for its proper use to have living hands, and for the enjoyment of life, is it not indispensable to possess life? "At the crossing of the transepts of Milan Cathedral has lain, for three hundred years, the embalmed body of St. Carlo Borromeo. It holds a golden crosier, and has a cross of emeralds on its breast. Admitting the crosier and emeralds to be useful articles, is the body to be considered as 'having' them? Do they, in the politico-economical sense of property (Mr. John Stuart Mill's, for instance) belong to it? If not, and if we may, therefore, conclude generally that a dead body cannot possess property, what degree and period of animation in the body will render possession possible?" Is it not enough to be physically dead, extended on an altar tomb with a sculptured dog at one's feet, like the lords and ladies of the fifteenth century? Has he any enjoyment of wealth, though he still breathe, when, crushed by the care and pleasures of money, he is extended on a couch with a living dog asleep at his feet? Surely not. To enjoy wealth a man must be erect and standing, and the dog too should be barking gaily in the thicket amid the flying birds, or among the flowing waters in the meadows.

We shall find then on reflection that health is the first of all riches. Now do money and the pleasures of money endow us with health? For health we must have pure water. The factory makes money but it poisons the streams around, till the manufacturer finds no natural water to drink. Is that wealth? But money enables our hands to remain idle, and our body to avoid all muscular toil. This is the great modern progress. True, but at the end of a few years the body, exhausted by cerebral action, becomes diseased, and the doctors prescribe in the name of hygiene that active exercise from which the engineers in the name of progress have triumphantly rescued man. Is this exhaustion wealth? Moreover, if there are no longer forests into which we can follow the birds, nor meadows where we can admire the flowers, what is the use of health? Natural beauty is destroyed in the pursuit of riches —it is preserved only in certain privileged parks.

What shall avail this beauty if man does not cultivate within him that enthusiastic spirit which can appreciate all its grace and be responsive to all its energies? Does the rich man possess this enthusiasm? No. It is a great error of the age to think that any one absorbed in money-making, who in the interval between two *coups* goes luxuriously to listen to the Opera, can hear anything. . . . He hears nothing. It is a great error to think that the collector appreciates the beauty of the works of the Master when he has only to hold out his hand to procure them. . . . He does not see them. The one hears only the sound of gold jingling on the international counter, or maybe the groans of the crowd ruined by his lucky speculation. The other perceives in the cloudscape of his pictures only the white of the bank-notes he gave for them, and his eyes scrutinise the corner of the canvas, as if it were a cheque, for the signature which makes it of value. "It is not by paying for them but by understanding them that we become the real possessors of works of art and of the enjoyment they give. It is not by opening our purse, but by opening our hearts, and for this we must have hearts to open. Money cannot procure the pleasures belonging to true wealth, only love."

Lastly, do we by accumulating gold obtain truer friends, more real sympathy, franker greetings, more enduring affections. Can gold give serenity of heart and soul, and that peace which sheds a brighter glow upon our lives? It would be absurd to say so. Money, while it seems to gather round the rich man more friends, sows the seed of doubt in friendship, and the hands offered to him in greeting are as the hands of statues—waiting to receive— cold hands of stone, unable to sustain or bestow. But peace and gladness, everything that renders life more beautiful, are these not riches to be desired next after our daily bread? "The economists seem to have a misgiving that there is other wealth than the gold found in Australia, since they speak of all 'useful articles' and proclaim that 'time is money.' Health is money, wit is money, knowledge is money; and all your health, and wit, and knowledge, may be changed into gold, but the gold cannot be changed in its turn back into health and wit."

And whatever is true of private wealth, is it not still more true of national wealth? Is it possible to estimate in figures or to measure by credit the true wealth of a country? There have been and there still are to be found countries which may be called poor. Are the people less happy there than elsewhere? Are they less prosperous, less healthy, less energetic, and, small though they be, is it not often these same people who, while rich countries hesitate (like the soldier mentioned by Horace with too much gold in his belt), lead all the others into the paths of justice and of liberty? "The strength of a nation is in its multitude, not in its territory; but only in its sound multitude. . . . It has been the madness of kings to seek for land instead of life." Is it necessarily a sign of strength for a nation to have a large revenue? For example, one of the reasons which makes France so rich relatively to the total of her population is her diminishing birth-rate. . . . The economists boast of this high level of fortune for each individual. But is it truly a national strength? Is it wealth?—One of the reasons which enables us to meet the expenses of our budgets is that each year the taxes on drink yield a greater return, exceeding often the optimistic forecasts of the financiers. This proves only that an increasing number of people leave their health and sometimes their reason in the gin-shops, but the economists triumph. Moreover, because ruined healths and darkened intellects add to revenue returns, do they therefore create national wealth? and can this be rightly termed wealth?

The absurdity of these propositions is enough to condemn them. The truth is that the indefinite accumulation of money for the sake of money, the production of capital for the sake of capital, without regard to the end attained by this accumulation, is in no sense the same thing either for a man or for a nation as the accumulation of things useful, necessary, and beneficent. "The best and simplest general type of capital is a well-made ploughshare. Now if that ploughshare did nothing but beget other ploughshares, in a polypous manner,—however the great cluster of polypous plough might glitter in the sun, it would have lost its function of capital. And the true

III. LIFE   251

home-question to every capitalist and to every nation, is not, 'how many ploughs have you?' but, 'where are your furrows?' not—'how quickly will this capital reproduce itself?'—but, 'what will it do during reproduction?' What substance will it furnish, good for life? what work construct, protective of life?" If it is used to make adulterated alcohol, to build suburban residences less healthy than cottages, to create an industry out of pure luxury, which destroys the lungs or blinds the eyes of the workmen, or a harmful literature, a restless and pessimistic art which enfeebles the soul of the intellectual classes, it is fatal. "Production does not consist in things laboriously made, but in things serviceably consumable; and the question for the nation is not how much labour it employs but how much life it produces."

"There is no Wealth but Life, Life including all its powers of love, joy, and admiration." Men were deceived "if in a state of infancy they supposed indifferent things such as excrescences of shell-fish, and pieces of blue and red stone, to be valuable, and spend large measures of the labour which ought to be employed for the extension and ennobling of life, in diving or digging for them, and cutting them into various shapes,—or if, in the same state of infancy, they imagine precious and beneficent things, such as air, light, and cleanliness, to be valueless,—or if, finally, they imagine the conditions of their own existence, by which alone they can truly possess or use anything, such, for instance, as peace, trust, and love, to be prudently exchangeable, when the markets offer, for gold, iron, or excrescences of shells.—In fact it may be discovered that the true veins of wealth are purple—and not in Rock, but in Flesh — perhaps even that the final outcome and consummation of all wealth is in the producing as many as possible full-breathed, bright-eyed, and happy-hearted human creatures. . . . It is open to serious question, whether, among national manufactures, that of souls of a good quality may not at last turn out a quite leadingly lucrative one? —The real science of political economy—or rather of human economy—is that which teaches nations to desire and labour for the things that lead to life and which teaches them to scorn and destroy the things that lead to destruction."

Wealth, then, as it is understood in the current language of financiers and economists, is an evil: the enemy, not only of the picturesque beauty of nature, but also of social happiness. Thus it is bad in every way and therefore not legitimate. What? it may be said, is there no legitimate wealth? Not very great wealth, replies Ruskin. "The lawful basis of wealth is, that a man who works should be paid the fair value of his work: and that if he does not choose to spend it to-day, he should have free leave to keep it, and spend it to-morrow. Thus, an industrious man working daily, and laying by daily, attains at last the possession of an accumulated sum of wealth, to which he has absolute right. . . . Therefore the first necessity of social life is the clearness of national conscience in enforcing the law — that he should keep who has JUSTLY EARNED." So far we agree with the economists and we admit readily the inequality of fortune. Great wealth is hardly to be acquired in this way. "No man ever became, or can become, largely rich merely by labour and economy. All large fortunes (putting treasure-trove and gambling out of consideration) are founded either on occupation of land, usury, or taxation of labour."— "But there is also a false basis of distinction: namely, the power held over those who are earning wealth by those who already possess it, and only use it to gain more." This is not to say that the labour-master is not permissible. This is not to say that there should only be workmen in the world, and no one to give them tools and to direct them. This is not to say that the socialists are right in maintaining that they can do without "captains of work." But the economists are wrong in maintaining that the masters may appropriate the whole profits of labour up to that extreme limit which causes a strike. "But I beg you to observe that there is a wide difference between being captains or governors of work, and taking the profits of it. It does not follow because you are general of an army, that you are to take all the treasure, or land, it wins." The profit due to the master by reason of his intellectual or moral labour is quite legitimate. But the excessive profit by this master or capitalist, solely by reason of his capital, is not legitimate. The Church denounced this as "the execrable multiplying of money." It is not wealth, it is the "too great riches" condemned by the saints when they spoke κατὰ τοὺς πλεονέκτας.

But, the economist may exclaim, what do you mean by "too great riches"? Is this a scientific formula? How can what is just at a certain figure become unjust when it passes beyond that figure? And what figure would you fix? It would be a strange miracle that could transform an action quite lawful for a working man who has economised several years of wages, into a wrongful action for his grandson whose fortune, increased by successive interests, arrives at several millions. Whatever is right in a financial operation remains right for this also, no matter what number of zeros you add to it. Yes, mathematically it is true, but humanly and socially speaking it can be infinitely less so. Human equations are not algebraic equations. There are certain moral elements which falsify all calculations, certain truths which pushed to a certain point become errors, and certain kinds of justice pushed to a certain point which become injustice: *summum jus, summa injuria*. In theory, a large capital lawfully acquired may also be lawfully employed. As a fact its power ruins and its weight crushes the small rival industries ready to grow up under its shelter. "In this respect, money is now exactly what mountain promontories over public roads were in old times. The

III. LIFE 255

barons fought for them fairly:—the strongest and cunningest got them; then fortified them, and made every one who passed below pay toll. Well, capital now is exactly what crags were then. Men fight fairly (we will, at least, grant so much, though it is more than we ought) for their money: but, once having got it, the fortified millionaire can make everybody who passes below pay toll to his million, and build another tower of his money castle. And I can tell you, the poor vagrants by the roadside suffer now quite as much from the bag-baron, as ever they did from the crag-baron."

And if we are told that this is no injustice because it is the immediate and necessary effect of "the struggle for life," we shall reply that the supreme injustice of our age lies precisely in this horrible fratricidal conflict which students complacently designate the struggle for life. We ought boldly to censure as cruel, cowardly, and pagan, this merciless rivalry by which the most intelligent and the most persevering and the most sagacious ruin the feeble in mind, will, and judgment. "Is it not wonderful, that while we should be utterly ashamed to use a superiority of body, in order to thrust our weaker companions aside from some place of advantage, we unhesitatingly use our superiorities of mind to thrust them back from whatever good that strength of mind can attain? You would be indignant if you saw a stout fellow thrust himself up to a table where some hungry children were being fed, and reach his arm over their heads, and take their bread from them. But you are not in the least indignant if, when a man has stoutness of thought and swiftness of capacity, and, instead of being long-armed only, has the much greater gift of being long-headed—you think it perfectly just that he should use his intellect to take the bread out of the mouth of all the other men in the town who are of the same trade with him."

But the economist will say this competition or, if you will, this struggle, is the very soul of commerce. Without it there would be no emulation, no progress, no effort, no business, and therefore no wages for working men. It is as sad as it is inevitable that here and there it should crush the imprudent and unskilful. It is the law of all progress. It is very praiseworthy of an owner to give, as Ruskin ordains, the whole of his actual profit to his workmen, when he has no means of making them suffer any of his loss. It is very edifying that he should abstain from all competition that might ruin rivals less wealthy or less skilful. Unfortunately these praiseworthy edifying practices extolled by Ruskin might possibly result in his gradual ruin: a crisis of difficult circumstances might arise in which he would be forced either to disobey the prophet of Brantwood or to die of hunger. . . .

Ruskin quietly replies: Let him die of hunger. "All which sounds very strange: the only real strangeness in the matter being, nevertheless, that it should so sound." Would it be the first time in the world that a man gave his life for his fellows in a time of public danger? "Why in the public estimate of honours is the soldier preferred before the merchant?" "Philosophically, it does not, at first sight, appear reasonable that a peaceable and rational person, whose trade is buying and selling, should be held in less honour than an unpeaceable and often irrational person, whose trade is slaying. Nevertheless the consent of mankind has always, in spite of the philosophers, given precedence to the soldier. And this is right.

"For the soldier's trade, verily and essentially, is not slaying, but being slain. This, without well knowing its own meaning, the world honours it for. A bravo's trade is slaying; but the world has never respected bravos more than merchants: the reason it honours the soldier is, because he holds his life at the service of the State. . . . The merchant is presumed to act always selfishly. His work may be very necessary to the community; but the motive of it is understood to be wholly personal. So that among the five great intellectual professions relating to the necessities of life" which have hitherto existed, his alone incurs no personal danger.

"The Soldier's profession is to *defend* life.
The Pastor's, to *teach* it.
The Physician's, to *keep it in health*.
The Lawyer's, to *enforce justice* in it.
The Merchant's, to *provide* for it.

And the duty of all these men is, on due occasion, to *die* for it.

> The Soldier, rather than leave his post in battle.
> The Physician, rather than leave his post in plague.
> The Pastor, rather than teach falsehood.
> The Lawyer, rather than countenance injustice.
> The Merchant—what is *his* 'due occasion' of death?

It is the main question for the merchant, as for all of us. For, truly, the man who does not know when to die, does not know how to live."

Well, for the merchant who becomes every day more important in the modern world, for the owner, for the manufacturer, who is in our days a real leader of men, there are occasions of devotion to the common welfare. "There are circumstances in which he can show a self-sacrifice equal to that of the soldier, and which would raise him to the level of the soldier, —if he could understand social duty as military duty is understood, and fulfil it. And when social duty calls upon him to sacrifice riches rather than cause ruin to his competitors, or a reduction of wages to the workmen, he is bound to do so."

For from whichever point of view we regard it, from the point of view of the Æsthetic of Nature, disfigured and defiled by industrial speculations, or from the point of view of the welfare of the lower classes who are pillaged and crushed by it, wealth of gold is an evil. "THERE IS NO WEALTH BUT

III. LIFE

LIFE. Life, including all its powers of love, of joy, of admiration. That country is the richest which nourishes the greatest number of noble and happy human beings: that man is richest who, having perfected the functions of his own life to the utmost, has also the widest helpful influence, both personal, and by means of his possessions, over the lives of others." A so-called wealthy country is not a happier nor a more beautiful country, and the worship of mammon is quite as impossible to reconcile with social justice as with the Religion of Beauty.

§ 3

There is a story of a famous æsthete who overtook a poor wretch begging on London Bridge in an aggressively inartistic costume. This beggar wore a filthy frock coat and a horrible tall hat. The æsthete, disgusted by the want of harmony between the garments of the wretch and his profession, took him to the cleverest tailor that he could find, and fitted him out at his own expense in correct begging clothes, copied from the pictures of the Old Masters in the National Gallery. He then took him back to the bridge, but the story does not relate that he gave him anything to eat. This æsthete was neither a follower of Ruskin nor an æstheticist.

The story goes on to say that an evangelist, coming along the same bridge, was indignant that the outward appearance of the hungry man had been cared for and his soul neglected. So he led him off to a chapel, and after showing him the way of eternal life, took him back again to his bridge. But the story does not say that he gave him anything to drink. This evangelist was not a disciple either. Ruskin would have taken the beggar not to a picture-gallery nor to a meeting-house, but into a pastry-cook's shop. He would have given heed not to his clothes, not to his soul, but first of all to his stomach.

For if too much "industrial enterprise" and wealth in a country destroys the beauty of nature, too much misery in a town destroys the beauty of the human form, and without plastic beauty no art and no visions of art are possible. "You cannot have a landscape by Turner, without a country for him to paint; you cannot have a portrait by Titian, without a man to be pourtrayed. The beginning of art is in getting our country clean, and our people beautiful. There has been art where the people were not all lovely, where even their lips, were thick—and their skins black, because the sun had looked upon them; but never in a country where the people were pale with miserable toil and deadly shade, and where the lips of youth, instead of being full with blood, were pinched by famine, or warped with poison."

For the human form, then, we must lay stress on the cultivation of the beautiful. "The body of each poor child must be made as beautiful and perfect in its youth as it can be, wholly irrespective of ulterior purpose." When he arrives at the age when he must earn his bread, his labour will perhaps deform, deface, debase, and distort the splendid pliant muscles, as we see them in the Vatican athletes who anoint themselves for the coming contest. But meanwhile, "let the living creature whom you mean to kill, get the full strength of its body first, and taste the joy, and put on the beauty of youth. . . . To this end, your schools must be in fresh country," and exercises of all sorts and music "should be the primal heads of this bodily education." Why are we forced to study and grow pale before headless and handless marbles in a museum? Our chests and shoulders should be as well worthy to be seen as those Elgin Marbles. We should listen neither to the ascetics nor to the preachers. We should not imprison the best among men in cloisters, that they may devote themselves to what they pompously term "the Service of God"; rather should they devote themselves to the service of man. "A woman should earnestly desire to be beautiful, as she should desire to be intelligent. The man and woman are meant by God to be perfectly noble and beautiful in each other's eyes."

Now the greatest obstacle to plastic beauty is poverty, and, in default of human sentiment, it is the æsthetical sentiment which urges us to fight and to vanquish it. But how? By all means in our power: by charity towards unmerited misfortune, by the repression of vice, by grace, by strength, by gold, and by iron. Gold scattered by handfuls as the poet scattered lilies on the ancient tomb, as Spring scatters the roses over Botticelli's grass. What we are in the habit of giving is nothing: we must give all. The economists are content with the remedies offered to the poor by public or private charity; they pride themselves on the hospitals, asylums, orphanages, and dispensaries. What avails it? And if it avails, whence come all the crippled limbs, the emaciated faces in our towns, the livid countenances in our prisons? How can society speak of charity while so much injustice remains, or of the fine arts while so much human misery exists? So long as human beings suffer cold and hunger in the country around us, not only is art not possible, but it cannot be denied that splendour of raiment and furniture is a crime. Better a hundred times that the marbles of Phidias should crumble and the colours of Leonardo's portraits fade, than that the features of living women should be defiled or tears fill the eyes of children who are living or who at least might live if poverty had not already tainted them with the hues of death. In the living Æsthetic all the gold given to art is lost when life is needing it, and it is shameful to find pleasure in the adornment of some women while other women lack sufficient clothing, and are despoiled of all human beauty by cold, sickness, and the weariness of unhealthy life.

Then the economists rise up with the ironical smile so often seen in Holbein's portraits of learned men.

III. LIFE 263

When we attack luxury by the plea of charity they defend it by that of science. One of their favourite theories, also the most questionable, is that it is of little importance how the rich man spends his gold provided he spends it, and the more he spends it even in useless articles of luxury, the more efficaciously he assists society. "Another erroneous idea," says a Report of the New York Council, "is that luxurious living, extravagant dressing, splendid turnouts and fine houses, are the cause of distress to a nation. No more erroneous impression could exist. Every extravagance that the man of 100,000, or 1,000,000 dollars indulges in adds to the means, the support, the wealth of ten or a hundred who had little or nothing else but their labour, their intellect, or their taste. If a man of 1,000,000 dollars spends principal and interest in ten years, and finds himself beggared at the end of that time, he has actually made a hundred who have catered to his extravagance, employers or employed, so much richer by the division of his wealth. He may be ruined, but the nation is better off and richer, for one hundred minds and hands, with 10,000 dollars apiece, are far more productive than one with the whole."

"Yes, gentlemen of the Common Council," replies Ruskin, "but what has been doing in the time of the transfer? The spending of the fortune has taken a certain number of years (suppose ten), and during that time 1,000,000 dollars' worth of work has been done by the people, who have been paid that sum for it. Where is the product of that work? By your own statement, wholly consumed; for the man for whom it has been done is now a beggar. . . . If a schoolboy goes out in the morning with five shillings in his pocket, and comes home at night penniless, having spent his all in tarts, principal and interest are gone, and fruiterer and baker are enriched. So far so good. But suppose the schoolboy, instead, has bought a book and a knife; principal and interest are gone, and bookseller and cutler are enriched. But the schoolboy is enriched also, and may help his schoolfellows next day with knife and book, instead of lying in his bed and incurring a debt to the doctor."

The study of expenditure, therefore, is not superfluous when we are investigating the causes of poverty and its remedies. And it is important not only to know whether the wealthy spend their money and whether it gives work, but also to define how they spend it and the use of this work. For good sense without the aid of science, and practical knowledge without the aid of political economy, show that the expenditure of this money in useless luxuries, which are rapidly consumed without any benefit to health or wealth, is not the same thing as the expenditure of it in making roads, ports, canals, and sanitary appliances, which will not only augment the wealth of the workmen but also that of the community. To plead for luxury because it gives work to the makers of luxury cannot be a solid argument till it can be shown that the makers of unnecessary articles are more interesting than others, or when it can be proved that they are more numerous, and that consequently the general well-being of workmen should be sacrificed to them—a thesis which the partisans of luxury are not yet in a position to establish.

Further, what is the meaning of "making workmen live"? There is only one way of making any one live; that is, to produce, or to help to produce, things useful to life, things which nourish, which clothe, which preserve from heat or cold, which heal, which purify. All the ingenuity of economists would not alter the fact that a hundred men employed in demolishing the insanitary hovels of a town so as to rebuild them, or in cleaning out the cesspools of a village, would do more for life than a hundred men transformed into footmen, spending the time waiting in antechambers during a hundred unnecessary conversations, or in figuring uselessly with folded arms by the side of a hundred coachmen.

"For instance," says Ruskin, "if you are a young lady, and employ a certain number of sempstresses for a given time, in making a given number of simple and serviceable dresses—suppose, seven; of which you can wear one yourself for half the winter, and give six away to poor girls who have none, you are spending your money unselfishly. But if you employ the same number of sempstresses for the same number of days, in making four, or five, or six beautiful flounces for your own ball-dress—flounces which will clothe no one but yourself, and which you will yourself be unable to wear at more than one ball—you are employing your money selfishly. You have maintained, indeed, in each case, the same number of people; but in one case you have directed their labour to the service of the community, in the other case you have consumed it wholly upon yourself. I don't say you are never to do so; I don't say you ought not sometimes to think of yourselves only, and to make yourselves as pretty as you can; only do not confuse coquettishness with benevolence, nor cheat yourselves into thinking that all the finery you can wear is so much put into the hungry mouths of those beneath you."

Neither let us confuse vanity with the love of art, nor plead for luxury on the pretext that it creates a taste for Beauty. The majority of the great works of the Middle Ages are not due by any means to the personal luxury of an individual, but on the contrary to the encouragement of combined artistic effort. And in the present day, for the true encouragement of art, it is not the treasure of a Maecenas but a "commonalty" of small purses that is needed. "Instead of the capitalist-employer's paying three hundred pounds for a full-length portrait of himself, in the attitude of investing his capital, the united workmen had better themselves pay the three hundred pounds into the hands of the ingenious artist, for painting, in the antiquated manner of Lionardo or Raphael, some subject more religiously or historically interesting to *them;* and placed where they can always see it."

Thus gold can do much to avert poverty. And society is responsible for many of the physical evils of its environment, but is it responsible for all? Those who attack society the most, do they produce the weapons needed to triumph over poverty? Not at all. They refuse them, on the contrary, so that the fiercest socialists are not any nearer the solution of the social problem than the most plausible among economists. For it is true that society is responsible, but it is only responsible for the things that it can prevent. And among miseries there are those which are not the result of an inadequate wage or insufficient education: there are those which result from misconduct, for example, alcoholism. Now can we prevent alcoholism? Have we the right to shut the public-houses? Have the socialists ever proposed any law to abolish three-fourths of the distilleries of alcohol? And without going as far as legislation, have the socialist municipalities used the means given them by law in order to reduce the number of these destructive and poisonous dens? These same socialists who make society responsible for the harm done by the gin-shop would, were the suggestion made, support these causes of the evil in the name of liberty. It is the duty of society to aid the drunkard coming out of the gin-shop, but it has not the right to stop him going in. How can it be responsible if it is not free, and why should it accept the duty of curing these wretched ones if it has no right of previous interference?

Ruskin assures us it has the right. It has especially such rights, for there is no remedy so good as prevention. "The right of public interference with their conduct begins when they begin to corrupt themselves;—not merely at the moment when they have proved themselves hopelessly corrupt. . . . It has been the manner of modern philanthropy to remain passive until that precise period, and to leave the sick to perish, and the foolish to stray, while it spent itself in frantic exertions to raise the dead, and reform the dust. "The recent direction of a great weight of public opinion against capital punishment is, I trust, the sign of an awakening perception that punishment is the last and worst instrument in the hands of the legislator for the prevention of crime. The true instruments of reformation are employment and reward;—not punishment. Aid the willing, honour the virtuous, and compel the idle into occupation, and there will be no need for the compelling of any into the great and last indolence of death."

To begin with, the State is to accustom the child to an intellectual and manual labour, compulsory and free:—"Go out into the highways and hedges, and compel them to come in." But at the same time it must not allow this work to be excessive. "In order that men may be able to support themselves when they are grown, their strength must be properly developed while they are young; and the State should always see to this—not allowing their health to be broken by too early labour, nor their powers to be wasted for want of knowledge." Later, it should not permit the health of man to be injured by the want of muscular toil, nor his mind to be distorted by too much knowledge. There is much talk of the *right of work*, but there is little talk of the *duty of working*. Again, if the workman has the right to insist that the State should keep him employed on Saturday because he has need of his wages that day, surely the State should have the right to say he must work on Monday instead of going to drink his wage at the gin-shop. You must do something for me, says the idle beggar. Good, replies society, but then you must do something for us. These clothes that you wear, this food that you eat, have been produced by some one's labour. What labour do you give us in return? None. This is not just. "Since for every idle person, some one else must be working somewhere to provide him with clothes and food, and doing, therefore, double the quantity of work that would be enough for his own needs, it is only a matter of pure justice to compel the idle person to work for his maintenance himself."

But here again the would-be reformer comes into collision with the protests of economists and radicals. They oppose the despoiling of the rich for the sake of the usefulness of luxury, and in like manner they oppose the compulsion of the poor in the name of liberty. Misery proceeds from two things, misfortune and vice. The unfortunate should not be succoured at the expense of the industries of luxury, the vicious should not be restrained at the expense of individual liberty.

What then is liberty? This word irritates Ruskin immeasurably, like a lie, a defiance, a hypocrisy, the laugh of a *crétin*. What is the liberty spoken of, and what the independence? And liberty from what? From eternal laws and venerable people? Then liberty is a privilege of the most insignificant, the most feeble, and the vainest of creatures. "The dog fastened to a chain is a good animal and strong. The fly is free. Throughout nature there is obedience, the laws of gravitation govern everything. The massive rock obeys more docilely than the miserable feather, falling in endless gyrations to the ground. When Giotto drew his circle, saying, 'You may judge my masterhood of craft by seeing that I can draw a circle unerringly,' did he give perfect freedom to his hand?" The radical doctrine is that, whatever use he may make of it, liberty is a good thing for man. "Folly unfathomable, unspeakable, unendurable to look in the full face of, as the laugh of a *crétin*. You will send your child, will you, into a room where the table is loaded with sweet wine and fruit—some poisoned, some not?—you will say to him, 'Choose freely, my little child. It is so good for you to have freedom of choice; it forms your character—your individuality. If you take the wrong cup, or the wrong berry, you will

III. LIFE

die before the day is over, but you will have acquired the dignity of a free child'?"

But there is a holy liberty which each man should possess: it is freedom from his own tyrannical instincts and from his absorbing prejudices. Before he can be free from others, he ought to be free from himself. What is the use of liberating him from all outside obligations if his power is always impeded by his own vicious tastes? Where is the use of space if we have no power to expand? We cry out against despotism. Are we capable of liberty? "Tintoret's touch, Luini's, Correggio's, Reynolds', and Velasquez's, are all as free as air, and yet right. . . . By the discipline of five hundred years they had learned and inherited such power. . . . and whereas all former painters could be right only under restraint, they could be right, free. . . . Obey, and you also shall be free in time; but in these minor things, as well as in great, it is only right service which is perfect freedom."

Right service alone can triumph in life over unhappiness, as in art it triumphs over ugliness. It is by assiduous work among the poor and the condemnation of all luxury and all unproductive spending among the rich that health, vigour, and grace, that is to say Beauty, can be restored to suffering mankind. And perhaps here again the worship of loveliness in all things is the surest guide towards the solution of those problems which are called social.

§ 4

Lastly, it would be of no advantage to restore their primitive beauty and grace to living human bodies, if man's soul is not able to find pleasure in their happiness. What is the use of the loveliness of things if man is not capable of appreciating it? What is the use of beautiful creatures and objects, unless there are souls able to take delight in them? Now have the minds of our fellow-men the capacity for such admiration? Some there are, no doubt, and they are the fortunate ones. But do not many of us pass by the beauties scattered in profusion throughout nature and art much as the attendants in a museum, or the policemen, walk about among the pictures of Van Dyck and Hobbema? Our education, our manners, our occupations, give no training in this sense. We have neither sufficient attention nor leisure for the higher joys of æsthetical life. "The whole force of education, until very lately, has been directed in every possible way to the destruction of the love of nature. The only knowledge which has been considered essential among us is that of words, and, next after it, of the abstract sciences; while every liking shown by children for simple natural history has been either violently checked, (if it looked an inconvenient form for the housemaids,) or else scrupulously limited to hours of play; and the love of nature has become inherently the characteristic of truants and idlers. While also the art of drawing, which is of more real importance to the human race than that of writing (because people can hardly draw anything without being of some use both to themselves and others, and can hardly write anything without wasting their own time and that of others),—this art of drawing, I say, which on plain and stern system should be taught to every child, just as writing is,—has been so neglected and abused, that there is not one man in a thousand, even of its professed teachers, who knows its first principles."

We must first cultivate the faculty of admiration among children. "Botanists have discovered some wonderful connection between nettles and figs," ... which is very interesting, but a cowboy had better learn "what effects nettles have on hay, and what taste they will give to porridge; and it will give him nearly a new life if he can be got but once, in a springtime, to look well at the beautiful circlet of white nettle blossom, and work out with his schoolmaster the curves of its petals, and the way it is set on its central mast." The scholars in primary schools should be told: "Draw such and such a flower in outline, with its bell towards you. Draw it with its side towards you. Paint the spots upon it. Draw a duck's head—her foot. Now a robin's —a thrush's,—now the spots upon the thrush's breast." But instead the contents of the bird's stomach are described. Children are not taught to

S

admire the beauties of the clouds or the mosses, they are taught the value of the air for heating furnaces, and that of textile fibres for use in looms. The object seems to be their "erudition" but not their education; for to educate a child is not to teach him "what he knew not, but to make him what he was not." And the beginning of all education is "Reverence, Compassion, Admiration." For what? No matter what. Let the child worship pebbles or vegetables if he has nothing else to reverence, but "reverence and compassion we are to teach him primarily." And above all that he should not learn analysis and dissection which chill and destroy. It is of no moment that he learns rather less. We do not live to learn any more than we live to eat. We live in order to love. As long as knowledge stimulates or increases this strength in us, it is serviceable, but it is fatal directly it diminishes it. What! Knowledge can be an evil? No, it is a good like light. But butterflies perish in seeking light, and man perishes in seeking knowledge. Men or butterflies, what we demand from light is less that it should explain things than that it should beautify them.

"In Reverence is the chief joy and power of life. . . . What I have suggested hitherto . . . you must receive throughout as merely motive of thought. . . . The feelings that I most desire to cultivate in your minds are those of reverence and admiration. . . . *This* is the thing which I KNOW—and which, if you labour faithfully, you shall know also. . . . Reverence, for what is pure and bright in your own youth; for what is true and tried in the age of others; for all that is gracious among the living,—great among the dead,—and marvellous, in the Powers that cannot die." This is the secret of happiness. For the disciple of Ruskin there is no pleasure to be compared to æsthetical pleasure, and it alone is sufficient to take the place of all others. If he should be rich he will undertake by intelligent patronage to furnish the people with something to admire. He will not make use of his resources for personal enjoyment of the moment, but for monuments serviceable for after ages. Should he have the good fortune to meet with a Michael Angelo, he will not command him to mould a statue out of snow like Pietro di Medici. His first duty on the contrary would be "to see that no intellect shall thus glitter merely in the manner of hoar-frost; but that it shall be well vitrified, like a painted window, and shall be set so between shafts of stone and bands of iron, that it shall bear the sunshine upon it, and send the sunshine through it, from generation to generation." If he be poor he would rejoice in seeing things of beauty possessed by others, by churches, by museums, surpassing all private collections in their manifold treasures. If he has the means of travelling and following up abroad the artistic relics of great creators of Art, he would do so constantly, marking with a white cross those days of his life when a new interpretation of beauty dawned upon him, or when in the solitude of a museum a new master was revealed to him. If he is stopped on the way by want of funds, he would recall the pilgrimages so often undertaken by poor artists of Poussin's time, who, leaving for Rome, stopped at Lyons or at Avignon, and paid for each stage by a picture, vainly stretching out their arms toward the Eternal City, and arriving at last better fitted by long expectation to feel its eternity, and by long desire to taste its joys. It is unnecessary for the enjoyment of æsthetical life, that he should visit every beautiful country: but it is essential that he should give heed to all loveliness in the country that he does see. If he sees a beautiful woman he would admire her beauty: if she is ugly he would admire her smile: if she does not smile he would reflect on her dignity or nobility. If only one note remains in his clavichord, the disciple would love this note. If the country where he dwells has only one river, like Zeeland, he would love this river: if his window is so small that at night he can see only one star, he would adore this star: and by dint of watching for the beauty that is in everything, he would create happiness for himself with the crumbs of the feast, where others, satiated, drink long draughts of boredom.

As it is not possible to admire anything that is inferior to him, he would desire to have many things and many people superior to him. In this way he would transform into happiness such things as are often secret causes of annoyance or discomfort to others. Walking he would wish to see handsome equipages passing along the roads; they are a pleasure to his sight which he is not to theirs. In a town he would dwell, not in a palace, but in a modest house opposite a palace, that he might admire at leisure the beautiful architecture. It is from the end of the table that the general effect of the dresses and flowers can be best observed. It is from the nameless crowd that the effect of a procession is the most appreciated. He would obey his king if he has a king; the elders of his family if he has elders; the laws of his country if his country has laws; but he will know how to become free, and being free inwardly, in spite of all his submission, he will experience the true joys of freedom. He would fear no greatness, no honour, no talent, for he fears only evil. He would be sceptical only on one point, viz. the reputed ease of the pillow of scepticism to a *teste bien faicte*. If he lacks pedigree, he would rejoice in the aristocracy, and still more that he does not belong to it, for in beholding it at a distance he can admire it the better and respect it the more. He would have rebellious thoughts only for ugliness. He would only find fault with great personages if they were too small, badly dressed, or appeared in assemblies in vulgar graceless costumes, or if they kept their fine collections from the public, and cut down their old oaks or olives. Against the wealthy he would only have one complaint; the ruin of old dwellings, and the construction of new buildings of which "the countenance is indifferent." But everything which honours what is ancient and beautiful he would honour. He would mock only at mockery. He would hate only hatred. He would contemn only contempt.

Thus by true reverence and with no thought of self he would be happy. We may judge whether many lives in history are happier than those of the great landscape-painters. These were often ill like Chintreuil, often poor like Corot, often misanthropic like Turner, often threatened with blindness like Troyon; and if, nevertheless, their lives have been as relatively happy as their letters and their autobiographies seem to indicate, the reason is, that they spent their life in reverent admiration. Unhappiness comes from envy; whoever admires with all his heart does not envy. Unhappiness proceeds also from regret—in revering, we no longer remember; or from rancour—in revering, we pardon; or from doubts—in revering, we believe.

The unhappiness not only of the individual but also of the community, proceeds from these evils and can be cured only by this antidote. This feeling of reverent admiration, which, while it is the sole and supreme necessity for æsthetical life, is at the same time the one remedy for social evils. It is the direct antidote to the foolish desire for praise, a desire which destroys all enthusiasm, a puerile conceit which consumes all love. We protest a great deal in these days against the power of money, but the social canker does not lie here; it is only one of its symptoms. Money is deeply coveted because the satisfactions it procures for vanity are the principal objects coveted. When we seek for gold rather than life, it is not to transform it into useful means of existence, but into the playthings of vanity and luxury. It is not that we should be able to say frankly and openly: Let us eat and drink, but to be able to think secretly and jealously: Let us be brilliant and admired, and above all let no one be more brilliant or more admired than ourselves! The passion of the capitalist for accumulation is one form which this desire takes, but it is not the only one; the other is the passion of the revolutionist. He who for his own advantage endeavours to extend the power of money because he has it, and he who asks to destroy it because he has none, are impelled alike by the same feeling: pride. It gleams in the eyes of the revolutionary apostle who arrays himself with the pomp of poverty, quite as much as in those of the pharisee resplendent in his luxury. Impatient of all inequality, dissatisfied with all superiority, and detesting all kinds of government, the one and the other have the same object: the wish to appear to the world in the same guise as the great. This is manifested quite as much by loud and vaunted contempt of money as by extreme and obstinate desire of it, and is reiterated by the onslaught of the Socialist prophets in their attempts to cut down the steps or the social ladder, and by the worshippers of Mammon in their clever manœuvres to hide each step by covering it with gold. A painting by M. Rochegrosse gives one of the truest pictures of our modern social system. It was exhibited at one of our recent Salons, and will not be easily forgotten. Upon the heights of a rich, ugly, unquiet manufacturing town, its sky darkened with smoky emanations from an unhealthy, profitless toil, a crowd of human beings, hungering for riches, honour, social advancement, and notoriety, is struggling, every man with his brother, in a kind of human pyramid. They hurtle and fight, fall and rise again, climbing regardless of peace, regardless of beauty, regardless of life, towards a gilded figure of Fortune which soars above, always out of reach, eluding the empty outstretched hands below.

For an idea of another and better life let us turn to a well-known picture by Burne-Jones, *The Golden Stairs*. In a high narrow frame, a golden staircase, spiral and without balusters, like a ladder in a dream, leads from an unknown floor up to an unseen landing. Maidens crowned with leaves and draped in delicate tunics, the folds as straight as the fluting of a column, are descending the steps, some holding violas, others cymbals or tambourines, others again the long trumpets which in the blue skies of Fra Angelico dart like sunbeams from the hands of angels. Their bare feet are standing on the golden steps, and the fingers of their tapering hands touch the silver strings of lutes, and press the stops

III. LIFE

of reeds. The gleaming stairs reflect their feet, and the vibrating chords the souls of the sad-faced minstrels. Sheaves of foliage stand below as in the porch of a church on Palm Sunday. Here and there a head is turned—as if in regret. Eye looks into eye as if to read a secret. A head is bowed as if in thought—lips smile to lips as if for a kiss. Here and there beneath the peaceful brows, deep-set eyes look forth beyond the frame, beyond the halls, beyond the house, perhaps beyond the world itself. They carol and they play. In truth, the music is weak, their raiment simple, and it is but a narrow dwelling. But there is grace in their light gestures, calm on their steadfast countenances. Quite at the top of the canvas doves have settled for a moment on the tiled roof, to draw as it seems the envy of the skies to this lovely spot on earth, or it may be, perhaps, to carry the olive branch gathered here to ambitious souls storm-tossed on the breakers of the world. Every ambition is appeased, all noise is hushed, and instead of climbing to grasp a Chimera, all step gladly and simply down the grades of social existence, descending the slopes of Fortune — the Steps of the Golden Stairs.

When Ruskin's dream is accomplished Humanity, instead of mounting to the assault of riches, will descend the Golden Stairs. Everything will be ordered for peace and for beauty. The rails of the railway will be buried in the fields: the remains of stations will be as rare as the vestiges of ancient

Roman camps: and the last of the locomotives will be on show in some museum, by the side of the coach that Louis XVI. had to wait for. No factory chimney will darken the sky with smoke. The hand of man will take the place of steam, so that we shall hear no more of work without workmen, or of workmen without work. Steam reaping-machines, monsters which devour the wage of the agricultural labourer, will no longer creak and scream in the fields, but "the curves of the scythe will dart forth blue lightnings as they catch the sunlight in the hands of the reapers." The illogical temper of the age which replaces as far as possible manual labour by newly invented machines, and at the same time is indignant at the number of hands it leaves unoccupied, will disappear. Iron will no longer be cast in unchanging moulds, it will be forged each time anew. Certain tasks will be performed less quickly, but they will be better accomplished. We shall no longer buy butter from unknown people who send it to us from a distance of two or three hundred miles. The purchaser will know his provider, and they will shake hands with each other. Perhaps also the suppression of the intermediary, "the middleman," will bring greater profit to both. Travellers will journey along the roads more observant if more dilatory than in these days, and the news they bring will be coloured by their imagination. It will probably be quite as true as accounts in newspapers. The social condition of the wayfarer will be recognised

III. LIFE

at the distance of a hundred yards, for the people of every caste and of every trade will have special costumes, designed and fitted to perfection, but not interchangeable. The glazier will have one as well as the haberdasher. There will be no fear of mistaking the senator for a hairdresser, or the Prime Minister for his youngest clerk. The clothes of all will be as spotless as those of the Horse Guards or of the Queen's dairymaids. But on high-days and holidays family chests will be ransacked for gorgeous apparel. "The women will have jewellery and uncut gems; the peasants will be dressed in pure colours, beautiful and bright. Those who nurse the sick and feed the poor will be clad in purple and gold: soldiers on the contrary in black, like public executioners, so that children, who are fond of bright uniforms, instead of playing at soldiers, should play at philanthropists. The nobles will keep all the insignia of their rank, but with gems uncut, their beauty not being increased by cutting, which disturbs the poor mineralogists in their researches and is very expensive. The money which the English habitually spend in cutting diamonds would, in ten years, if it were applied to cutting rocks instead, leave no dangerous reef nor difficult harbour round the whole island coast."

The great nobles, possessors of ancestral estates, will not be despoiled by others, but they will set to work to despoil themselves. They will live constantly on their properties, teaching the peasants dancing, music, with the history of their provinces, even to that of their old clock-tower. The landowner will no longer live in Piccadilly and spend on racecourses the money produced by the labour of the workman in the country. He will live in his own park and scatter his money on the fields of corn and flowers. He will indeed only retain of this money the just rent due for the directing of the labour of his workmen, that is, if he is capable of so directing them. The remainder he will restore to its owner. If it is asked: To whom, and how? —To the land, in manure to renew it; and to the workmen, in works of art to educate them. For example, "he would give the parish school precious minerals or books or beautiful Greek vases, Lecythi, Œnochoes, or those little Tanagra figures so full of teaching from having dwelt so long among the dead." The schools will be decorated from top to bottom with images of the highest art or specimens of the most serviceable objects, for it is "just in the emptiest room that the mind wanders most, for it gets restless like a bird for want of a perch, and casts about for any possible means of getting out and away."

Not only in school but everywhere we shall gain all our knowledge from the eye. Art will penetrate into all the nooks and corners of life, for the cowl truly makes the monk, and "to teach taste is inevitably to form character." Everything around will speak first to the eye and then to the heart. A traveller who visits an unknown town will be greeted, not by colossal advertisements of chocolate merchants or bicycles, but by some such inscription as formerly met the eyes of wearied wayfarers on entering the north gate of Siena:

"Cor magis tibi Sena pandit."

So, too, when standing for a moment or leaning against the pillars of a shop door, where some poet —Roumanille or William Morris—may be offering for sale books or candlesticks, these pillars will recall to us something well worth the memory touching the marble or stone quarries of Italy, or Greece, of Africa, or Spain,—for "even the unsculptured walls of our streets will become to us volumes as precious as those of our libraries." The metallic currency will also address the eye by its chasing, the touch by its "delicacy, and the heart by its purity; there will be ducats and half-ducats, in gold, florins, penny, halfpenny, and one fifth of penny in silver": the smaller coins being "beat thin and pierced with apertures." The gold ducat "will bear the figure of the archangel Michael: on the reverse, a branch of Alpine rose: above the rose-branch, the words '*Sit splendor*'; above the Michael, '*Fiat voluntas*'; . . . round the edge of the coin, '*Domini.*'" The coin will be not only up to standard but absolutely pure metal, so as to teach honour to the nation. In this way the State will speak of beauty to the multitude by all means in its power, by the temples, by the walls, by the bells, by the costumes, by the arms, and especially by public ceremonies which will be luxurious — of a luxury for all and by the help of all — and by national festivals.

One of these festivals will be that of marriage. "In every year there should be two festivals, one on the first of May, and one at the feast of harvest home in each district," at the time when heaven promises, and at the time when it has given. The authorities will proclaim the permission to marry, before the assembled people, for they alone may marry who have attained a vigorous physical and moral existence. This permission will be given to them "as the national attestation that the first portion of their lives has been rightly fulfilled." The young girls will receive the title of "rosière" and the youths that of "bachelor," "and so be led in joyful procession, with music and singing." Nothing must be done impromptu or by chance. "When a youth is fully in love with a girl, and feels that he is wise in loving her, he should at once tell her so plainly, and take his chance bravely, with other suitors. No lover should have the insolence to think of being accepted at once, nor should any girl have the cruelty to refuse at once; without severe reasons. If she simply does not like him, she may send him away for seven years or so — he vowing to live on cresses, and wear sackcloth meanwhile, or the like penance; if she likes him a little, or thinks she might come to like him in time, she may

III. LIFE

let him stay near her, putting him always on sharp trial to see what stuff he is made of, and requiring, figuratively, as many lion-skins or giants' heads as she thinks herself worth. The whole meaning and power of true courtship is Probation; and it ought not to be shorter than three years at least,—seven is, to my own mind, the orthodox time. And these relations between the young people should be openly and simply known, not to their friends only, but to every one who has the least interest in them: and a girl worth anything ought to have always a dozen or so of suitors under vow for her."

When she has chosen her companion for the journey she will await the national feast of marriage, for there will be but one marriage-day, as at Venice in the tenth century. "This day will be a festival for all,—an actual festival for some, a commemorative festival for others. There will be a great display of magnificence, and no one will be envious that every bride is *vestita, per antico uso, di bianco, e con chiome sparse giu per le spalle, conteste con filo d'oro.*" On other days the villagers will be enacting scenes depicted by Le Nain or by Millet, but on that day scenes such as Lancret or Watteau would love to paint. Perfect equality will exist between all as the same sun shines upon all, and the couples there united will not start along different paths in life according to their social conditions. When they leave the church one will not, as nowadays, find in readiness a softly-cushioned coupé full of flowers, while another has to climb the rude staircase of a hovel. No. The State will provide every poor bachelor and rosière with a fixed income for seven years, and will withhold from every rich "bachelor" and every rich "rosière" all their wealth for the same period, allowing them an equal sum with the poor, "so that the rich and poor should not be sharply separated in the beginning of the war of life; but the one supported against the first stress of it long enough to enable them to secure their footing, the others trained somewhat in the use of moderate means," and therefore disposed to acquire greater abundance by the exercise of a handicraft and also to find pleasure in work.

It will be said: That is impossible. Ruskin has never said it was possible: he only said it was to be desired. He never speaks of these things except as of a picture for which both canvas and colours are lacking, and has never put them elsewhere than in the Island of Barataria. Ruskin does not look to the reason of man to move the world,—he puts his trust in love,

"L'amor che muove il sole e l'altre stelle,"

and he appeals for aid to the queenly power of women. She is the *Dea ex machinâ* in this sweet fable of humanity that he puts into the place of the world. When he despairs of ugly and perverse man, he turns to her "whose first duty is to charm," and he begs her openly to be strong where man is

III. LIFE

weak, to be modest where he is boastful, devoted where he is egotistical. In the portrait he paints we do not recognise the sumptuous and learned women of the Renaissance, the Isabella d'Este of Lionardo or of Lorenzo Costa, as depicted in the Louvre picture, nor even the Marchesa di Pescairo of Paolo Veronese, nor yet St. Anna's visitor, who in the frescoes of Santa Maria Novella advances with measured step, all sparkling with gems, and garlanded by Ghirlandajo, the man of gems. No, it is the woman of the primitive pictures and of the old Flemish or Tuscan masters of the first period, sitting erect and calm on a queenly chair and "governing her house by her glance, pale like the faces in tapestry, bewitching as a fairy, tranquil and glowing as a torch." She knows everything, but she does not deck herself with knowledge as with a jewel. She learns many languages in order that she may "understand the sweetness of a stranger's tongue." She also knows how to sew, to prepare the daily meal, to keep accounts, and to tend the sick. Her clothing is not luxurious, but she thinks of that of others—the poor and needy in workhouses, asylums, and hospitals. When she dresses in costly garments it is for a great public ceremony of traditional solemnity, like the maidens who follow St. Ursula in Carpaccio's picture, or that her beauty may do homage to some great idea and be a gracious spectacle for the people who have no other spectacles. She enters into no contests or struggles, but she buckles the armour on the

T

shoulder of her husband for the battle. She does not speak of emancipation nor go to women's meetings in rivalry with men, but she becomes the last appeal of man's action and accords the prize of the tournament. "A true wife, in her husband's house, is his servant; it is in his heart that she is queen. . . . From her, through all the world's clamour, he must win his praise; in her, through all the world's warfare, he must find his peace." She will not be at her mirror like Titian's picture of *Laura Dianti*. The pure simple lines of her face will be reflected in the polished copper on the dresser or in the deep blue of the cuirass. Above all she is joyous. She does not dwell upon the pious pictures of Mothers weeping beneath a crucifix. If she has sorrow, if she has tears, she shakes them off like a "roseleaf shakes off rain," and reappears the brighter. She "follows after righteousness," but she does not preach sermons. Her hands are busy, not folded. She stays in her house as a queen in her kingdom—she watches and beautifies it, active in the morning, tired at night. Her life flows onward amidst work, love, and beauty. And when it is in part run out "the perfect loveliness of a woman's countenance will consist in that majestic peace which is founded in the memory of happy and useful years." She will thus shed light on everything around her and on the path of her husband and son. In her eyes there will be light as well as fire, in her soul there will be reverence as well as pity. She will have no imaginary grievances against the decrees of fate, as she will not expect of life more than it can bestow, or of death any certain promise. No sadness will float across her sweet uncovered brow; none, unless perhaps now and then when she wanders through this Ruskinian Arcadia circled by blue mountains, and discovers some simple tomb beneath an olive tree revealing some forgotten life with the melancholy thought of Poussin's shepherdess scarce expressed: *Et in Arcadia ego*.

And the future? The future need not concern us. Our duty in this life is enough. It is puerile to deny the next; and to discuss and argue about it is presumptuous. What is there to affirm? Let us be content to admire and love what we can see and not to expect any material reward. "The purest forms of our own religion have always consisted in sacrificing less things to win greater; time, to win eternity; the world, to win the skies." Let us expect no other recompense from the skies but their splendour, from the earth but its peace. Let us adopt our notion of heroism from the young Greek of old, who would give his life for a kiss and not obtain it. It is not well to disturb seers when they speak to us of a marvellous land where "the ocean breezes blow round the Blessed Islands, and golden flowers burn on their bright trees for evermore." Let us listen to the prophets as we listen to the singing of the birds. They form part of the heritage of Beauty. Let us not imagine "the sight of any thrones in heaven but the rocks, or of any spirits but the clouds." In the flowers among the rocks, in the broideries of the clouds, so intensely loved, we may acknowledge "the mystery of Power, Beneficence, and Peace which underlies them," and not deny the personality of their Maker. Life has no reward but life itself, veneration for the Unknown artist none but veneration, love for all His works none but Love itself.

"But if this life be *no* dream, and the world no hospital, but your palace-inheritance;—if all the peace and power and joy you can ever win, must be won now, and all fruit of victory gathered here, or never; —will you still, throughout the puny totality of your life, weary yourselves in the fire for vanity? If there is no rest which remaineth for you, is there none you might presently take? was this grass of the earth made green for your shroud only, not for your bed? and can you never lie down *upon* it, but only *under* it? The heathen, in their saddest hours, thought not so. They knew that life brought its contest, but they expected from it also the crown of all contest: No proud one! no jewelled circlet flaming through Heaven above the height of the unmerited throne; only some few leaves of wild olive, cool to the tired brow, through a few years of peace. It should have been of gold, they thought; but Jupiter was poor; this was the best the god could give them. Seeking a better than this, they had known it a mockery. Not in war, not in wealth, not in tyranny, was there any happiness to be found for them—only in kindly peace, fruitful and free. The wreath was to be of *wild* olive, mark you:—the tree that grows carelessly, tufting the rocks with no vivid bloom, no verdure of branch; only with soft snow of blossom, and scarcely fulfilled fruit, mixed with grey leaf and thorn-set stem; no fastening of diadem for you but with such sharp embroidery! But this, such as it is, you may win, while yet you live; type of grey honour, and sweet rest.[1] Free heartedness, and graciousness, and undisturbed trust, and requited love, and the sight of the peace of others, and the ministry to their pain; these,—and the blue sky above you, and the sweet waters and flowers of the earth beneath; and mysteries and presences, innumerable, of living things,—may yet be here your riches; untormenting and divine: serviceable for the life that now is; nor, it may be, without promise of that which is to come."

This might be called the metaphysic of the landscape-painter. "The sun is God," said the dying Turner, and Corot also on his deathbed cried: "Look, look at these landscapes." In admiration and gratitude, they prayed in their last hour that the beauty of Nature might remain their reward beyond the grave. Their happiness had been in things seen far from the haunts of men, by the banks of rivers, on the slopes of the hills, in the solitude of the woods and in the caves of the earth, and when the time came for them to leave this world they desired only to

---

[1] μελιτόεσσα, ἀέθλων γ' ἕνεκεν.

find its image in heaven. Or might we say this earth had been indeed their heaven?

For Ruskin also passionate love of nature has been Alpha and Omega. It has controlled every feature of his personality, dictated all his words, dominated every thought. This was the fire which illuminated, animated and purified him, preserving him from the meanness of hatred, and prevailing over the sorrows of human love. It led him by the path of analysis to a truer knowledge of his mistress, and over the highest regions of synthetic thought to a deeper love of her he had learned to know. It sent him in quest of science, that he might dive deep into the secrets of Nature; but it shielded him against the futilities of that science by revealing those æsthetic relations of things which science neither explores nor admits, if only for the very reason that they belong to the domain of Art. It determined his conception of Art and was the foundation of all his definitions. Lastly, it armed him against those presumptuous men who would fain improve upon Nature, and imbued him with the deepest sympathy for those who live laboriously amidst her joys, or for those who, in our artificial nineteenth-century cities, are for ever deprived of them. Though in our opinion he may not have attained to absolute Truth, we are not therefore alarmed either for him or for ourselves. It may be in the darkness of our night the "Wise Men" are led astray by Will-o'-the-wisps, and only the poor shepherd marks the guiding star. But speaking of these kingly

III. LIFE

wanderers, of whom Ruskin has been one, let us say that it is not the light in their sky but the power in their heart which prevails. The star may lead them to the oasis of faith or to the desert of doubt, but if they have prayed for Truth and sought her honestly, disinterestedly, and humbly, oasis or desert will be alike for them a Bethlehem. And for this aged man who for sixty years of his life has chanted, "Glory to Beauty in the highest," there must surely be some angels of the Holy Night who tarry still to answer, "On earth Peace, Goodwill towards men."

APPENDICES

APPENDIX A

Pp. 28, 29, 30.—Referring to the meeting at Sheffield of some members of the St. George's Guild—the occasion was the inauguration of the new Museum at Meersbrook Park. Mr. Ruskin could not be present, owing to ill-health; he had previously visited Sheffield as the guest of some friends who were not members of St. George's Guild. The journey by postchaise did not take place on any of these occasions, but was undertaken purely as an experiment in travelling, and was wholly unconnected with any operations of St. George's Guild. For the history of the tea-shop, see *Fors Clavigera*, Letter 48.

G. A.

APPENDIX B

P. 32.—Mr. George Thomson, one of the Trustees for St. George's Guild, comments as follows on the account of the mill at Laxey: "Not true to fact—all machine carding and spinning;" and he substitutes "weaving" for "bleaching." His remark on the mode of payment to the farmers for their wool is: "Not true now—conducted on ordinary business lines."

The letter from Mr. Thomson to me, appended below, speaks for itself:—

"*Jan.* 18/99.

"You give me a somewhat difficult task. The whole statement should be reduced to a very simple paragraph, as the matter is an exaggerated view of *Fors*—entirely misleading and really not true in fact.

"My first active association with Ruskin economies arose through Swan showing me some patterns—which I had previously been led from reading *Fors* to believe were made under such conditions as the writer describes. To my amazement I found they were really produced upon very antiquated machinery, and badly made machine goods; and being very anxious for the Master's reputation I at once condemned them as frauds on the public, which would sooner or later lead to failure. Swan told the Master, and he wrote asking me to take the whole thing off his hands, as it had been a great bother to him. I went over and found the place exactly what I had imagined from seeing the goods; neither hand-spinning or hand-weaving—about three persons employed, two men including Rydings and one old woman doing odd jobs. I saw at once the only way to save the Guild money was to put the place upon a business footing, and it has continued ever since to just manage to keep the few people employed in a more or less satisfactory manner; but I never saw either hand-spinning or weaving, and the demand for the goods arises almost entirely from 'sentimental' considerations for the Master, and not from any special virtue in them. This has been a difficulty, *i.e.* keeping up the sentiment, since the Master withdrew from activity."

G. A.

APPENDIX C

LIST OF RUSKIN'S WORKS QUOTED:

Mornings in Florence—Præterita—Modern Painters—Sesame and Lilies—The Oxford Museum—Fors Clavigera—The Seven Lamps of Architecture—General Statement explaining the Nature and Purposes of St. George's Guild—Val d'Arno—Arrows of the Chace—The Queen of the Air—Deucalion—Time and Tide—The Crown of Wild Olive—The Relation between Michael Angelo and Tintoret—Aratra Pentelici—The Harbours of England—Letter to Young Girls—Unto this Last—Munera Pulveris—Frondes Agrestes—The Eagle's Nest—The Stones of Venice—The Elements of Drawing—Lectures on Art, 1870—Ethics of the Dust—Love's Meinie—St. Mark's Rest—Ariadne Florentina—The Laws of Fésole—The Art of England—Lectures on Architecture and Painting—A Joy for Ever.

WORKS BY JOHN RUSKIN

THE UNIFORM COMPLETE EDITION

Crown 8vo, per Vol. net; cloth, gilt top, 5s. Roan, gilt edges, 7s. 6d. Half-parchment, gilt top, 6s. 6d.

SESAME AND LILIES. Containing the Three Lectures, "Kings' Treasuries," "Queens' Gardens," and "The Mystery of Life." With Long Preface and Index. 40th Thousand. Complete Edition.

MUNERA PULVERIS. Six Essays on the Elements of Political Economy. With Index.

The EAGLE'S NEST. Ten Lectures on the Relation of Natural Science to Art. With Index.

TIME and TIDE, by WEARE and TYNE. Twenty-five Letters to a Working Man of Sunderland on the Laws of Work. With Index.

The CROWN of WILD OLIVE. Four Essays on Work, Traffic, War, and the Future of England. With Articles on the Economy of the Kings of Prussia. Ninth Edition. With Index.

The QUEEN of the AIR: A Study of the Greek Myths of Cloud and Storm. Sixth Edition. With Index.

The TWO PATHS. Lectures on Art and its Application to Decoration and Manufacture. Delivered 1858-9. With New Preface and added Note. Third Edition. With Index.

"A JOY FOR EVER" (and its Price in the Market). The Substance of Two Lectures on the Political Economy of Art. With New Preface and added Articles. Third Edition. With Index.

LECTURES on ART, delivered at Oxford in 1870. Revised by the Author. With New Preface and Index. Seventh Edition.

The ETHICS of the DUST. Ten Lectures to Little Housewives on the Elements of Crystallisation. Ninth Edition. With Index.

The ELEMENTS of DRAWING. In Three Letters to Beginners. Illustrated. Sixth Edition. With Index.

GEORGE ALLEN, 156, CHARING CROSS ROAD, LONDON

WORKS BY JOHN RUSKIN

IN THE UNIFORM EDITION

Crown 8vo, per Vol. net; cloth, gilt top, 5s. Roan, gilt edges, 7s. 6d. Half-parchment, gilt top, 6s. 6d.

The STONES of VENICE: Selections for the Use of TRAVELLERS. 2 vols. Eighth Edition. With Index.

LOVE'S MEINIE. Lectures on Greek and English Birds. With Index.

OUR FATHERS HAVE TOLD US. Sketches of the History of Christendom. THE BIBLE OF AMIENS, with the 4 Engravings and Plan of the Western Porches of Amiens Cathedral. With Index.

The ART and the PLEASURES of ENGLAND. The Courses of Lectures Delivered at Oxford during 1883 and 1884.

PRÆTERITA. Outlines of Scenes and Thoughts Perhaps Worthy of Memory in my past Life.

> Vol. I.—Consisting of Twelve Chapters, with Engraving of "My Two Aunts"—1819 to 1839.
>
> Vol. II.—Consisting of Twelve Chapters, with Plates of "Old Dover Packet Jib," and "The Castle of Annecy."—1839 to 1849.
>
> Vol. III.—Containing Chapters I. to IV., together with Parts I. and II. of "Dilecta," and a third hitherto unpublished Part, in addition to a comprehensive and elaborate Index to the whole work, and a Plate of "The Grand Chartreuse," from a drawing by Mr. Ruskin —1850 to 1864.

On the OLD ROAD. A Collection of Miscellaneous Articles and Essays on Literature and Art. In 3 vols. (Sold separately.)

SELECTIONS from RUSKIN. 2 Vols., crown 8vo, each with Index and Portrait (sold separately). Cloth, 6s. each; roan, gilt edges, 8s. 6d. each. Third Edition.

FRONDES AGRESTES. Readings in "Modern Painters." Thirteenth Edition. Cloth, 3s.; roan, gilt edges, 4s.

FORS CLAVIGERA. Letters to the Labourers and Workmen of Great Britain. A New Edition, in 4 vols., each with an Index. With all the Illustrations. Crown 8vo, cloth, 6s. each; roan, gilt edges, 8s. 6d. each.

GEORGE ALLEN, 156, CHARING CROSS ROAD, LONDON

WORKS BY JOHN RUSKIN

IN THE UNIFORM EDITION

Crown 8vo, per Vol. net; cloth, 7s. 6d. Roan, gilt edges, 10s. Half-parchment, gilt top, 9s. With all the Plates.

ARATRA PENTELICI. Seven Lectures on the Elements of Sculpture. With 1 Engraving on Steel and 20 Autotype Plates.

ARIADNE FLORENTINA. Six Lectures on Wood and Metal Engraving, and Appendix. With 4 Full-page Facsimiles from Holbein's "Dance of Death," and 12 Autotype Plates.

VAL D'ARNO. Ten Lectures on Art of the Thirteenth Century in Pisa and Florence. With 1 Steel Engraving and 12 Autotype Plates.

LECTURES on ARCHITECTURE and PAINTING. Delivered at Edinburgh in November 1853. With 15 Full-page Illustrations drawn by the Author.

The HARBOURS of ENGLAND. With the 12 Illustrations by TURNER, reproduced in Photogravure; and an Introduction by T. J. WISE.

GIOTTO and his WORKS in PADUA. A New Small Edition of the work formerly in the possession of "the Arundel Society." With 50 Illustrations.

The SEVEN LAMPS of ARCHITECTURE. The 14 Plates for this Edition have been specially prepared from the larger work. Seventh Edition.

The STONES of VENICE. In 3 Vols., cloth, gilt top, crown 8vo, 30s. net. With the 119 Woodcuts, the 6 Plates in Colour, the other 47 Full-page Illustrations, Reproduced in Photogravure and Half-tone, and the Text as originally issued. Each Volume sold separately.

    Vol. I.—THE FOUNDATIONS. With 21 Full-page Plates and 72 Woodcuts, cloth, gilt top, 10s. net.

    Vol. II.—SEA STORIES. With 20 Full-page Plates and 38 Woodcuts, cloth, gilt top, 10s. net.

    Vol. III.—THE FALL. With 12 Full-page Plates and 9 Woodcut and Index, cloth, gilt top, 10s. net.

MODERN PAINTERS. A New Cheap Edition in 5 Vols. and Index. Crown 8vo, cloth, gilt tops, £2, 2s. net. With the 225 Woodcuts, the 1 Lithograph, and the 89 Full-page Illustrations reproduced in Photogravure and Half-tone. The Text is complete, and includes the "EPILOGUE," written by Mr. RUSKIN in 1888.

    Vols. I. and II. (not sold separately), 11s. net.
    Vol. III., 8s. net.
    Vols. IV. and V., 9s. each net; Index Vol., 5s. net.

GEORGE ALLEN, 156, CHARING CROSS ROAD, LONDON

WORKS BY JOHN RUSKIN

IN THE UNIFORM EDITION

The NATURE of GOTHIC. Reprinted from "The Stones of Venice," with Preface by WILLIAM MORRIS. Crown 8vo. 96 Pages, paper covers, 1s. net.; cloth, 1s. 6d. net.

LETTERS TO THE CLERGY: On the Lord's Prayer and the Church. Edited by Rev. F. A. MALLESON. Third Edition, with Additional Letters by Mr. RUSKIN, crown 8vo, cloth, 5s. net.

THREE LETTERS and AN ESSAY on LITERATURE, 1836-1841. Found in his Tutor's Desk. Crown 8vo, cloth, 3s. net.

LETTERS TO A COLLEGE FRIEND, 1840-1845, including an Essay on "Death before Adam Fell." Crown 8vo, cloth, 4s. net.

HORTUS INCLUSUS. Messages from the Wood to the Garden. Being Letters to the Sister Ladies of the Thwaite, Coniston. Second Edition. Cloth, 4s. net.

EXAMPLES OF THE ARCHITECTURE OF VENICE. With the Text and the 16 Plates as originally published. Cloth cover (unbound), atlas folio (about 25 in. by 17 in.), £2, 2s. net.

THE POETRY OF ARCHITECTURE; or, The Architecture of the Nations of Europe considered in its Association with Natural Scenery and National Character. With Frontispiece in Colour, 14 Plates in Photogravure, and 9 Full-page and other Woodcuts. 4to, cloth, 21s. net.

VERONA, AND OTHER LECTURES. Delivered principally at the Royal and the London Institutions between 1870 and 1883. With Frontispiece in colour and 11 Photogravure Plates. Med. 8vo, cloth, 15s. net.

LECTURES ON LANDSCAPE. Given at Oxford in January and February, 1871. With 20 Plates in Photogravure and 2 in colour. 15 by 11 in., buckram, gilt top, £2, 2s. net.

UNTO THIS LAST. Four Essays on the First Principles of Political Economy. Tenth Edition. Fcap. 8vo, cloth, 3s.; roan, gilt edges, 4s. net.

READINGS IN "FORS CLAVIGERA." Fcap. 8vo, cloth, 2s. 6d. net.

ARROWS OF THE CHACE: being a Collection of the Scattered Letters of JOHN RUSKIN (1840-1880). With Preface. In 2 vols., cloth, 8vo, 20s. net. (Not sold separately.)

GEORGE ALLEN, 156, CHARING CROSS ROAD, LONDON

MISCELLANEOUS PUBLICATIONS

THE OXFORD MUSEUM. By Sir HENRY ACLAND. With Letters from JOHN RUSKIN and Preface by Sir HENRY ACLAND. Also Portrait of Mr. Ruskin, taken in 1893, an Engraving of a Capital, and a Plan. Crown 8vo, cloth, 4s. net.

RUSKIN ON MUSIC: being Extracts from the Works of JOHN RUSKIN. Intended for the Use of all interested in the Art of Music. Edited by Miss A. M. WAKEFIELD. With Frontispiece in Colour. Med. 8vo, cloth, 5s. net: Half-parchment, 6s. 6d. net.

STUDIES IN RUSKIN: Some Aspects of Mr. Ruskin's Work and Teaching. By EDWARD T. COOK. With 13 Woodcuts. Crown 8vo, cloth, 5s.; roan, gilt edges, 7s. 6d. Second Edition.
Also a Large-Paper Edition, crown 4to, price 12s. 6d. Containing, in addition to the Woodcuts, 13 Autotypes of Drawings by Mr. RUSKIN, with Descriptive Text.

RUSKIN AND THE RELIGION OF BEAUTY. A French view of Ruskin. By R. De La SIZERANNE. Translated by Lady GALLOWAY. Crown 8vo, 5s. net.

RUSKIN: ROSSETTI: PRE-RAPHAELITISM. Containing Sixty Letters of Mr. Ruskin, and Letters and Documents of Rossetti, Millais, Ford Madox Brown, and others concerned with the Pre-Raphaelite Movement in England, 1854-1862. Edited by W. M. ROSSETTI. Illustrated with numerous Plates in Photogravure. Crown 8vo, cloth extra, 10s. 6d. net.

THE BIBLE REFERENCES OF JOHN RUSKIN. Selected (by permission of Mr. Ruskin) and arranged in Alphabetical Order by MARY and ELLEN GIBBS. Crown 8vo, 320 pp., cloth gilt top, 5s. net.

READER'S COMPANION TO "SESAME AND LILIES." Paper covers, 1s. net.

WISDOM AND DESTINY. By MAURICE MAETERLINCK. Translated, with an Introduction, by ALFRED SUTRO. Crown 8vo, cloth, gilt top, 6s. net.

THE TREASURE OF THE HUMBLE. By MAURICE MAETERLINCK. Translated by ALFRED SUTRO. With an Introduction by A. B. WALKLEY. Second Edition. Crown 8vo, cloth, 5s. net.

SPENSER'S "FAERIE QUEENE." With 231 Illustrations by WALTER CRANE. Edited from the Original Editions, with Preface and Bibliography, by THOMAS J. WISE. A Limited Edition on Arnold Unbleached Hand-made Paper, in 19 Parts, large post 4to, £9, 19s. 6d. net; or in 6 vols., cloth, gilt tops, £10, 15s. net.

GEORGE ALLEN, 156, CHARING CROSS ROAD, LONDON

MISCELLANEOUS PUBLICATIONS

THROUGH the DOLOMITES from VENICE to TOBLACH.
By the Rev. ALEXANDER ROBERTSON, D.D. A Practical, Historical, and Descriptive Guide-Book. With 42 Full-page Illustrations and a Map of the District, and an Appendix giving Railway and Diligence Stations, Times, Fares, Carriage Tariffs, Guides, Hotels, &c. Small crown 8vo, cloth, 7s. 6d.

The BIBLE of ST. MARK, the ALTAR and THRONE of VENICE. By Rev. ALEXANDER ROBERTSON. A History of St. Mark's Church, Venice, and a Description and Interpretation of its Sculptures and Mosaics. With 80 Full-page Illustrations from Photographs specially taken by NAVA, and Plans of the Atrium and Interior. Large crown 8vo, cloth, Designed Cover, gilt top, 10s. 6d. net.

THE HOMERIC HYMNS. A New Prose Translation, with Essays Literary and Mythological. By ANDREW LANG. Illustrated with 7 Photogravure Plates and 7 Half-tone Subjects from old Greek Sculptures. Crown 8vo, 272 pp., cloth, gilt top, 7s. 6d. net.

GOOD CITIZENSHIP. Twenty-three Essays by Various Authors on Social, Personal, Political, and Economic Problems and Obligations. Edited by Rev. J. E. HAND. With Preface by the Rev. CHARLES GORE, M.A., D.D. Crown 8vo, cloth, 6s. net.

THE BOOK OF THE ART OF CENNINO CENNINI. A Handbook for Artists. Newly Translated, with Copious Notes, and additional Technical Information. By Mrs. HERRINGHAM. Crown 8vo, cloth, gilt top, 6s. net.

TALES FROM BOCCACCIO. Rendered into English by JOSEPH JACOBS, with an Introduction. Also 20 Full-page Designs, Illustrated Borders to each Story, and a Cover by BYAM SHAW. Pott 4to, cloth, 7s. 6d. net.

THE REDEMPTION OF EGYPT. By W. BASIL WORSFOLD. With 4 Illustrations in Colour, and 20 Full-page and 70 Text Illustrations from Sketches and Photographs by the Author. Cloth, gilt top, extra fcap. 4to, 25s. net.

PEG WOFFINGTON. By CHARLES READE. A New Edition, with 74 Illustrations, besides Initials and Cover, by HUGH THOMSON, and an Introduction by AUSTIN DOBSON. Crown 8vo, cloth, gilt, 6s.

PRIDE AND PREJUDICE. By JANE AUSTEN. With 100 Illustrations by HUGH THOMSON, and an Introduction by GEORGE SAINTSBURY. Crown 8vo, cloth, gilt, 6s.

GEORGE ALLEN, 156 CHARING CROSS ROAD, LONDON

WORKS BY AUGUSTUS J. C. HARE

LIFE AND LETTERS OF FRANCES, BARONESS BUNSEN. Third Edition. With Portraits. 2 vols., crown 8vo, 21s.

MEMORIALS OF A QUIET LIFE. 3 vols., crown 8vo. Vols. I. and II., 21s. (Nineteenth Edition); Vol. III., with numerous Photographs, 10s. 6d.

DAYS NEAR ROME. With more than 100 Illustrations by the Author. Third Edition. 2 vols., crown 8vo, 12s. 6d.

WALKS IN ROME. Fourteenth Edition, revised. With Map. 2 vols., fcap. 8vo, cloth limp, 10s.

WALKS IN LONDON. Sixth Edition, revised. With additional Illustrations. 2 vols., fcap. 8vo, cloth limp, 12s.

WESTMINSTER. Reprinted from "Walks in London," as a Handy Guide. Paper covers, 6d. net; cloth, 1s.

WANDERINGS IN SPAIN. With 17 Full-page Illustrations. Fifth Edition. Crown 8vo, 7s. 6d.

CITIES OF SOUTHERN ITALY AND SICILY. With Illustrations. Crown 8vo, 10s. 6d.

CITIES OF NORTHERN ITALY. Second Edition. With Illustrations. 2 vols., crown 8vo, 12s. 6d.

CITIES OF CENTRAL ITALY. Second Edition. With Illustrations. 2 vols., crown 8vo, 12s. 6d.

SKETCHES IN HOLLAND AND SCANDINAVIA. Crown 8vo, with Illustrations, 3s. 6d.

STUDIES IN RUSSIA. Crown 8vo, with numerous Illustrations, 10s. 6d.

FLORENCE. Fourth Edition. Fcap. 8vo, cloth limp, 3s. With 22 Illustrations.

VENICE. Fourth Edition. Fcap. 8vo, cloth limp, 3s. With 23 Illustrations.

THE RIVIERAS. Fcap. 8vo, cloth limp, 3s. With 67 Illustrations.

PARIS. With Illustrations. New Edition, revised. Fcap. 8vo, in 2 vols., cloth limp, 6s.

DAYS NEAR PARIS. With Illustrations. Crown 8vo, cloth, 10s.; or in 2 vols., cloth limp, 10s. 6d.

GEORGE ALLEN, 156, CHARING CROSS ROAD, LONDON

WORKS BY AUGUSTUS J. C. HARE

NORTH-EASTERN FRANCE. Crown 8vo, cloth, 10s. 6d. With Map and 86 Woodcuts.
Picardy—Abbeville and Amiens—Paris and its Environs—Arras and the Manufacturing Towns of the North—Champagne—Nancy and the Vosges, &c.

SOUTH-EASTERN FRANCE. Crown 8vo, cloth, 10s. 6d. With Map and 176 Woodcuts.
The different lines to the South—Burgundy—Auvergne—The Cantal—Provence—The Alpes Dauphinaises and Alpes Maritimes, &c.

SOUTH-WESTERN FRANCE. Crown 8vo, cloth, 10s. 6d. With Map and 232 Woodcuts.
The Loire—The Gironde and Landes—Creuse—Corrèze—The Limousin—Gascony and Languedoc—The Cevennes and the Pyrenees, &c.

NORTH-WESTERN FRANCE. Crown 8vo, cloth, 10s. 6d. With Map and 73 Woodcuts.
Normandy and Brittany—Rouen—Dieppe—Cherbourg—Bayeux—Caen—Coutances—Chartres—Mont St. Michel—Dinan—Brest—Alençon, &c.

SUSSEX. With Map and 45 Woodcuts. Crown 8vo, cloth, 6s. Second Edition.

SHROPSHIRE. Illustrated with 50 Woodcuts, and a specially engraved Map of the County. Crown 8vo, cloth, 7s. 6d.

THE STORY OF TWO NOBLE LIVES: CHARLOTTE, COUNTESS CANNING, and LOUISA, MARCHIONESS OF WATERFORD. In 3 vols. Crown 8vo, cloth, £1, 11s. 6d. With 32 Plates in Photogravure from Lady Waterford's Drawings, and 32 Woodcuts.
Also a Special Large-Paper Edition, with India Proofs of the Plates. Crown 4to, £3, 3s. net.

THE GURNEYS OF EARLHAM: Being Memoirs and Letters of the Eleven Children of JOHN and CATHERINE GURNEY of Earlham, 1775-1875, and the Story of their Religious Life under Many Different Forms. Illustrated with 33 Photogravure Plates and 19 Woodcuts. In 2 vols., crown 8vo, cloth, 25s.

BIOGRAPHICAL SKETCHES: Being Memorial Sketches of ARTHUR PENRHYN STANLEY, Dean of Westminster; HENRY ALFORD, Dean of Canterbury; Mrs. DUNCAN STEWART; and PARAY LE MONIAL. Illustrated with 7 Portraits and 17 Woodcuts. 1 vol., crown 8vo, cloth, 8s. 6d.

THE STORY OF MY LIFE: 1834-1870. Together with Recollections of Places, People, and Conversations, extracted chiefly from Letters and Journals. Illustrated with 18 Photogravure Portraits and 144 Woodcuts from Drawings by the Author. Crown 8vo, cloth, £1, 11s. 6d. In 3 vols.

GEORGE ALLEN, 156, CHARING CROSS ROAD, LONDON

www.ingramcontent.com/pod-product-compliance
Lightning Source LLC
Chambersburg PA
CBHW030012240426
43672CB00007B/925